*Trapped in Thought*

IRISH STUDIES
James MacKillop, *Series Editor*

# TRAPPED IN
# THOUGHT

*A Study of the Beckettian Mentality*

ERIC P. LEVY

*Syracuse University Press*

First Edition 2007
07   08   09   10   11   12        6   5   4   3   2   1

Parts of this book were previously published in modified form in the following publica-
tions: "False Innocence in *Waiting for Godot*," *Journal of Beckett Studies* 3, no. 2 (1994):
19–36; "*The Unnamable*: The Metaphysics of Beckettian Introspection," *Journal of
Beckett Studies* 5, nos. 1–2 (1996): 81–105; "Living Without a Life: Disintegration of
the Christian-Humanist Synthesis in *Molloy*," *Studies in the Novel* 33, no. 1 (2001):
80–94; "To be is to be deceived: The Relation of Berkeley and Plato to *Waiting for
Godot*," *Journal of English and Germanic Philology* 101, no. 2 (2002): 222–37; "The
Beckettian Mimesis of Absence," *Colby Quarterly* 39, no. 2 (June, 2003): 137–50;
"*Krapp's Last Tape* and the Beckettian Mimesis of Regret," *Sydney Studies in English* 28
(2002): 51–69; "*Malone Dies* and the Beckettian Mimesis of Inexistence," *Studies in
Twentieth Century Literature* 27, no. 2 (Summer 2003): 291–312; "The Beckettian
Absolute Universal," *University of Toronto Quarterly* 72, no. 2 (2003): 660–78; "The
Beckettian Mimesis of Seeing Nothing," *University of Toronto Quarterly* 70, no. 2
(2001): 620–32; "Disintegrative Process in *Endgame*," *Samuel Beckett Today/
Aujourd'hui* 12 (2002): 263–81; "The Beckettian Mimesis of Pain," *Philological
Quarterly* 80, no. 3 (2001): 271–89.

The paper used in this publication meets the minimum requirements of American
National Standard for Information Sciences—Permanence of Paper for Printed Library
Materials, ANSI Z39.48–1984.∞™

For a listing of books published and distributed by Syracuse University Press,
visit our Web site at SyracuseUniversityPress.syr.edu.

ISBN-13: 978-0-8156-3102-6
ISBN-10: 0-8156-3102-2

**Library of Congress Cataloging-in-Publication Data**
Levy, Eric P.
Trapped in thought : a study of the Beckettian mentality / Eric P. Levy.—1st ed.
    p. cm.—(Irish studies)
Includes bibliographical references and index.
ISBN 0-8156-3102-2 (hardcover : alk. paper)
1. Beckett, Samuel, 1906–1989—Philosophy. I. Title.
PQ2603.E378Z763 2006
848'.91409—dc22                      2006032692

*Manufactured in the United States of America*

*To my daughter, Emi Novelle*

**Eric P. Levy,** who earned an M.A. and Ph.D. at Stanford, is associate professor of English at the University of British Columbia in Vancouver. He has published a book on Beckett's fiction as well as many articles on writers ranging from Shakespeare, Dickens, and Woolf to James Joyce and Frank McCourt.

# Contents

# Abbreviations

References to Beckett's works are abbreviated and cited parenthetically. For full facts of publication, consult the references.

| | |
|---|---|
| AFAR | "Afar A Bird" |
| ATF | All That Fall |
| BVV | "Bram Van Velde" |
| CAL | "The Calmative" |
| CAS | *Cascando* |
| COM | *Company* |
| D | *Disjecta: Miscellaneous Writings and a Dramatic Fragment* |
| DBVJ | "Dante . . . Bruno . . . Vico . . . Joyce" |
| E | "Enough" |
| EJ | Eh Joe |
| END | *Endgame* |
| EXP | *The Expelled* |
| F | *Film* |
| FAAW | "From an Abandoned Work" |
| FL | "First Love" |
| FTEYA | "For To End Yet Again" |
| HCA | "Horn Came Always" |
| HD | *Happy Days* |
| HIB | "He is barehead" |
| HOW | *How It Is* |
| IDI | "Imagination Dead Imagine" |

| | |
|---|---|
| IGUBB | "I Gave Up Before Birth" |
| ISIS | *Ill Seen Ill Said* |
| KLT | *Krapp's Last Tape* |
| LO | *The Lost Ones* |
| MAL | *Malone Dies* |
| MC | *Mercier and Camier* |
| MOL | *Molloy* |
| MPTK | *More Pricks Than Kicks* |
| MUR | *Murphy* |
| NI | *Not I* |
| OE | "Old Earth" |
| OI | *Ohio Impromptu* |
| P | *Proust* |
| PL | *Play* |
| ROCK | *Rockaby* |
| S | "Still" |
| TFN | *Texts for Nothing* |
| UN | *The Unnamable* |
| W | *Watt* |
| WFG | *Waiting for Godot* |
| WM | *Words and Music* |

*Trapped in Thought*

# Introduction

Every critic, perplexed by the notoriously enigmatic passages or situations that comprise Beckettian art, confronts the problem of meaning, succinctly formulated in *Watt*: "great formal brilliance and indeterminable purport" (W, 74). Indeed, Beckettian texts often challenge—or perhaps even taunt—the reader or audience regarding the task of interpretation. Examples are plentiful: *Watt*: "and he wondered what the artist intended to represent" (W, 129); *Texts for Nothing*: "let him understand who can" (TFN, 97); *How It Is*: "let him understand who has a wish to" (HOW, 55); *Play*: "looking for sense where possibly there is none" (PL, 55). Yet, however cogent his or her hermeneutic probing might be, no critic can escape the risk of fallibility to which Beckettian texts frequently refer: *Molloy*: "And perhaps I understood all wrong" (MOL, 59); *The Unnamable*: "In any case all these suppositions are probably erroneous" (UN, 345); *Texts for Nothing*: "That is why one must not hasten to conclude, the risk of error is too great" (TFN, 110). Faced with such exegetical difficulty, some critics have concluded that, in this literature, there ultimately is no purport, only formal brilliance. For example, according to Richard Begam, Beckett constructs "a universe of pure linguistic *aesthesis*, a universe where words come together and fall apart according to principles of permutation and transmutation . . . his sentences arrange themselves into shapely but increasingly meaningless patterns" (1997, 310). Leslie Hill makes a similar observation concerning *The Unnamable*: "There exists no intentional message that may be extracted from the verbal motions of the text" (1990, 120). His

remark echoes one made much earlier by Hugh Kenner on *How It Is:*
"Built phrase by phrase into a beautifully and tightly wrought structure, a few dozen expressions permuted with deliberate redundancy
accumulate meaning even as they are emptied of it" (1968, 189). Yet,
while the assertion that a text has no meaning—or, at best, an indeterminable and self-canceling meaning—eludes the danger of erroneously attributing meaning, it cannot advance our understanding of
Beckett's work very far *if* we construe the project of understanding to
include the achievement of meaning.

But many critics do not view the interpretive project in these
terms. Convinced that Beckettian art reflects the linguistic environment in which expression, regardless of import, necessarily partici-
pates, they address Beckettian texts—or portions of texts—as pure
verbal structures, abstracted from any meaning that their constitutive
language might communicate. Such readings effectively appropriate
as a hermeneutic principle *The Unnamable*'s formulation of his own
predicament: "It all boils down to a question of words" (UN, 335).
Here the concern is to analyze linguistic forms, abstracted from the
content in which they inhere. For example, Dina Sherzer views *The
Unnamable* as "a text about language" (1998, 89), while J. E.
Dearlove studies the "dual processes of fragmentation and tessellation" in what he terms Beckett's "non-relational art" (1982, 61).
Steven Connor construes *The Unnamable*'s utterance in terms of the
"hymeneal suture between cessation and continuance" (1988, 75).
Offering one of the most jargon-rich exegeses in this school of criticism, Edouard Morot-Sir interprets *The Unnamable* in terms of "language destructing bound variables and reducing grammatical deictics
to anaphoric relations" (1984, 239). In contrast, Julia Kristeva interprets the emphasis on "unnamable" meaning in terms of a postmodern preoccupation with "multiple, heteroclitic and unrepresentable
idiolect" (1980, 141).

The exegetical assumption that interpretation entails determination of meaning is challenged not just by practitioners of linguistic
analysis but also by adherents of postmodern literary theory who in
many instances seek not to recuperate meaning but to deconstruct it.

As Begam notes, postmodern analysis is often concerned with textual strategies involving "the breakdown of the signifying chain, and the deferral of meaning," not with the disclosure or affirmation of meaning (1996, 14). Another recent exponent of this breakdown is Anthony Uhlmann, who, in *Beckett and Poststructuralism,* locates his approach in the wake of Derrida's deconstructionism and construes Beckett's art in terms of an anti-Platonism that privileges "ambivalence or indeterminacy" in place of fixed and immutable truth (1999, 7). There can be no doubt that ambivalence and indeterminacy figure prominently in Beckett's art. Indeed, a quintessential formulation occurs in *Molloy:* "[O]ne knows already or will never know it's one or the other" (MOL, 45). But ambivalence and indeterminacy ultimately indicate not merely an epistemological condition but a psychological preference: "And I said with rapture, Here is something I can study all my life, and never understand" (MOL, 169). *The Unnamable* foregrounds the same predilection: "I don't know. I could know. But I shall not know" (UN, 301).

The deeper implications of this willed indeterminacy entail a stratum of anti-Platonism that Uhlmann overlooks, but which nevertheless is central to Beckettian art. The fundamental concern of Platonic philosophy is morality, construed as right conduct of life. In the *Euthydemus,* Plato argues that the basis of that morality is epistemological: to know the good is to do the good, for here the object and the result of knowledge coincide *(Euthydemus,* 281b). Wilhelm Windelband elaborates: "[H]e only will be able to act right who has the right knowledge of things and of himself" (1958, 1:77). No amount of knowledge of things will suffice to ensure right conduct of life, for to implement knowledge appropriately, the individual must first know himself. According to Plato, the initial step in achieving self-knowledge is to acknowledge ignorance. Self-knowledge, he asserts, requires a "man to know what he knows, and what he does not know" *(Charmides,* 167a). Once the defect of ignorance is recognized, increasing self-knowledge becomes the supreme purpose of life. Indeed, according to Socrates' celebrated dictum in the *Apology,* "[L]ife without this sort of examination is not worth living" *(Apol-*

*ogy,* 38a). As Karl Jaspers indicates, such continuous examination, by which the self is related to the good that it knows, enables a "transcending of one's own nature through thinking, guided by whatever is revealed in thought" (1955, 119).

The Platonic inheritance in Beckettian mimesis will be investigated more fully and from various angles in portions of chapters 4 and 8. But at this point, for purposes of introduction, it is sufficient to note that the Platonic connection provides a different way of interpreting indeterminacy. Whereas, in the Platonic schema, ignorance is the precondition for knowledge, in the Beckettian schema ignorance is exemption from knowledge. In the context of self-examination, not knowing is not being knowable, and not being knowable is to be excused from responsibility to use self-knowledge to determine (to invoke a phrase from Plato's *Gorgias*), "in what way one can best live the life that is to be his" *(Gorgias,* 512e). In the Beckettian schema, not knowing ensures not the best way to live but the worst: "For anything worse than what I do, without knowing what, or why, I have never been able to conceive" (MOL, 46). That is, not knowing enables a mode of existence—or, more precisely (as discussed in chapter 5), a mode of "inexistence"—exempt from life: "I have ceased to live" (MOL, 25). It concerns the paradoxical project, examined later in chapter 4, to live without a life—to live without the sense of purpose ordinarily informing the enterprise of living: "I wither as the living cannot" (MOL, 40).

Perhaps the most profound gloss on this project occurs in *How It Is:* "I have suffered must have suffered morally hoped more than once despaired to match your heart bleeds you lose your heart drop by drop" (HOW, 23). The demand to be beyond vulnerability to moral suffering is central to the representation of experience that constitutes Beckettian mimesis. As the passage just quoted shows, moral suffering arises from the conflict not between vice and virtue, but between hope and despair. That is, the suffering results from the thwarting of personal goals or ends, occasioning disappointed hopes and the eventual abandonment of hope that constitutes the state of despair. Such suffering is properly termed "moral" because, as Etienne Gilson indicates, morality concerns ends or purposes and the means of achieving them: "Morality consists in ordering all human acts in view of the true good, which is the true end" (1955, 715n. 118). In the Beckettian universe, ends or purposes are abandoned so that moral suffering can never rend: "What can it matter to me, that I succeed or fail?" (UN, 347). In their place is conviction in futility—a state that recurs with variations throughout the Beckettian canon. Futility becomes purpose because it protects from the moral suffering of botched purpose: "I have never been disappointed, and I often was in the early days, without feeling at the same time, or a moment later, an undeniable relief" (EXP, 13). In alternate formulation, the purpose of purpose is not to achieve an end, but to prolong conviction in its impossibility: "impossible to stop, impossible to go on" (UN, 395). What appears as perseverance is instead the prolongation of surrender: "I'll have gone on giving up, having had nothing, not being there" (TFN, 125).

Closer examination of the passage in *How It Is* concerning moral suffering will clarify this crucial notion. Though no textual proof of derivation is available, the passage corresponds to a famous utterance in Aeschylus's *Agamemnon*, epitomizing the ancient Greek view of tragedy: "And even in our sleep pain that cannot forget, falls drop by drop upon the heart, and in our own despite, against our will, comes wisdom to us" (qtd. in Hamilton 1930, 156). Whereas in Aeschylus's formulation pain engenders insight, in Beckettian mimesis pain engenders anesthesia: "your heart bleeds you lose your heart drop by drop" (HOW, 23). Instead of adding wisdom, drop by drop, suffering drains the capacity to feel, drop by drop, and in consequence depletes the capacity to learn from pain. More precisely, what is learned is the determination to found awareness on the principles of sameness and repetition, to ensure that "the same things recur" (TFN, 117) so that the only goal is to do again what has already been done: "Whereas to see yourself doing the same thing endlessly over and over again fills you with satisfaction" (MOL, 133). Reiteration guarantees that the only purpose is recapitulation of the irrelevance or absurdity of purpose—a sure defense against the moral suffering of thwarted purpose. Yet regardless of local circumstance or strategy, the fundamental purpose represented by Beckettian mimesis is to have no purpose: "stay for ever in the same place never had any other ambition" (HOW, 39).

At the deepest level, the purpose of purposelessness is to perpetuate perplexity so that self-knowledge can never be achieved: "Always the same thing proposing itself to my perplexity" (HOW, 121). Correspondingly, the most profound mode of repetition in Beckettian mimesis concerns reiteration of the vain effort to understand experience and the subject undergoing it. The ultimate purpose of perplexity is to dissolve the identity of the subject suffering it: "Where I am there is no one but me, who am not" (UN, 355). The pain of being oneself fuses with the pain of not knowing oneself in "the hell of unknowing" (FL, 32). For to know oneself would be to risk the intolerable moral suffering of hope and despair in the effort to fulfill intrinsic identity through finding, according to the Platonic dictum indicated earlier, "in what way one can best live the life that is to be his." The purpose is not to live the best life, but to *de-teleologize* (deprive of purpose) life, in various modes, by various means—for example, to reduce life to (a) a state of comatose abandonment, as in *The Lost Ones*; or (b) the inability to know that of which awareness is aware, as in *The Unnamable*; or (c) the iteration of trivial episodes whose "maxima and minima" coincide in one interminable tedium, as in "He is barehead" (HIB, 30); or (d) the waiting for direction that never arrives, as in *Waiting for Godot;* or (e) the preordained declension of automatist process, as in *Endgame*. The list of variations is as long as the list of items comprising the Beckettian canon: "what vicissitudes within what changelessness" (TFN, 118). For the reduction of life to modes of "coming and being and going in purposelessness" is central to Beckettian mimesis (W, 58).

We reach here the great paradox of Beckett's art. On the one hand, it manifests remarkable consistency and conservation, while on the other hand it displays extraordinary change and development, exploring different literary forms. Although chapter 2 briefly considers one aspect of stylistic development as it informs the project of minimalism, the mode of analysis of the present study is interpretive, not stylistic. The impetus for this is provided by Beckett's 1948 essay, "Peintres de l'empêchment" (Painters of Impediment): "Heureusement il ne s'agit pas de dire ce qui n'a pas encore été dit, mais de redire, le plus souvent possible dans l'espace le plus reduit, ce qui a été dit déjà" (Fortunately it is not a question of saying what has not yet been said, but of *repeating, as often as possible in the most reduced space, what has already been said*) (67; my emphasis).

Beckettian mimesis is indeed characterized by the tendency toward "repeating . . . what has already been said," especially in terms of recapitulating and reformulating the same fundamental concerns: "the same old questions and answers" (TFN, 78). Yet, like literary fractals, these concerns disclose increasingly complex conceptual patterns with increasingly intricate subdivisions, the more minutely they are analyzed. Moreover, each Beckettian text foregrounds a different aspect of the conceptual nexus constituting the core of meaning expressed in the canon as a whole. Thus, Beckett's work displays both continuity and novelty. The continuity is reinforced by the tendency of Beckettian mimesis to formulate itself as a "closed system" (MUR, 109) as through references in later texts to characters in earlier ones—for example, when the narrator of *Texts for Nothing* alludes to Molloy, Malone (TFN, 92), and Pozzo (TFN, 96); when Molloy refers to Watt (MOL, 76); and when the narrator of the late work "He is barehead" compliments Murphy's "first-rate legs" (HIB, 27). The novelty preeminently arises through the particular predicaments and resources that each text respectively expresses and deploys.

The term *closed system* can clarify the combination of sameness and difference in the Beckettian canon. In its original context, the term refers to Murphy's mind: "His mind was a closed system, subject to no principle of change but its own" (MUR, 109). At bottom, through the manifold texts by which it is expressed, Beckettian mimesis involves the representation of an anonymous mind or, more precisely, a *mentality,* a mode of construing experience that seeks only the reinforcement of its own preconceptions. The world in which awareness is situated ultimately contains nothing but these inveterate limitations of thought—a circumstance frequently suggested by the texts themselves and epitomized by the narrator of *The Calmative*: "[W]e are needless to say in a skull" (CAL, 38). On a preliminary level, this mental location indicates that what is perceived is no more than subjective fabrication: "Saying is inventing" (MOL, 32). But more profoundly, the emphasis on containment in the mind foregrounds the "laws of the mind" (MOL, 13) as they apply to the directing of what might be labeled *Beckettian awareness*. In this context, the criterion of truth is not what things are but what they seem to be from the point of view considering them: "For Watt's concern . . . was not after all with what the figure was, in reality, but with what the figure appeared to be, in reality. For since when were Watt's concerns with what things were, in reality?" (W, 227). A similarly anti-Platonic privileging of appearance over reality informs the response of Malone's mother to his query whether "[t]he sky is further away than you think": "It is precisely as far away as it appears to be" (MAL, 268).

The defining attribute of the attitude represented in Beckettian mimesis is its refusal to recognize its own status *as* an attitude: a subjective outlook or disposition limited to the subject in whom it inheres. Instead, Beckettian attitude claims universal validity: "from this point of view, but there is no other" (IDI, 65). To clarify this dispensation, it is useful to contrast it with Hamlet's melancholy—perhaps the most celebrated example of negative attitude in literature: "And indeed it goes so heavily with my disposition that this goodly frame the earth *seems to me* a sterile promontory, this most excellent canopy the air, look you, this brave o'erhanging firmament, this majestical roof fretted with golden fire, why it *appeareth nothing to me* but a foul and pestilent congregation of vapours" *(Hamlet,* 2.2.297–303; my emphasis).

As the italicized phrases in this passage show, Hamlet distinguishes between reality and his own perspectival distortion of it. That is, he assumes the distinction between subjective and objective perception. But in Beckettian mimesis, this distinction lapses: Perspectival idiosyncrasy becomes a first principle, determining the nature of all that is: "I place myself at my point of view" (HOW, 114). Here we find represented a mentality or cognitive orientation toward experience that, to interpolate phrases from *More Pricks Than Kicks,* is "final, uniform and continuous, unaffected by circumstance, assigned without discrimination" to everything it perceives (MPTK, 105). Within the confines of the Beckettian universe, there is no escape from this mentality or attitude, for that universe ultimately contains nothing but awareness ("inside an imaginary head" [TFN, 112]) bounded by its own range of registration: "where nothing obstructs your vision, wherever you turn your eyes, but the limits of vision itself" (EXP, 13).

But another factor ensures the insularity or confinement within its own boundaries of the Beckettian attitude: the tendency of that attitude to express itself through conspicuous reference to the terminology and "the spirit of method" (UN, 303) proper to philosophy. An immediate consequence of this tendency is the readiness of critics to interpret Beckett's thought in terms of concepts derived from extraneous—and frequently philosophical—sources. A more insidious result of the formalizing tendency is its aptitude to elevate mere attitude to "the plane of pure knowledge," where propositions are verified by "reasonings, based on analysis" (MOL, 91, 64): "I did conceive that system" (HOW, 94). In other words, the sheer technical proficiency through which the attitude finds verbal expression assures that the attitude itself will never be questioned, though it questions everything else: "so on it reasoned . . . vain questionings" (NI, 80).

According to Alfred North Whitehead, "Philosophy is the self-correction by consciousness of its own initial excess of subjectivity" (1978, 15). Yet in Beckettian mimesis, consciousness can no longer correct its own excess of subjectivity, because nothing remains of subjectivity but preoccupation with its own distress: "[H]e intensified the pressure and the pangs, they were a guarantee of identity" (MPTK, 65). Self-preoccupation becomes an autonomous mechanism, revolving incessantly the same concerns with "self-immersed indifference to the contingencies of the contingent world" (MUR,

168). Ultimately, in Beckettian mimesis, self-preoccupation is abstracted from the self to which it belongs. That is, self-preoccupation is heightened to the point of obsession with the need for "flight from self": "[T]here is no one here, neither me nor anyone else" (UN, 367; TFN, 102). This paradoxical dissolution of the subject, in the midst of the exercise of subjectivity, is at once the most startling and baffling achievement of Beckettian mimesis. But its roots lie in the reduction of subjectivity to automatism and repetition compulsion, by which awareness is divested of the need for the subject in which it inheres. The analogue of this dispensation concerns investing the body with the principle of locomotion ordinarily pertaining to the mind animating it: "my body doing its best without me" (FAAW, 49). In Beckettian mimesis, just as the body is reduced to an autonomous principle of locomotion, capable of executing the motions of life without the attention of the mind, so the mind is reduced to an autonomous principle of thought, enabled to think without the attention of its own awareness: "I should turn away from it all, from the body, away from the head, let them work it out between them" (TFN, 75). Beckett further explores subjectivity in *The Unnamable* and *Endgame* (examined respectively in chapters 6 and 9). The former constitutes a spectacular exposition of the alienation of subjectivity from its own subject, while the latter, in equally spectacular fashion, reduces subjectivity to autonomist process. In each case, Beckett's art deploys extraordinary intellectual resources, involving either the dismantling of renowned philosophical systems or the inversion of celebrated logical arguments (known as *reductiones ad absurdum*—reductions to logical impossibility), to express the mentality with which his art is concerned.

A signal triumph of Beckettian mimesis (here construed as the representation, by literary means, of a mentality or mode of delimiting experience) concerns a unique species of what Samuel Coleridge, in a general definition of beauty, termed "Multëity in Unity" (Coleridge 1952, 370). In the Beckettian context, multëity in unity becomes diversity in sameness, as epitomized by a passage quoted earlier: "what vicissitudes within what changelessness" (TFN, 118).

The diversity is evident not only in the array of textual forms achieved by Beckettian mimesis, but also by the plurality of angles from which the same mentality is viewed and expressed. To address this diversity, the present study deploys a dual method of analysis, combining thematic interrogation from different perspectives (in the first three chapters) with exegesis of specific texts (in the subsequent chapters). But the texts themselves constitute particular angles of representation and modes of conceptualization regarding the nodal concerns of Beckettian art. For this reason, the method of analysis involves placing the specific works under consideration in the context of related concerns in the entire canon. Beckettian mimesis is at once centripetal (moving toward the center by contracting the field of attention) and centrifugal (moving away from the center by expanding its implications). That is, at bottom, Beckettian mimesis reiterates the same core matters while enriching their sense and reference.

Yet this characterization of Beckettian mimesis in terms of centripetal and centrifugal tendencies of movement toward and away from a central cluster of concerns requires further refinement. Viewed from a certain angle, Beckettian mimesis represents an attitude that seeks to *repudiate* the center: to circle round and round a center that is no longer there or that, in being there, simply serves as a focal point of pointlessness. The processes of recurrent cycling or revolving depicted in the Beckettian canon ultimately confirm the pointlessness of their own revolution: "Itself it went nowhere, only round and round, like the spheres, but mutely" (MPTK, 37). The principle of movement—the center around which the circumference is constructed—negates the purpose of movement. Cycle reduces the function of cycle to recapitulation of the same fatuity or futility: "the endless April showers and the crocuses and then the whole bloody business starting all over again" (W, 47). At bottom, preoccupation with purposeless reiteration confirms the pointlessness of "the customary cycle of birth, life and death" (MOL, 52), thereby assuring exemption from moral suffering—the suffering of hope and despair that derives from purpose. When the purposeless reiteration concerns obsessions, not life events, their cyclic revolution progressively evacuates the content of the subject entertaining them, until self-awareness is reduced to modalities of emptiness—a Beckettian escape from the pain of identity (a problem interrogated, on various levels, in chapter 1). The subjective center is replaced by the registration of nothingness, absence, or inexistence—complex notions involving complex strategies, investigated in chapters 2, 3, and 5 respectively.

A passage in the "Proteus" chapter of James Joyce's *Ulysses* suggests the invitation and challenge that Beckettian mimesis proposes to the reader: "In. Come. Red carpet spread. You will see who" *(Ulysses, 59)*. Beckettian mimesis beckons the reader inside a mentality—an attitude of cognitive apprehension—never before represented in literature. The mentality is not itself a character, but it has the aptitude to inhere in characters or in their witness. Beckettian mimesis chooses both alternatives, in different texts: to express the mentality through its instantiation—one might almost say its incarnation—either in a character or a narrator, or in the narratorial perspective on other characters. Beckettian mimesis also pursues a third alternative. In certain works, such as *The Unnamable* and *Texts for Nothing*, it represents the mentality *personified*, without the mediation of a character, properly speaking, in which to inhere. That is, the relation between subject and its own experience, underpinning the very notion of selfhood, which in turn underpins the notions of character and first-person narrator, is categorically rejected: "If I speak of a head, referring to me, it's because I hear it being spoken of" (UN, 353). Yet, regardless of the diverse means applied, the consistent aim in Beckettian mimesis is to evacuate experience of any content but conviction in the excruciating futility of enduring it: "The syndrome known as life is too diffuse to admit of palliation" (MUR, 200). That is, at bottom, nothing remains of experience—and, *a fortiori*, nothing remains to mimesis in the representation of experience—but the negative attitude toward experience: "[Y]ou would do better, at least no worse, to obliterate texts than to blacken margins, to fill in the holes of words till all is blank and flat and the whole ghastly business looks like what it is, senseless, speechless, issueless misery" (MOL, 13). In alternate formulation, no matter what happens, the negative attitude toward it never changes.

The notion of unvarying attitude is enunciated in *Watt*: "For it was an attitude become, with frequent repetition, so part of his being" (W, 32). The predisposition to register only misery in experience—to reduce experience to what in *Watt* is termed "the inner lamentation"—symptomizes the Beckettian wound, a notion also articulated in *Watt*: "[W]hy then a wound had perhaps been opened, never again to close, never, never again to close" (W, 217, 32). But the great paradox of the Beckettian mentality is that the wound it perseverates must never be allowed to close—or, in alternate formulation, the wound is allowed to close only to be opened again: "[T]he little wounds have time to close before being opened again" (HIB, 26). The wound ultimately concerns the need to persist in registering pain, and the pain ultimately concerns the persistence of futility: "I gave rein to my pains, my impotence" (MAL, 210). The sheer constancy—or obstinacy—with which Beckettian mimesis pursues its defining project raises three perplexing questions: (a) What caused the wound? (b) Why cannot the wound be allowed to close? (c) What fuels or perpetuates obsession with the wound? No certain answers can be given to any of these queries, but some informed hypotheses can be tendered for the purposes of introduction.

The wound cannot be allowed to close, because it affords protection from more suffering: "I shall not speak of my sufferings. Cowering deep down among them I feel nothing" (MAL, 186). To heal would be to risk vulnerability to another wound. In the context of moral suffering, to heal would be to take the notion of purpose seriously, with resultant exposure to the pangs of disappointed hope. In Beckettian mimesis, what seems on the surface to concern hopeful straining toward a goal is, at bottom, the project to sustain hopelessness. See, for example, *Texts for Nothing*: "I'll have gone on giving up, having had nothing, not being there" (TFN, 125). Keeping the wound open protects not just against the risk of more wounds, but also against the threat of change—a hazard fundamental to several Beckettian texts. Obsession with pain is a bulwark against the passage of time: "They were perhaps not so much reflections as a dark torrent of brooding where past and future merged in a single flood and closed, over a present for ever absent" (MC, 32). According to the

Beckettian mentality, to think that the future will just involve more of the same condition in which the present languishes now is to find refuge from the risk of hope. Refusal to close the wound—to accept healing or salvation regarding it—remains unremitting and implacable: "[H]ad I only the little finger to raise to be wafted straight to Abraham's bosom I'd tell him to stick it up" (HOW, 38). As the quotation suggests, there appears to be a further motive for keeping the wound open, one that concerns suffering as mode of revenge. This notion can be clarified by reference to Hamlet's "To be or not to be" soliloquy, where suicide is construed as a means of revenge or retaliation "against a sea of troubles" *(Hamlet,* 3.1.58). In the tortured logic of Beckettian mimesis, suffering itself is revenge against suffering. There are references in the Beckettian canon, for example, to Vanni Fucci, the figure in Dante's *Inferno* (canto 25) who makes an obscene gesture and defiant utterance in the direction of the Heaven, indicating his contempt for the Power that damned him. The most dramatic of these references occurs in *Mercier and Camier,* when Mercier, enraged by incessant rain, dashes his umbrella—his only protection from pain—"to the ground," and screams "to the sky": "As for thee, fuck thee" (MC, 26).

This study will examine these and other motives for perpetuating pain. Yet whatever the reasons for the need to keep the wound open, the project can succeed only if there are means to remain obsessed with suffering. This illustrates a first principle of the Beckettian mentality—the tendency to formulate itself as an awareness of lack and deprivation, even in the act of mimesis: "But my notes have a curious tendency, as I realize at last, to annihilate all they purport to record" (MAL, 259). To grasp this tendency, we must refer to the role of abstraction in the act of intellectual conception or cognition. To identify an object is to determine by abstraction the universal, type, or form inhering in it, by virtue of which the object can be identified as what it is. In other words, to identify an object is always to determine what type of object it is—to determine the property or properties this object has in common with other objects of the same type. Whatever is unique to the object is left out, in order that the essential core of qualities characterizing it as a certain type of object (a pot, a man) can be known.

Bishop Berkeley—whose philosophy has unexpected and hitherto unseen correspondences with Beckett's (discussed in chapter 8 and the conclusion)—formulates the process of abstraction compactly:

> For example, the mind, having observed that Peter, James, and John resemble each other in certain common agreements of shape and other qualities, leaves out of the complex or compounded idea it has of Peter, James, and any other particular man that which is peculiar to each, *retaining only what is common to all*, and so makes an abstract idea wherein all the particulars equally partake—abstracting entirely from and *cutting off all those circumstances and differences which might determine it to any particular existence*. And after this manner it is said we come by the abstract idea of man or, if you please, humanity, or human nature; wherein it is true there is included color, because there is no man but has some color, but then it can be neither white, nor black, nor any particular color wherein all men partake. (Berkeley 1957, 8–9; my emphasis)

Watt's difficulty with the pot that refuses to be identified as a pot (discussed in the conclusion) foregrounds the need for abstraction of the form or universal in determining the identity of an object, and indicates that the process of abstraction undergoes a transformation in Beckett's art: "[T]his indefinable thing that prevented him from saying, with conviction, and to his relief, of the object that was so like a pot, that it was a pot, and of the creature that still in spite of everything presented a large number of exclusively human characteristics, that it was a man" (W, 82–83). Abstraction continues to operate, but with a slippage from its ordinary function—a slippage formulated by the gentleman with whom Watt converses: "Something slipped" (W, 42). After the slippage, nothing is perceived in the same way. "At the same time my tobacco-pipe, since I was not eating a banana, ceased so completely from the solace to which I was inured, that I took it out of my mouth to make sure it was not a thermometer, or an epileptic's dental wedge" (W, 44). The same slippage applies when the object perceived is life itself: "Life, we dare almost say, in the abstract" (MPTK, 105). In this context, awareness always abstracts the same properties of confusion, misery, futility, and exhaustion. No matter what is experienced, it is always construed as the same experience, in virtue of the core of properties—the "common agreements of . . . qualities" (Berkeley's term above)—abstracted from it. Just as physical science, when dealing with the question of momentum, considers objects only in terms of the properties of mass and velocity common to them, excluding all other characteristics, so the Beckettian mentality, when construing the nature of life, addresses only the same essential characteristics: "The essential doesn't change" (WFG, 14).

Yet there is another dimension to Beckettian abstraction—one that points not toward the tendency of the mind or the awareness to understand experience in terms of only some of its essential aspects, but toward conviction in what Roger Penrose, in a different context, terms "an entirely abstract world" (Penrose 1994, 413)—the Beckettian equivalent of the Platonic world of Pure Ideas or Forms: "the voice is of a world collapsing endlessly, a frozen world" (MOL, 40). As Penrose indicates, Plato's world of Forms subsists in its own ontological realm without necessary relation to human knowledge or action: "To Plato, the world of perfect forms is primary, being timeless and independent of ourselves" (Penrose 1994, 417). The endlessly collapsing world noted by Molloy corresponds to the world of Pure Forms posited by Plato. Moreover, it enjoys the same heuristic relation to the mind as does the world of Pure Forms in the epistemology of Plato. That is, just as, in the Platonic epistemology, the world of Pure Forms can function as the goal toward which philosophical contemplation rises, in its search for the immutable and self-identical truth by which the knowing function of the mind is exalted and fulfilled so, by implication at least, the world of Beckettian forms can focus the Beckettian mentality on that which consummates its negative attitude toward experience.

This matter can be clarified through examination of the notion of "a world collapsing endlessly." A world that collapses endlessly is a world of unbecoming, in perpetual transit between being and nothing. But here the poles of being and nothing have been bracketed or eliminated from consideration, leaving only the process of unbecoming, whose unfolding presupposes them. This paradigm of endless collapsing or unbecoming, with no determinate content and neither *terminus a quo* nor *terminus ad quem* (poles from which and toward which), informs much of Beckettian mimesis. Two opposite tactics in the representation of endless collapsing can be noted here. In one, formulated by Molloy, life continues, but it is without relation to either origination or termination, so that its unfolding simply accumulates superfluity: "[F]or at the same time it is over and it goes on, and is there any tense for that?" (MOL, 36). In another, formulated by Pozzo, the process of collapsing has itself collapsed, resulting in the coincidence of the contraries, beginning and end, by which it was bounded: "[O]ne day we were born, one day we shall die, the same day, the same second, is that not enough for you? They give birth astride a grave, the light gleams an instant, then it's night once more" (WFG, 57). In fact, these contrary formulations of Molloy and Pozzo constitute reciprocal expressions of the same abstraction. According to the Beckettian mentality, the property common to all life is disintegration, construed as unremitting collapsing. The particular content of this endless collapsing has no ultimate value or significance. All that stands out is the property of continuous disintegration common to all lives. But if life is thus construed as continuous collapsing with no significant content, then the boundaries—birth and death—of this process have nothing to contain, and therefore fuse, with the result that their proper function in demarcating life is forfeited: "I'm dead and getting born, without having ended, helpless to begin, that's my life" (TFN, 119).

Construing life in terms of the inability to begin that which has not yet ended or to end that which cannot begin epitomizes the Beckettian mentality. Nothing remains of life but awareness of futility. Yet futility here entails not merely uselessness of action but uselessness of existence. There is not only nothing to be done but also nothing to be. This is not, however, a case of existential absurdity, where existence unfolds in the absence of intrinsic or prior purpose, ordinarily derived from an antecedent creative power or originary dispensation. Instead, the inability to be—the Beckettian plight of "inexistence"—derives from existential incapacity or ineptitude: "who could not be and gave up trying" (UN, 347). This incapacity results from and expresses a mentality that, refusing to regard life as anything but an imposition and an injustice, prefers to preoccupy attention with versions of absence or oblivion, whose supreme modality is amnesia: "[T]ime to forget all lose all ignorant of all whence I come whither I go" (HOW, 110). We reach here the quintessential inversion of Platonism in Beckettian mimesis. Whereas in the Platonic schema anamnesis or recollection is the means of recuperating knowledge innate in the soul and thus perfecting self-knowledge, in the Beckettian schema amnesia or the inability to recollect is the means of excusing awareness from the very possibility of self-knowledge. To be without self-knowledge is to lack the principle of what to be. According to the Beckettian mentality, the ultimate refuge from the demands of being is fixation on nothingness: "[W]ho having nothing will wish for nothing, except to be left the nothing he hath" (MC, 114).

The Beckettian refusal of being appears to find its ontological root in a defective parent-child relationship in childhood (discussed in depth in chapter 9). A typical reference occurs in *The Unnamable*: "[F]ather and mother, both dead, at seven months interval, he at the conception, she at the nativity, I assure you, you won't do better" (UN, 377). Without the nurturing influence proper to love, life becomes a process of disintegration, with no goal but its own elapsation, and no content but reiteration of the pain of loss. Ironically, though life without love is reduced to a process of disintegration, obsession with that disintegration becomes a means of protection against the risk that the need for love will intrude on awareness. Indeed, on registering with "dismay" that he has fallen in love, the narrator of "First Love" refers explicitly to the stratagem of keeping thoughts of love at bay by thinking only of his own suffering: "I who had learned learnt to think of nothing, nothing except my pains" (FL, 21, 22). Molloy provides a ribald example of the link between preoccupation with disintegration and protection against vulnerability to the need for love: "And if they had removed a few testicles into the bargain, I wouldn't have objected" (MOL, 35). In this context, the supreme desire is to identify with the process of disintegration, so that the only need remaining concerns more disintegration: "[T]he most you can hope is to be a little less, in the end, the creature you were in the beginning, and the middle" (MOL, 32). Here the ultimate fulfillment is loss of desire for it: "where provisions are dwindling but not so fast as appetite" (HOW, 132). As formulated in *Watt,* the cardinal desideratum is "the need never to need" (W, 202) in order, as *The Unnamable* says, to "feel nothing, know nothing" (W, 202; UN, 307). Only in this state of abandonment does the Beckettian mentality feel safely at home.

# 1

# The Beckettian Mimesis of Pain

In his study of Beckett, Leslie Hill complains that "the critical response to the task of interpreting Beckett's work has been, to a large degree, bland and unconvincing" (1990, x). Whether or not Hill's assessment is correct, criticism of Beckett's work is characterized by a pronounced tendency toward abstraction, such that character is often construed as the mere site of subjectivity that, in turn, is analyzed not as mimetic (representative of individually lived experience) but *meta*mimetic or transcendental (expressive of basic structures common or fundamental to all subjectivity, wherever instantiated).[1] These structures are themselves construed in various ways, including the (a) psychological, (b) linguistic, and (c) philosophical, with the last category splintering into many variants, such as the Cartesian, the Husserlian, and the Heideggerean.[2] Poststructuralist abstractive

---

1. According to Ruby Cohn, "The Unnamable seeks himself, and by extension the essence of all selfhood" (1973, 108). Livio Dobrez construes the Unnamable as "the eternal fretting of consciousness" (1973, 221). To Paul Foster, "Beckett suggests that the nature of 'I' is ineffable" (1989, 211). With reference to the Unnamable, Wolfgang Iser argues that "the self can only experience its own reality through an unending sequence of unintegrated and unintegratable images" (1974, 175). David Hesla insists that the Unnamable epitomizes the subject-object duality of introspection: "It is impossible . . . that I should speak of 'I', for I can speak only of 'me' " (1971, 118).

2. (a) Psychological: On the relation of Beckett's work to Freud, see O'Hara (1992, 47–63). On repetition compulsion, see Meche (1995) and Baker (1997,

readings are also prominent, focusing on what Daniel Katz refers to as the "deconstruction" of "the metaphysical subject," and what Anthony Uhlmann terms the undermining of "the Platonic order of representation from within, by arguing that the very concept of imitation/representation is infected with the same kind of ambivalence or indeterminacy found in other terms" (Katz 1999, 192; Uhlmann 1999, 7).

Yet, the critical emphasis on abstraction collides with the recurrent textual emphasis on *pain*—perhaps the most private of all experiences and hence the one that most resists abstraction. A short list of examples includes (a) the narrator's concern for the suffering of a boiling lobster in "Dante and the Lobster" (MPTK, 23); (b) the Unnamable's query, "What makes me weep so?" (UN, 293); (c) the narrator of "From an Abandoned Work" complaining of "feeling awful" (FAAW, 39); Watt's "tears of mental fatigue" (W, 88); (e) the desperate panting of the narrator lurching across the mud in *How It Is* (HOW, passim); (f) the suffering of Estragon who "hurts his foot" when kicking Lucky in *Waiting for Godot* (WFG, 56); (g) Molloy's reference to "senseless, speechless, issueless misery" (MOL, 13); (h) Macmann's sense of "punishment" while "[i]ncommoded by the rain" in *Malone Dies* (MAL, 239); and (i) Hamm's bleeding heart in *Endgame*: "There's something dripping in my head. A heart, a heart in my head" (END, 18). But the most methodical reference to pain in the Beckettian canon occurs in *First Love*, where the narrator provides a partial inventory of all the ills that flesh is heir to, "beginning

128–44). (b) Linguistic: For a Lacanian linguistic interpretation of the Unnamable's introspection, see Cousineau (1979, 2): "[L]anguage allows a corrupt culture to seduce the individual with a distorted conception of himself." For analysis of verbal patterns, see Dearlove (1982, 61–74), Moorjani (1982, 56–60), and Morot-Sir (1984, 225–39). (c) Philosophical: For Cartesian readings, see note 3 below. For a Heideggerean reading of *The Unnamable*, see Thiher (1983, 82). For an application of Husserl to Beckett's *Company*, see Locatelli (1990, 162–66). For an application of the Husserlian device of "bracketting" to Beckett's fiction, see Butler (1984, 78). Regarding Derrida's critique of Husserl, see Trezise (1990, 10–13) and Uhlmann (1999, 166–69).

with the hair and scalp and moving methodically down, without haste, all the way down to the feet beloved of the corn, the cramp, the kibe, the bunion, the hammer toe, the nail ingrown, the fallen arch, the common blain, the club foot, duck foot, goose foot, pigeon foot, flat foot, trench foot and other curiosities'" (FL, 20). Similarly, Molloy offers an inventory of afflictions, emphasizing malfunctions of the genito-urinary tract (MOL, 81), while Malone cites "the furies and frenzies happily too numerous to be numbered of the body including the skull and its annexes, whatever that means, such as the club foot" (MAL, 242–43).

As Max Scheler has argued, pain—or, more generally, sensory feeling—resists abstraction because of its involvement in the immediacy of experience, localized in a concrete body: "Its only mode of being is that of its time and place *on* the body" (Scheler 1967, 23). But pain in the Beckettian canon is never merely physical, even when it concerns physical pain. Instead, pain is intermingled with mind, for the mind seeks to understand suffering: "imagining I had grasped at last the true nature of absurd tribulations" (MAL, 224). Yet, the effort to understand pain only compounds distress in ways that we shall now examine.

## Five Levels of Paradox in the Beckettian Mimesis of Pain

A series of paradoxes unfolds at this point. Inability to understand increases pain, but understanding of pain can be achieved only when the pain concerned reaches sufficient intensity: "I'm not suffering enough yet . . . not suffering enough to be able . . . to understand" (UN, 412). Yet, while the only way to understand pain is to increase its intensity, the prime factor increasing its intensity is the inability to understand: "strange pain" (UN, 414) suffered "in obedience to the unintelligible terms of an incomprehensible damnation" (UN, 308). Hence, though pain must increase in order to be understood, the more it increases, the less meaning it has—and the less relevant it becomes to its victim: "The tears stream down my cheeks from my unblinking eyes. What makes me weep so?" (UN, 293). In other words, the more pain intensifies, the less personal content it retains, until it becomes the abstraction of suffering—that is, pain abstracted from the subject suffering it: "All is inexplicable, space and time, false and inexplicable, suffering and tears, and even the old convulsive cry, It's not me, it can't be me" (TFN, 113). But pain abstracted from its subject negates the very foundation of pain: "But am I in pain, whether it's me or not, frankly now, is there pain?" (TFN, 113). Conversely, to suffer pain abstracted from its subject is to lose one's identity: "Nothing to do but stretch out comfortably on the rack, in the blissful knowledge that you are nobody for the rest of eternity" (UN, 338). Thus, in the Beckettian mimesis of pain—to transpose the extraordinarily apt comment of Paul Ricoeur on Kierkegaard—"[T]he intimacy of the most individual confession coincides with the generality of the barest abstraction" (Ricoeur 1978, 79).

The paradoxical coincidence of individuality and generality in the Beckettian mimesis of pain can be viewed on a different level—one that invokes what the Oxford philosophers of ordinary language term *incorrigibility*, or the impossibility of verifying the accuracy of statements concerning the private object (sensations, feelings, or thoughts of which inwardness is aware). Ludwig Wittgenstein epitomizes this problem of verification through an example: "Always get rid of the idea of the private object in this way: assume that it constantly changes, but that you do not notice the change because your memory constantly deceives you" (1958, 207e). In this context, there can be no genuine knowledge of the private object (e.g., pain) because there is no criterion by which truth and falsehood, accuracy and error regarding it can be distinguished. Since first-person statements regarding private objects cannot be validated by any objectively reliable principle of verification, they cannot be evaluated in terms of correctness (Malcolm 1966, 101). Hence, first-person pain statements are *incorrigible*.[3]

The *locus classicus* regarding the problem of incorrigibility in the Beckettian mimesis of pain concerns Moran's leg: "My leg was no better, but it was no worse either. That is to say it was perhaps a little

---

3. For a more detailed discussion of incorrigibility (in the context of *Hamlet*), see E. Levy (1999, 712–14).

worse, without my being in a condition to realize it, for the simple reason that this leg was becoming a habit, mercifully" (MOL, 147). Here Moran himself acknowledges the impossibility of verifying his own pain sensations. But in the Beckettian universe, the problem of incorrigibility involves not merely the impossibility of verifying the accuracy of private-object statements but also the impossibility of verifying the distinction between private objects and public objects: the distinction between what is internal to the subject and what is external. Molloy's encounter with the sheep will introduce this difficulty. "The bleating grew faint, because the sheep were less anxious, or because they were further way, or because my hearing was worse than a moment before" (MOL, 29). In this instance, it is impossible to determine whether the factor responsible for a change in auditory sensation is internal or external. In *The Unnamable,* the distinction between internal and external objects (private and public) becomes meaningless and is no more than vestigial: "For the visibility, unless it be the state of my eyesight, only permits me to see what is close beside me" (UN, 297). The ultimate formulation of this predicament concerns the impossibility of determining whether vision is objectively or subjectively oriented: "I sometimes wonder if the two retinae are not facing each other" (UN, 301). In these circumstances, incorrigibility ensures "the *absurdity* of . . . verification" (MOL, 142; my emphasis).

Thus, Beckettian mimesis compounds the problem of incorrigibility. On the one hand, incorrigibility concerns the impossibility of verifying statements about experience. But on the other hand, experience itself ultimately concerns incorrigibility or the unavailability of distinctions between accuracy and error: "Let it be assumed then that I am at rest, though this is unimportant, at rest or forever moving, through the air or in contact with other surfaces, or that I sometimes move, sometimes rest, since I feel nothing, neither quietude nor change, *nothing that can serve as a point of departure towards an opinion on this subject*" (UN, 306–7; my emphasis).

At this level of uncertainty, pain can be neither verified nor even suffered: "labyrinthine torment that can't be grasped, or limited, or felt, or suffered, no, not even suffered" (UN, 314). Here pain cannot be suffered because experience concerns not an awareness sustained or undergone by a subject, but an awareness deprived of a subject: "I seem to speak, it is not I, about me, it is not about me" (UN, 291). Awareness is deprived of a subject because the possibility of distinguishing between what in experience pertains exclusively to a subject and what pertains to the world it inhabits or occupies no longer applies. Hence, in this context, the inability to suffer is paradoxically the cause of pain.

We have considered two aspects of the coincidence of individuality and generality in the Beckettian mimesis of pain, pertaining respectively to (a) the abstraction of pain from its subject, and (b) the problem of incorrigibility. In the first, pain is divested of personal reference; in the second, pain ultimately entails the inability to suffer as a subject who can distinguish inner from outer experience. We can now address a third aspect: one concerning the reciprocals of Beckettian narration. On the one hand, the narrator refers to himself as the source of the voices with which his "creatures" (UN, 371) speak: "I think Murphy spoke now and then, the others too perhaps, I don't remember, but it was clumsily done, you could see the ventriloquist" (UN, 348). On the other hand, the narrator construes his experience as the echoing of a voice that is not his: "I say it as I hear it" (HOW, 7).

Here individuality is generalized or depersonalized from opposite directions. Individuality is construed from one direction as depersonalizing invention, designed to enable its creator to achieve "the alleviations of flight from self" (UN, 367): "I thought I was right in enlisting these sufferers of my pains. I was wrong. They never suffered my pains, their pains are nothing, compared to mine, a mere tittle of mine" (UN, 303–4). From the opposite direction, however, it is construed as the impersonal repetition of first-person statements that are not the speaker's own: "[I]t's not I" (UN, 407). But this predicament constitutes the Beckettian mimesis of "impossible sorrow" (UN, 393)—a category of suffering expressed nowhere else in literature. To understand this aspect of the Beckettian mimesis of pain, we must first clarify its reciprocal poles: identifying as an originary "ventriloquist" (UN, 348) manipulating "mannikins" (UN, 306) versus identifying as the echo or "parrot" (UN, 335) of a voice not one's own.

Here individual existence unfolds with no distinction between the reciprocal modalities proper to it: "action" and "passion" (UN, 228). That is, the distinction between agency (that which moves itself), and response (that which is moved by something else) is meaningless. The only action is speaking of "futility" (UN, 389). The only reaction is listening to "all this babble" (UN, 348) or "flow of inanity" (UN, 352), which provokes the futile effort to understand: "trying to cease and never ceasing, seeking the cause, the cause of talking and never ceasing, finding the cause, losing it again, finding it again, not finding it gain, seeking no longer, seeking again, finding again, losing again, finding nothing, finding at last, losing again, talking without ceasing . . . wondering what it's all about, seeking what it can be you are seeking" (UN, 385).

The passage just quoted is remarkable for its ambiguity concerning the task of seeking "the cause of talking and never ceasing." The task can be interpreted to refer to the *listening* or reactive mode of awareness, vainly trying to understand what it hears. But the task equally pertains to the *speaking* or active mode of awareness, trying vainly to determine the reason for its act of expression. This ambiguity is compactly formulated in *Texts for Nothing*: "one who speaks saying, without ceasing to speak, Who's speaking?, and one who hears, mute, uncomprehending, far from all" (134). In this context, action and response (agency and passion) coincide, for to speak is to enable listening: "If I were silent I'd hear nothing" (TFN, 111). And to listen is to repeat the content of speech: "Hearing too little to be able to speak, that's my silence" (UN, 393). But action and response are also respectively self-negating. To act (here, to speak) is to problematize the very meaning of agency: "what am I doing, I must find out what I'm doing" (UN, 387). To be passive (here, to listen) is to undertake the futile action of trying to understand: "I hear, to understand, not that I ever understand" (UN, 393). In this predicament or "state of affairs" (UN, 386), individuality is no more than the membrane or "partition" between contrary poles: "I'm neither one side nor the other" (UN, 383). In alternate formulation, it is both poles at once and neither in isolation.

Paradoxically, this "supreme aberration" (UN, 385) constitutes the Beckettian "paradigm of human kind" (TFN, 108), and hence another level on which individuality and generality coincide in the Beckettian mimesis of pain. On all three levels that we have investigated, pain is associated with the deconstruction of the subject suffering it. On the first level, pain is associated with *unintelligibility,* with the result that the more intense it grows, the less relevant to the sufferer it becomes, until to suffer is to be separated from one's own identity. On the second level, pain is associated with *incorrigibility,* with the result that its registration entails problematizing not only its own presence but also the possibility of distinguishing between what pertains exclusively to the subject and to the world occupied by the subject. On the third level, pain is associated with *reciprocity* or, more precisely, with the confusion of the reciprocal poles of existence: action and passion (here, speaking and listening).

The coincidence of individuality and generality in the Beckettian mimesis of pain can be examined on a fourth level. This stratum concerns the need to assuage inward pain through outward expression. Brief explication of relevant Thomistic doctrine will facilitate analysis. Aquinas is directly quoted in *Malone Dies* (MAL, 218): *nihil in intellectu.* This is a fragmentary citation of the Thomistic formula regarding the primacy of sense data (phantasms) in the acquisition of knowledge—a doctrine opposed to "innate knowledge" (UN, 297): *nihil in intellectu quod prius non fuerit in sensu (Summa Theologica,* 1, Q84, A7). But the Thomistic doctrine entrained by the Beckettian mimesis of pain concerns the relation not between sense and intellect, but between pain and the need to relieve it. According to this doctrine, inward pain seeks relief through outward expression. Without such release, inward pain intensifies:

> Tears and groans naturally assuage sorrow . . . because a hurtful thing hurts yet more if we keep it shut up, because the soul is more

intent on it; but if it be allowed to escape, the soul's intention is dispersed as it were on outward things, so that the inward sorrow is lessened. This is why *when men, burdened with sorrow, make outward show of their sorrow, by tears or groans or even by words, their sorrow is assuaged. (Summa Theologica,* 1–2, Q38, A2, resp.; my emphasis)

In the Beckettian mimesis of pain, the relation between inward pain and its outward expression is reversed. Instead of relieving pain, the outward expression of suffering only increases it. The Unnamable frequently refers to his tears: "The tears stream down my cheeks from my unblinking eyes" (UN, 293). Yet instead of affording relief, they slide uselessly "down along the neck" (UN, 394–95). But the predicament is worse than this. For the tears that express pain are also associated with words: "[M]y words are my tears" (TFN, 111). Yet words both express and *cause* pain. The "muted lamentation" of "impossible sorrow" (UN, 393) necessitates the excruciating task of listening to and repeating the pain: "I say them as I hear them murmur them in the mud" (HOW, 7).

This predicament, where suffering is engendered and perpetuated by the universal reflex to relieve pain through its outward expression, leads us to the fifth level of the coincidence of individuality and generality in the Beckettian mimesis of pain. Here individual pain is construed as the result of universal punishment: "I was given a pensum, at birth perhaps, as a punishment for having been born perhaps" (UN, 310). This notion of birth as original sin is derived from Pedro Calderon de la Barca, whose idea of "the sin of having been born" is quoted in Spanish in *Proust* (P, 67). Beckett's application of this idea involves a paradox. Pain signifies punishment, but punishment signifies innocence. The sufferer is not responsible for his own parturition: "[I]t's nobody's fault, what's nobody's fault, this state of affairs" (UN, 386). Hence, through punishment for sin, the sufferer remains innocent: "But whom can I have offended so grievously, to be punished in this inexplicable way[?]" (TFN, 113). Thus, the coincidence of individuality and generality in the Beckettian mimesis of pain here concerns the displacement of individual guilt by "innocence" (UN, 403) through the universal implication of all individual human life in antecedent birth.

## The Relation Between Thought and Pain

Having carefully excavated five superimposed strata in the Beckettian mimesis of pain, we can now proceed to analyze the factor responsible for the suffering that this mimesis concerns. The first step in this enterprise is to recognize that the suffering represented is self-inflicted: "[I]t's I who do this thing and I who suffer it" (UN, 402). More precisely, the suffering derives from a mentality or way of thinking. The relation between thought and pain can be clarified by another aspect of the Thomistic paradigm, one that distinguishes between two kinds of pain: outward and inward. Outward pain is sensory; inward pain (also termed *sorrow*) is mental: "[O]utward pain arises from an apprehension of sense, and especially of touch, while inward pain arises from an interior apprehension, of the imagination or of the reason" (*Summa Theologica*, 1–2, Q35, A7, resp.). Hence, thought (i.e., the operation of reason or imagination) is the *sine qua non* of inward pain. But insofar as thought is the cause of inward pain, the only way to alleviate that pain is to understand and then modify the mentality that causes it.

Yet far from being able to understand how thought causes pain, "experienced existence" (to appropriate F. H. Bradley's phrase) in the Beckettian universe lacks understanding or correct identification of the pain felt: "I don't know what I feel, *tell me what I feel and I'll tell you who I am*, they'll tell me who I am, I won't understand" (UN, 382–83; my emphasis; Bradley 1930, 360). As the italicized portion of this passage suggests, the "unintelligible" (UN, 308) pain to be understood concerns confusion about identity. That is, the pain derives from *thinking* about identity without the ability to achieve clarity: "the confusion of identities being merely apparent and due to my inaptitude to assume any" (UN, 330). This predicament reverses the customary relation between a feeling and the subject undergoing it.

Ordinarily, as Alfred North Whitehead explains, a feeling "is one aspect of its own subject" and cannot be construed apart from that subject: "A feeling cannot be abstracted from the actual entity entertaining it" (1978, 221). But with Beckett, the subject becomes an aspect of his feeling and can be defined only in terms of it. Whereas for Whitehead "it is in virtue of its subject that the feeling is one thing," for Beckett only in virtue of determining its feeling can the subject discover its own identity or what one thing it is (1978, 221).

It is evident now how inaccessible is the celebrated Cartesian formula "I think, therefore I am"—in the Beckettian universe. Here, instead of assuring existence of the *cogito* or thinking subject, thought provokes feeling, but feeling, through its unintelligibility, obscures or problematizes the identity of the subject to whom it belongs. Hence, in place of "I think, therefore I am," the Beckettian formula for individual existence is much more complicated: "I think therefore I feel; so 'tell me what I feel and I'll tell you who I am.' "[4]

## The Inversion of Schopenhauer

But the philosopher whom the Beckettian mimesis of pain most spectacularly controverts is neither Whitehead nor René Descartes, but Arthur Schopenhauer. It has become a convention of both literary critics and biographers to link Beckett with Schopenhauer.[5] Whereas

---

4. For discussion of the Beckettian disintegration of the relation between the Cartesian *cogito* and *cogitatum*, see chapter 6, p. 000. For the seminal treatment of the Cartesian inheritance in Beckett's fiction, see the "The Cartesian Centaur" in Kenner (1968, 117–32). For a deconstructionist rendering of the Beckettian *cogito*, see Katz: "If there is one Beckettian cogito, 'I hear, therefore, I am,'" which involves an inversion of Cartesian originary causality, there is also another that inverts the cogito's logical temporality, as many of The Unnamable's enunciations could be glossed as, 'Therefore I am, I think' " (1999, 116). Yet Katz's claim that the Beckettian cogito is never originary but always citational (i.e., repeating what is heard) is demonstrably incorrect.

5. For a recent example, see Uhlmann, who prefaces his own application of Schopenhauer to Beckett with references to two biographies: "On a number of occa-

critics often insist that Beckett transposes ideas proper to Schopenhauer, closer inspection reveals how he actually inverts them. In
Schopenhauer's pessimism, life entails inevitable pain because its
principle is the will or ceaseless striving for satisfaction. Wilheim
Windelband brilliantly summarizes: "All human life flows on contin-
ually between willing and attaining. But to will is pain, is the ache of
the 'not-yet-satisfied.' Hence *pain is the positive feeling*, and pleasure
consists only in the removal of a pain" (1958, 2:620).

Yet in *The Unnamable*, pain is caused not by movement intrinsic
to the will but by the refusal of such movement. Here the satisfaction
willed entails stasis, not dynamism: "[T]he metamorphosis is accomplished, of unchanging future into unchangeable past" (UN, 367).
By thinking obsessively on the confusion of thought, the Unnamable
perpetuates a state of immutable pain. But pain here results not from
the Schopenhauerian movement between willing and attaining, but
from the Beckettian need to resist movement: "But within, motionless, I can live, and utter me for no ears but my own" (UN, 325).
Whereas the Schopenhauerian will tends ceaselessly toward fulfillment and satisfaction, the Beckettian will tends relentlessly toward
futility and frustration: "No, one can spend one's life thus, unable to
live, unable to bring to life, and die in vain, having done nothing,
been nothing" (UN, 358). In contrast to Schopenhauer, who construes the will as "endless *striving*" (1967, 101; my emphasis), Beckett construes it as endless *lapsing*: "He goes down . . . falls . . . on
purpose or not" (CAS, 11). Unlike the Schopenhauerian will, which
strives for possession, the Beckettian will tends toward lessness, "dis-
memberment" (UN, 330), "decomposition" (UN, 322), "evacuation" (UN, 349), "supineness in the mind" (FL, 18) "exhaustion"
(MOL, 163), "backsliding" (MOL, 61), "collapse" (UN, 325), "relapse" (MAL, 195), "discouragement" (MAL, 255), and "resignation" (MOL, 149). In fact, the celebrated Beckettian tendency
toward contradiction and retraction—the plunging of "no's knife in

---

sions in Knowlson's and Cronin's biographies of Beckett, we are told of Beckett's close
attention to and admiration for Schopenhauer" (1999, 15).

yes's wound"—expresses, on the epistemological level, this self-negating will: "yes, a new no" (TFN, 139, 131).[6]

The inevitable consequence of the Beckettian will to lapse is "tedium" (MAL, 187, 217). For here tedium results from willing the "impotence" (MOL, 105; MAL, 188, 210) that can or will do nothing: "powerless to act, or perhaps strong enough at last to act no more" (MOL, 161). According to Immanuel Kant, tedium is a pain that entails "an *emptiness* of sensations" (1963, 62). As such, it is opposed to "vitality," which "aims at filling this emptiness, and even though there be no positive pain to incite activity, this pain, tedium, may so affect a man that he will feel the urge to do something damaging to himself rather than nothing at all" (1963, 62). Kant's doctrine of tedium as a pain that seeks relief by creating more pain is epitomized in Molloy's statement: "[T]he mind cannot always brood on the same cares, but needs fresh cares from time to time" (MOL, 64).

## The Import of the Beckettian Mimesis of Pain

The most unusual feature of the Beckettian mimesis of pain is that despite—or perhaps in virtue of—all its complications, pain is viewed as the preeminent means of simplification: "To be nothing but pain, how that would simplify matters!" (FL, 20). We reach now a fundamental paradox: to be a pure awareness of pain would afford simplification, but the very attempt to understand pain introduces complication. At bottom, pain and futile effort to understand it are inextricably intermingled, for pain in the Beckettian context is both the object of obsessive thought and that which derives from thought. In fact, the fundamental Beckettian project is to preoccupy thought with the futile effort to understand "unintelligible" (UN, 308) pain. By this means, the burden of individuality is relieved: "I, of whom I know nothing" (UN, 304).

The paradox of pain as simplification and the effort to under-

6. For representative discussions of retraction and denial in Beckett's art, see Uhlmann (1999, 84–90); Trezise (1990, 102n. 33); and Federman (1970, 103–17).

stand pain as complication rests on a basic ambiguity in the Beckettian mimesis of pain. On the one hand, the predicament regarding "incomprehensible" pain (UN, 308) seems to be universal and to derive from the original "sin of having been born" (UN, 67). But on the other hand, this predicament seems to be quintessentially particular and to pertain to acquired guilt about personal identity: "I was given a pensum, at birth perhaps, as a punishment for having been born perhaps, or for no particular reason, *because they dislike me,* and I've forgotten what it is" (UN, 310; my emphasis). That is, the sin of having been born can be construed as referring to either a universal condition (as in the poetry of Calderon) or a unique one, applying to a single individual who is made to feel guilty for being himself. The ambiguity remains intractable. Nevertheless, some speculation regarding it can be pursued.

Beckettian art prominently construes love as threat: "love fear of being abandoned a little of each no knowing" (HOW, 66). In *Company,* the newborn in its crib is viewed unlovingly by its parents: "No trace of love" (COM, 66). In this context, the sin of having been born clearly pertains not to a universal condition, but to a painfully specific one: *this* infant being made to feel unwanted and deserving of abandonment or banishment. The Beckettian response to this predicament is to transform *individual* identity (the site of the sin of being who one is) into *universal* identity. The transformation is accomplished or, more precisely, approximated by reducing individual identity to preoccupation with unintelligible pain. Through this incessant preoccupation, the individual is reduced to universality in virtue of recourse to rational activity: "perhaps even regret being a man under such conditions, that is to say *a head abandoned to its ancient solitary resources*" (UN, 361; my emphasis). Moreover, at the same time that the effort to understand reduces individuality to universality, the *inability* to understand drains individual identity of its individual content—the content that has made it deserving of punishment for the sin of having been born.

But in the Beckettian mimesis of pain, the sin of having been born can also, with equal intensity, enable the *assertion* of individuality, not its erasure. For example, in *Mercier and Camier*, Mercier succumbs to a paroxysm of blasphemous rage when his umbrella fails to open in a sudden rainstorm: " 'And to crown all, lifting to the sky his convulsed and streaming face, he said, As for thee, fuck thee' " (MC, 26).[7] Mercier's imprecation recalls that of the thief, Vanni Fucci, down in the seventh *bolgia* or pouch of Dante's *Inferno* (canto 25): "At the end of his words the thief raised up his hands with both the figs [obscene gesture made with thumb and first two fingers], crying, 'Take them, God, for I aim them at you!' " (1970, 1:259). A muted allusion to the same passage occurs in *Molloy*, when Moran stands under the tattered "canopy" of his umbrella: "And the long spike of my umbrella was like a finger" (MOL, 171–72). In these examples, the suffering of pain enables the vigorous expression of individuality, not its repression or displacement.

These two examples concerning rain are crucial in the Beckettian mimesis of pain. In *Malone Dies,* when Macmann lies exposed ("now supine, now prone") in a sustained downpour, rain provokes a meditation on suffering:

> And in the midst of his suffering . . . he began to wish that the rain would never cease nor consequently his sufferings or pain, for the cause of his pain was almost certainly the rain, recumbency in itself not being particularly unpleasant, *as if there existed a relation between that which suffers and that which causes to suffer.* For the rain could cease without his ceasing to suffer, just as he could cease to suffer without the rain's ceasing on that account. (MAL, 242; my emphasis)

The passage is remarkable for its deconstruction of the causal "relation between that which suffers and that which causes to suffer" in a circumstance where that relation seems incontrovertible. In this context, the cause of suffering is negated even as it is affirmed. The upshot of this paradox is that pain is rendered causeless or self-causing

---

7. For further commentary regarding the superimposition of this novel on *The Divine Comedy*, see E. Levy (1980, 39–53).

and self-originating, like the God whom Vanni Fucci and his Beckettian descendants revile. The technical term for the state of self-derivation ascribed to divinity is *aseity*.

If, like God, pain has absolute self-sufficiency and autonomy, then the wish (in *First Love*) "[t]o be nothing but pain" (FL, 20) gains deeper meaning. It now signifies not only the desire to "simplify matters," but also the desire to be without cause. To be without cause is to solve the problem of individuality. At bottom, in the Beckettian mimesis of pain, the problem of individuality is the problem of not knowing the cause of suffering. But if pain is self-causing, then it includes its own explanation, allowing thought at last to desist. Yet, the Beckettian wish "[t]o be nothing but pain" concerns the ultimate "pain-killer" (END, 71) above all other "pain-killers" (UN, 320) on another level as well. For if pain is self-causing, then to be nothing but pain is to be the cause of one's own pain, and hence, to be anesthetized to all other causes of suffering. As such, pain enables "inexistence" (TFN, 91; UN, 344; HOW, 69)—a state of "animation" (UN, 353) concerned with neither the vulnerabilities of living nor the inevitability of death: "There never was anything, never can be, life and death all nothing, that kind of thing, only a voice dreaming and droning on all round, that is something, the voice that was once in your mouth" (FAAW, 49).

The fantasy of listening uncomprehendingly to a voice whose forgotten origin is the auditor's own thought is the Beckettian simulacrum of self-causing pain: "But it is solely a question of voices, no other image is appropriate" (UN, 347). By this means, pain achieves aseity, and "experienced existence" (to retrieve Bradley's phrase) becomes "inexistence."

# 2

## The Beckettian Mimesis
## of Seeing Nothing

The aesthetic of lessness, espoused by Beckett in his seminal essay "Peintres de l'Empêchment" (Painters of Impediment), quoted in the introduction, formulates the task of the artist in terms not of originality but of reductive reformulation, repeating, as often as possible in the most reduced space, what has already been said. In mimetic terms, this aesthetic principle has two immediate consequences. First, it requires the representation of experience defined by futile repetition: "Whereas to see yourself doing the same thing endlessly over and over again fills you with satisfaction" (MOL, 133). Second, the principle dictates that each successive work by a given artist represent the same experience of futile repetition in progressively impoverished or contracted circumstances: "as if to grow less could help, ever less and less and never quite be gone" (TFN, 112). Beckettian art conforms relentlessly to its defining principle with the result that, in the last works such as "Still," reductive repetition eventually achieves a mimetic spareness almost beyond expression: "Or anywhere any ope staring out at nothing just failing light quite still till quite dark though of course no such thing just less light still, when less did not seem possible" (S, 20).[1]

The mimetic reduction in the passage just quoted, where exis-

1. For a study of Beckett's aesthetic of minimalism, see Brater (1987). For comment on the "progressive shrinking of scale" in Beckettian art, see Knowlson and Pilling (1980, 103). For reference to "the movement toward simplicity," see Gontarski (1985, 3). For comment on Beckett's "regressive reduction," see Amiran (1993, 13).

tence concerns "staring out at nothing," is the quintessential Beckettian experience. Celebrated analogues include (a) Murphy's vision of Nothing: "Murphy began to see nothing, that colourlessness which is such a postnatal treat, being the absence . . . not of *percipere* but of *percipi*" (MUR, 246); (b) Watt's nocturnal vigil in the train station: "There was now no longer a dark part and a less dark part, no, but all now was uniformly dark, and remained so, for some time" (W, 225); (c) the Unnamable's eyes that "must remain forever fixed and staring on the narrow space before them where there is nothing to be seen, 99 percent of the time" (UN, 301); (d) the narrator of *Texts For Nothing* "begging in another dark, another silence, for another alm, that of being or of ceasing, better still, before having been" (TFN, 115); (e) Hamm's prediction in *Endgame*: "You'll be sitting there, a speck in the void, in the dark, for ever, like me" (END, 36); (f) Krapp, at the end of *Krapp's Last Tape*, "motionless staring before him" (KLT, 28); (g) Mr. Slocum in *All That Fall*: "Gazing straight before me, Mrs. Rooney, through the windscreen, into the void" (ATF, 47); (h) the narrator in *Company* describing the experience of "one on his back in the dark" (COM, 7); (i) the narrator of "He is barehead" describing one "staring before him, and even all about him, hour after hour, day after day, and never seeing a thing" (HIB, 26); and (j) Winnie's anxiety, in *Happy Days*, about her plight should Willie ever depart: "Simply gaze before me with compressed lips. *(Long pause while she does so. No more plucking.)* Not another word as long as I drew breath, nothing to break the silence of this place. *(Pause.)* Save possibly, now and then, every now and then, a sigh into my looking-glass" (HD, 21).

As the last phrase ("a sigh into my looking-glass") of Winnie's utterance suggests, a mirror relation obtains in Beckettian mimesis between apprehending the void and self-preoccupation. The relation is similarly emphasized by the Unnamable, who associates gazing at the void with obsessive introspection: "I sometimes wonder if the two retinae are not facing each other" (UN, 301). That is, the external void is ultimately a reflection of inner emptiness. The difficulty of distinguishing outer from inner recurs in "Horn Came Always": "It is in outer space, not to be confused with the other, that such images develop" (HCA, 34).[2] A cognate example occurs in *Texts for Nothing*, where the distinction between reality and reflection is no longer relevant, for the same vacancy applies equally to each: "in the eyes of a mute, an idiot, who doesn't understand, never understood, who stares at himself in a glass, stares before him in the desert, sighing yes, sighing no, on and off" (TFN, 117).

In these examples, *seeing nothing* is associated with a subject (or, in the case of the Unnamable, a quasi-subject) gazing at the void whose emptiness is ultimately a reflection of his or her own emptiness, construed in turn as the refusal to attend to anything but interior distress: "I who had learnt to think of nothing, nothing except my pains" (FL, 22). But in *Texts for Nothing*, the mirror relation between *seeing nothing* and self-preoccupation is sometimes reversed. There, *seeing nothing* is occasionally associated not with the subject, but with his reflection, for the reflected image that a subject contemplates in a mirror cannot itself see: "I must have been twelve, because of the glass, a round shaving-glass, double-faced, faithful and magnifying, staring into one of the others, the true ones, true then, and seeing me there, imagining I saw me there, lurking behind the bluey veils, *staring back sightlessly,* at the age of twelve, because of the glass, on its pivot" (TFN, 103; my emphasis).

This transposition of *seeing nothing* from the subject to its reflection epitomizes the mimetic project of reductive repetition that Beckettian art pursues. That is, the recurrent motif of seeing nothing or "staring out at nothing" not only signifies perception of the outer void and, by extension, perception of inner emptiness, but also assimilates the staring subject to the status of a reflection, "staring back sightlessly" from the mirror it inhabits.[3] As this crucial point can eas-

2. Compare with Moorjani: "Beckett's novels from *Watt* onward . . . undermine the classic project of the novel to mirror outer and inner reality, the fiction of transparency" (1982, 45).

3. The most recurrent critical approach to the motif of nothing in Beckettian art emphasizes Sartre's notion of nothingness. See Butler (1984, 74–113); Hesla (1971,

ily be misunderstood, further clarification is necessary. By definition, the reflection in a mirror is identified with the subject it reflects. By identifying the reflection as its own, the subject confirms a self-image. But the situation obtaining in Beckettian mimesis is not the same as the paradigm just described. For instead of identifying the reflection as its own, here the subject approximates the condition of its own reflection. That is, the subject paradoxically seeks to exchange its own identity for that of its reflection. In other words, the subjective project is to become one's own reflection, and to be freed from the strains of identity or selfhood outside of the mirror.[4]

The most explicit formulation of this project occurs in "The Calmative," where the narrator expresses the aim to shatter the unity of his physical identity into a universe of fragmentary reflections: "[T]his old body to which nothing ever happened, or so little, which never met with anything, loved anything, wished for anything, in its tarnished universe, except for mirrors to shatter, the plane, the curved, the magnifying, and to vanish in the havoc of its images" (CAL, 30; my emphasis).

A related formulation occurs in *Texts for Nothing*, where the narrator represents his "hero" as existing "under glass"—that is, as a reflection in a reflected world that imposes "no limit to his movements

---

184–92); Cohn (1973, 111). Alan Astro associates "nothing" with "[t]he meaninglessness of life" (1990, 119). Stephen Barker links it with both the Freudian unconscious and the Heideggerian negation of the totality of beings" (1996, 125–56). John Leeland Kundert-Gibbs relates the Beckettian notion of nothing to Zen Buddhism for which "the Void" (*Mu*), or emptiness (or *Sunya* in Sanskrit), is a 'maelstrom,' or chaos around our puny constructed order, but this maelstrom is at the heart a 'source'—the source, in fact, of the universe" (1999, 19). A broad spectrum of critics link Beckettian Nothing with varieties of chaos theory. Uhlmann invokes the chaos theory of Deleuze and Guattari (1999, 21). John Pilling provides a serviceable account of Beckett's debt to Democritus (1976, 124). Regarding applications of the chaos theory of James Gliek, see Meriwether (1994, 95–108), and S. Levy (1996, 81–95). More conventional discussions of chaos are developed by Dearlove (1982) and Federman (1965).

4. For a differently oriented study of the mirror motif, see E. Levy (1982, 95–104).

in all directions," but that remains just a reflection sustained by the surface of a mirror: "Between them [i.e., "the sky and earth"] where the hero stands a great gulf is fixed, while all about they flow together more and more, till they meet, so that he finds himself as it were under glass, and yet with no limit to his movements in all directions, let him understand who can, that is no part of my attributions" (TFN, 97).

The prototype in Beckettian art for the identification of the subject with its reflection occurs in *Watt*, when the narrator, Sam, does a mirror dance with *Watt*: "Then I took a single pace forward, with my left leg, and he a single pace back, with his right leg (he could scarcely do otherwise). Then I took a double pace forward with my right leg, and he of course with his left leg a double pace back. And so we paced together between the fences" (W, 63).[5]

A more complex example occurs in *Molloy*, when Moran, like a decrepit Narcissus, beholds his "reflection" (MOL, 145) in a pool and, as an immediate result, acknowledges his "growing resignation to being dispossessed of self" (MOL, 149): "And then I saw a little globe swaying up from the depths, through the quiet water, smooth at first, and scarcely paler than its escorting ripples, then little by little a face, with holes for the eyes and mouth and other wounds, and *nothing to show if it was a man's face or a woman's face, a young face or an old face*, or if its calm too was not an effect of the water trembling between it and the light" (MOL, 148–49; my emphasis).

Here two kinds of identity oppose each other. On one side is conventional identity—or its remnant—defined in terms of unique individuality: This is the one and only Moran, distinct from all that is not Moran. On the other side is the reflection with no individual identity at all, but instead only a "global" ("I saw a little globe") or abstract general identity, displaying attributes common to all human faces insofar as they are identifiable as human faces, yet without any *individualizing* characteristics. Hence, this global face is no one's

---

5. For discussions of inversions involved in the mirror imagery in *Watt*, see Katz (1999, 51) and Ramsay (1985, 31–34).

face. That is, to identify with that face, as an individual ordinarily identifies with his or her reflection, is to identify not as an individual but as a type or species. Paradoxically, therefore, Moran's encounter with his reflection entails not affirmation of personal and particular identity, but loss of it. But in losing personal identity, Moran gains "a sharper and clearer sense of [his] identity than ever before, in spite of its deep lesions and the wounds with which it was covered" (MOL, 170).

This deepened sense of identity no longer concerns identity in the Aristotelian-Thomist sense as "in itself undivided, but . . . distinct from others" *(Summa Theologica,* 1, Q29, A4, resp.). That is, identity is now defined in terms not of unique and distinct *individuality* but of a *universality* in which all particularizing distinctions have been obliterated. Here, all that remains of identity is its "humanity" (UN, 325). And all that remains to *signify* humanity are wounds: "a face, with holes for the eyes and mouth and other wounds." Thus, in Beckettian mimesis, identity concerns not individuality per se but the universality of the pain ("wounds") caused by the need to have an identity. This pain is construed in reciprocal ways. On the one hand, it derives from the need to retrieve identity that has already been lost: "All I can say is for my part is that for me they are not what they were when I was young and . . . foolish and . . . (Faltering, head down) . . . beautiful . . . possibly . . . lovely . . . in a way . . . to look at. (Pause. Head up.) Forgive me, Willie, sorrow keeps breaking in" (HD, 34). On the other hand, the pain derives from the need to gain an identity that can never be achieved but at best "asymptotically approach[ed]" (MOL, 149) in the future: "[I]t will be I" (UN, 414).

This opposition between two kinds of pain—one arising from the loss of identity in the past, the other from the "inaptitude" (UN, 330) to assume an identity in the future—constitutes another version of the mirror motif. For here the divestiture of identity in the past is reflected as the groping toward identity in the future. Preoccupation with movement toward the future becomes a reflection of preoccupation with movement toward the past because the same awareness of divestiture of identity pertains to both. In alternate formulation, that which remains unvarying in movement toward the future reflects or duplicates that which remains unvarying in movement toward the past: "[T]he metamorphosis is accomplished, of unchanging future into unchangeable past" (UN, 367). In Beckettian mimesis, movement toward the future entails loss of the identity that pertained to the past: "aged out of recognition" (HOW, 107). But the pain entailed in this loss of identity caused by movement toward the future and away from the past can be neutralized by identifying not through the identity that has been lost (as in the mode of "regretting" [UN, 371]), but through the identity that cannot yet be found: "[I]t's not my turn to know what, to know what I am, where I am, and what I should do to stop being it" (UN, 412).

On the level now under consideration, Beckettian mimesis treats the same awareness of emptiness in reciprocal modes in order to void identity of the pain of its own emptiness. One experience of emptiness (regret) is exchanged for another (indeterminacy). But the project can succeed only at the cost of converting memory of the past into loss of the sense of temporal continuity. Beckettian art abounds in examples of temporal discontinuity. Of these, a first category concerns simple erasure of the past: (a) "All that goes before forget" (E, 53); (b) "I'll never have a past never had" (HOW, 54); (c) "Where now? Who now? When now?" (UN, 291); (d) "As to the events that led up to my fainting and to which I can hardly have been oblivious at the time, they have left no discernible trace, on my mind" (MAL, 183). A second category of temporal discontinuity concerns sudden change that renders the past irrelevant: "Then one day, suddenly, it ends, it changes, I don't understand, it dies, or it's me, I don't understand, that either" (END, 83). A third category appears in contrary versions, each nullifying the distinction between past and present. The first version reduces temporality to "one enormous second" (TFN, 82) that sustains indefinitely the same unchanging duration. The second version reduces temporality to one fleeting second, too brief for continuity to have any meaning: "[O]ne day we were born, one day we shall die, the same day, the same second, is that not enough for you?" (WFG, 57).

In Beckettian mimesis, life is reduced to a reflection of its own vacuity. More precisely, life is represented in terms of the excruciating pointlessness of its own relentless continuation: "one can't go on one can't stop put a stop" (HOW, 90). But this reflection of life depends on the mimetic means producing it. That is, just as in reality the existence of a reflection presupposes the existence of a mirror, so in the world of art the mode of reflecting or representing life presupposes an interpretive perspective on life. Beckettian art not only foregrounds this interpretive perspective but also insists on its unique authority: "[F]rom this point of view but there is no other" (IDI, 65). Yet at the same time as the unique authority of this perspective is asserted, it is also satirized, as when the idiot, whom we encountered earlier in *Texts for Nothing*, "stares at himself in a glass" without comprehending. Here the perspective reflected *in* the mirror is one that cannot distinguish between reflection and the reality reflected. The same limitation operates in Beckettian art, which undertakes to reflect or represent life from a perspective defined in terms of what it omits, excludes, or refuses to see: "Islands, waters, azure, verdure, one glimpse and vanished, endlessly, *omit*" (IDI, 63; my emphasis). In this context, Andrew Renton refers to the "deliberate impulse towards exclusion" in Beckettian art (1994, 173).

At bottom, the preoccupation in Beckettian mimesis with seeing nothing derives from a mentality that cannot bear loss and would rather have nothing forever than have something and risk losing it: "I shall lose nothing more see nothing more" (HOW, 35). Here, loss, in all its modes, becomes the habitual state and inalienable possession: "Loss of spirits . . . lack of keenness . . . want of appetite" (HD, 13; ellipsis in original). Indeed, on moving into a room adjacent to his lover, the first action of the narrator in "First Love" is to rid the room of all furniture: "I began putting out the furniture through the door to the corridor" (FL, 29). Similarly, no sooner does he confirm his love than it begins to dissipate: "Already my love was waning, that was all that mattered" (FL, 30).

The mimesis of loss also informs the celebrated Beckettian narrative device of echolalia, wherein the narrator compulsively repeats what he hears: "[S]o many words so many lost one every three two every five first the sound then the sense same ratio or else not one not one lost I hear all understand all" (HOW, 95). In this predicament, there is no criterion by which to distinguish between (a) losing (or not hearing) the words to be repeated, and (b) accurately repeating all. Hence, the contraries of loss and retention coincide, and to repeat what is heard is to express its loss. As the Unnamable says of the voice he echoes, "[I]t is truly at a loss" (UN, 411). A related coincidence of contraries in Beckettian art concerns the opposition between plethora and paucity. Whereas the Unnamable's suffering stems from a superabundance of words, Winnie's plight concerns the fear that her limited stock of words and her limited number of things to do will run out: "Ah yes, so little to say, so little to do, and the fear so great, certain days, of finding oneself . . . left, with hours still to run, before the bell for sleep, and nothing more to say, nothing more to do, that the days go by, certain days go by, quite by, the bell goes, and little or nothing said, little or nothing done" (HD, 35; ellipsis in original). The longer Winnie goes on, the more she dreads the inevitability of stopping. The longer the Unnamable yearns to stop, the more he suffers the obligation to persevere.

As we have noted, Beckettian mimesis represents different modes of seeing nothing: (a) seeing nothing outside: the void; (b) seeing nothing inside: the sense of deprivation, regret, and sorrow; (c) identifying as the "sightless" reflection in the mirror; (d) not seeing individual identity but instead assuming a universal one; (e) not seeing past identity but endlessly seeking a future one; (f) not seeing temporal continuity; (g) problematizing the distinctions between loss and retention, plethora and paucity, and continuation and closure. Underlying these multiple modes of representation is a fundamental ambiguity regarding the consequence of seeing nothing. In one interpretation, seeing nothing involves "the *positive peace* that comes when something gives way, or perhaps simply adds up, to the Nothing, than which in the guffaw of the Abderite naught is more real" (MUR, 246; my emphasis).[6] In the contrary interpretation, seeing nothing involves "deep trouble for the mind" at the spectacle of emptiness or "wilderness" (HD, 51, 50). That negative perturbation can, in turn, be expressed through either pointless endurance ("Woburn . . . hang on . . . don't let go" [CAS, 17; ellipsis in original]) or equally pointless capitulation: "[W]eary to death one is almost resigned to—I was going to say to the immortality of the soul" (MAL, 229).

The ambiguity of "seeing nothing" has profound moral implications. As F. H. Bradley has noted, "[M]orality implies that there 'is not only *something to be done,* but something to be done by me' " (1951, 10; my emphasis). But in Beckettian art, as a result of the primacy of seeing nothing, the moral notion of "something to be done" collides with that of "Nothing to be done" (WFG, 7). Whereas in *Murphy,* Nothing is construed in positive terms as the supreme reality, elsewhere in the Beckettian canon "nothing" (in the lower case) is construed in negative terms as the irrelevance of reality: "No, no souls, or bodies, or birth, or life, or death, you've got to go on without any of that junk" (TFN, 125). All that remains is absence ("Absent, always. It all happened without me" [END, 74])—a state where subjectivity is "[b]uried in who knows what profounds of mind" (OI, 18), and objectivity is inaccessible: "[T]he subject falls from the verb, and the object lands somewhere in the void" (MAL, 234).

The opposition between the two kinds of nothing—positive and negative—represented by Beckettian mimesis remains intractable.[7] But some attempt at its explication can be undertaken. A useful tool in this enterprise is provided by Winnie in *Happy Days.* On many occasions, when deploying terms that no longer apply to her contemporary experience, she uses the phrase "to speak in the old style." For example, in her present mode of interminable existence, death is no

---

6. For comment on "positive nothingness," see Buttner (1984, 30n. 57).

7. Compare with Uhlmann: "Derrida's deconstruction . . . affirms the importance of ambivalence, of the relation between terms rather than the choice of one term over another" (1999, 7).

longer an eventuality: "What if you were to die—*(smile)*—to speak in the old style. . . ?" (HD, 21). Perhaps a similar distinction between former and current reality applies to the Beckettian mimesis of seeing nothing. In one phase, or on one level, seeing nothing entails or offers a quasi-mystical subsumption of awareness in a universal reality that is the "absence" (MUR, 246) of reality. But in another phase or on another level, seeing nothing entails or offers the withdrawal of awareness from concern with presence in any of its modes: "I am the absentee again . . . who has neither body nor soul" (UN, 413). The distinction can be further clarified. In one mode, seeing nothing refers to the absence *of* reality and can be construed in the deconstructive sense as the erasure of "the metaphysics of the logos, of presence and consciousness" (Derrida 1976, 73). In the other mode, seeing nothing refers to absence *from* reality and can be construed as the Beckettian equivalent to salvation: "the blessedness of absence" (MAL, 222).

Though the tension between these contrary modes of seeing nothing cannot be removed, it can certainly be reduced. References in the Beckettian canon to the absence *from* reality quantitatively overwhelm those to the absence *of* reality. Additional inquiry will further minimize this opposition. In Beckettian mimesis, presence is a mandatory condition of life: "What counts is to be in the world, the posture is immaterial, so long as one is on earth. To breathe is all that is required" (TFN, 93).

In this context, absence *from* reality is the only way to exist immune to "the crass tenacity of life and its diligent pains" (MAL, 216). But absence *from* reality implies more than merely insulation from a hostile element. At bottom, it permits communication with the deepest principle of inwardness in Beckettian mimesis—a principle founded on inaccessible withdrawal and "unmakable being" (TFN, 140). The only approach to this principle is absence, construed as "the relapse to darkness, to nothingness":

> the rapture of vertigo, the letting go, the fall, the gulf, the relapse to darkness, to nothingness, to earnestness, to home, to him waiting

for me always, who needed me and whom I needed, who took me
in his arms and told me to stay with him always, who gave me his
place and watched over me, who suffered every time I left him,
whom I have often made to suffer and seldom contented, whom I
have never seen. (MAL, 195)

Here, the term *nothingness* does not pertain to a metaphysical
principle negating all reality, as in Murphy's vision. Instead, *nothingness* now refers to an inward state enabling communication with a region of identity that paradoxically negates the very notion of identity:
"this being which is called me and is not one" (TFN, 131). All the resources of Beckettian mimesis are deployed to express this region of
identity-as-non-identity and thus to represent "an absence less vain
than inexistence" (TFN, 131).

But even at this point, ambiguity intrudes. On the one hand,
Beckettian mimesis represents the unattainable region of identity-as-
non-identity from the perspective of the self seeking it: "to him waiting for me always, who needed me and whom I needed, who took me
in his arms and told me to stay with him always." But on the other
hand, the same region is represented from the perspective of its own
reception of the self seeking reunification with it: "I'm in my arms,
I'm holding myself in my arms, without much tenderness, but faithfully, faithfully" (TFN, 76). This reciprocity is compactly formulated
by the narrator of *Texts for Nothing*: "I'm up there and I'm down
here, *under my gaze,* foundered, *eyes closed,* ear cupped, against the
sucking peat, we're of one mind, all of one mind, always were, deep
down, we're fond of one another, we're sorry for one another, but
there it is, there's nothing we can do for one another" (TFN, 77; my
emphasis).

We reach now the ultimate ambiguity in the Beckettian mimesis
of seeing nothing. The union of the two aspects of identity (that
which seeks identity and that which eludes it) is itself represented in
terms of seeing and not seeing: "under my gaze" with "eyes closed."
Here we are beyond the reaches of conceptual explanation. For in
this context, seeing nothing has become no more than a metaphor

for an interiority so recessed that it has withdrawn even from its own content. At this depth, all that interiority contains is commiseration for the impossibility of "ceasing . . . before having been"—the shared "dream, of being past" and achieving at last "the extinction of this black nothing and its impossible shades" (TFN, 115, 139).

# 3

## The Beckettian Mimesis of Absence

Beckettian mimesis insists on the primacy of perspective: "seen from a certain angle" (LO, 13, 16; MAL, 245). But it is a perspective that paradoxically claims exclusive validity ("from this point of view but there is no other" [IDI, 65]) while acknowledging its own limitation and fallibility: "for the visibility, unless it be the state of my eyesight, only permits me to see what is close beside me" (UN, 297). Moreover, it is a perspective that, through recognizing its futility ("To be on the watch and never sight" [UN, 368]), repudiates its own function: "I don't believe in the eye either, there's nothing to see, nothing to see with" (375). In this context, the ultimate object seen from the Beckettian perspective is the reduction of sight to redundant reflex with neither stimulus nor registration: "Then the eyes suddenly start afresh as famished as the unthinkable first day until for no clear reason they as suddenly close again or the head falls" (LO, 32). Similar linkages of perspective with unprovoked and unregistering reflex occur in *Not I* ("[O]n and off . . . shut out the light . . . reflex they call it" [NI, 79]), and *Company* ("Only the eyelids stirring on and off since technically they must. To let in and shut out the dark" [COM, 37]). A more emotive description occurs in *The Unnamable*: "[M]y eyes, they're not mine, mine are done, they don't even weep any more, *they open and shut by the force of habit,* fifteen minutes exposure, fifteen minutes shutter, like the owl cooped in the grotto in Battersea Park, ah misery, *will I never stop wanting a life for myself?*" (UN, 392–93; my emphasis).

As the italicized portions of the passage just cited suggest, the mimetic function of this reduction of perspective to unnoticing mechanism or "force of habit" is to represent a mode of animation unable to achieve the coherence and continuous sequence proper to life: "[W]ill I never stop wanting a life for myself?" The fundamental task of Beckettian mimesis is to imitate life not as conventionally construed but as a paradoxical mode of experience founded on awareness of unawareness: "I didn't know where I was, nor in what semblance, nor since when, nor till when" (TFN, 130). The Beckettian term for this mode of experience is "absence" (TFN, 131; W, 207; MAL, 222; ISIS, 22, 51)—a condition that deprives experience of engagement with the circumstances of its own presence: "[H]ow is it nothing is ever here and now?" (TFN, 102). A short list of examples will illustrate: (a) "Absent, always. It all happened without me" (END, 74); (b) "[A] space with neither here nor there where all the footsteps ever fell can never fare nearer to anywhere nor from anywhere further way" (FTEYA, 15); (c) "my mind absent, elsewhere" (TFN, 108).

As the last quotation suggests, to be absent is to be "elsewhere," and the elsewhere in question concerns enclosure in the "closed system" (MUR, 109) of the mind (termed, in *Eh Joe*, "that penny farthing hell you call your mind" [EJ, 17] or, in *Ill Seen Ill Said*, "the madhouse of the skull" [ISIS, 20]). That mental system is "subject to no principle of change but its own" (MUR, 109), and its primary object of attention is the autonomous movement of its own content, which in each Beckettian text is described in terms of a presiding "metaphor" (UN, 325). But in Beckettian mimesis, the state of absence, whereby characters are "sunk in themselves" (CAL, 38), is represented on diverse levels and from conflicting angles, with the result that the very notion of absence is profoundly problematized.

The mimesis of absence in postmodern literature is a topic that, according to Yuan Yuan, has provoked "only isolated sporadic studies" (1997, 124–41). Most of these forays have invoked conceptual schemes constructed by structuralist and poststructuralist theory. Relevant examples include Todorov's foregrounding of the problematics of causality ("[t]he absence of the cause") in postmodern narrative (1989, 900–917); Derrida's emphasis on erasure *(la rature)* and the trace *(le trace)* (1976); and Lacan's construction of the Real as that which abides extraneous to the signifiers whose function is to express it (1978).[1] But aesthetic theory has also been invoked from two directions. One involves reference to the doctrine of minimalism, which formulates the artistic project as the asymptotic approach to absence resulting from what Andrew Renton terms the "deliberate impulse toward exclusion" (1994, 167–83).[2] The other allusion to aesthetic theory derives directly, according to Eyal Amiran, from Beckett's essay "Peintres de l'empechment," where the task of art is to "acknowledge, as Bram van Velde's painting does, the absence of rapport and the absence of the object" (1993, 46). Modern acting theory has made its own contribution to the notion of absence through its emphasis on what William Worthen calls the "histrionic antithesis between absence and presence, role and self" (1983, 419). More conventional or literal interpretations of absence, specifically in Beckett's art, include Mary Catanzaro's notion of absence in *Krapp's Last Tape* as "the absence of the other" or the "unavailability of a partner" (1989, 405); Barbara Becker's and Charles Lyons's interpretation of *Waiting for Godot* in terms of the "absence of context" for the given "dramatic environment" characteristic of postmodern drama (1985–86, 292); and Maria Brewer's reading of Godot as occupying "the absent space outside of the performance space" (1987, 151).

In Beckett's earlier novels, absence is sometimes epitomized by characters so hermetically insulated from awareness of external stimuli that they are hardly more than *personifications* of that condition. For example, in *Murphy,* Mr. Endon is portrayed exclusively in terms of his "immunity from seeing anything but himself" (MUR, 250). In *Watt,* the same characteristic applies to Mr. Knott, who inhabits a state of complete oblivion. But an ironic factor is introduced with the figure of Mr. Knott, for the perpetuation of his state of absence presupposes presence—in this case, the presence of a "spectator" (UN,

1. For a representative Derridean interpretation of absence, see Barker (1990, 181–205).

2. See also Brater (1987).

375) or witness: "[O]f himself he knew nothing. And so he needed to be witnessed. Not that he might know, no, but that he might not cease" (W, 202–3). Here the presence of the witness sustains the absence of what is seen: "That with his need he might witness its absence. That imperfect he might witness it ill. That Mr Knott might never cease, but ever almost cease. Such appeared to be the arrangement" (203).[3]

Yet, the perspective of the witness is extremely ambiguous in Beckettian mimesis. On the one hand, as the example from *Watt* indicates, the role of the witness is supportive or corroborative. Related examples occur in *Ohio Impromptu* ("I have been sent by—and here he named the dear name—to comfort you" [OI, 16]) and *Waiting for Godot* ("You did see us, didn't you?" [WFG, 34]; "Do you think God sees me?" [49]). But on the other hand, the role of the witness can be threatening and invasive, as in the description in *Film* of a photograph of a mother and an infant: "Her severe eyes devouring him" (F, 43). The most explicit account of the danger posed by the witness occurs in the Unnamable's reference to Basil, whose witnessing modifies or adulterates that which he sees: "Without opening his mouth, fastening on me his eyes like cinders with all their seeing, *he changed me a little more each time into what he wanted me to be. Is he still glaring at me, from the shadows?*" (UN, 298; my emphasis). Hence, in its positive capacity, the role of witness facilitates "the blessedness of absence" (MAL, 222), such as Mr. Knott seems to enjoy. Conversely, in its negative function, the role of witness induces "the agony of perceivedness" (F, 34).

3. Regarding the related notion of Mr. Knott's need "not to need" (W, 202), see Katz: "The need to need nothing is precisely the need that can never be met, as every abolition of need becomes no more than a reinforcement of its law. In order to finally achieve state of needing nothing, one would also have to reach the state where one no longer needed to need nothing, which would then open the door to all the needs one wished to exclude" (1999, 63).

The need for "the blessedness of absence" derives from "the agony of perceivedness." Vulnerability to negative witnesses, who impose their moral judgments on those they see, engenders or renews the recoil into absence that, in turn, entrains the presence of a positive witness whose function we can clarify by analyzing absence into its constituent poles: autonomous interiority and the unremitting self-preoccupation that sustains that interiority as a refuge. In the passage quoted earlier, Mr. Knott and Watt respectively represent each of those poles: Mr. Knott is associated with the state of autonomous interiority, while Watt is connected with the act of unremitting attention focused on that state. In later phases of Beckettian mimesis, instead of respective association with distinct characters, the two poles of absence are collapsed inside the same state of awareness that, in turn, paradoxically concerns its own lack of unity: "this being which is called me and is not one" (TFN, 131). Here we encounter "the question of voices" in *The Unnamable* (UN 347), wherein a single interiority is represented by an originary voice and the uncomprehending auditor-witness who repeats its utterance. Related versions occur in *How It Is* ("I say it as I hear it" [HOW, 7]); "From an Abandoned Work" ("the voice that was once in your mouth" [FAAW, 49]); and *Not I* ("and now this stream . . . not catching the half of it . . . not the quarter . . . no idea . . . what she was saying . . . imagine! . . . no idea what she was saying! . . . till she began trying to . . . delude herself . . . it was not hers at all . . . not her voice at all" [NI, 81]).[4]

In the last two examples, without any ambiguity, the auditor-witness is simply the original subject at one remove from his or her own thought (or verbalization thereof). That is, one subjective awareness is rendered in polar terms: autonomous interiority (represented by the originary voice) and its sustaining witness (represented by the auditor). The Unnamable's formula for this predicament is "in yourself, outside yourself" (UN, 385). This complex configuration—

4. Paul Lawley construes "the Mouth as an *emblem of absence*" (1983, 412; original emphasis): that is, as a hole.

perhaps Beckett's most spectacular innovation in narrative form—is the same as that informing the conjunction of Mr. Knott and Watt—except that now the "real separateness" (to interpolate F. H. Bradley's term) of characters has been replaced by the internal relations between reciprocal aspects of the same ambient experience (1930, 24).

This fission of awareness into insular experience and its estranged witness translates the Beckettian mimesis of absence to a new level. As noted earlier, the goad for absence is the need to avoid "the agony of perceivedness." But here the perceivedness to be escaped ironically concerns the very act of self-preoccupation by which absence itself is defined: "immunity from seeing anything but himself" (MUR, 250). That is, the motive for imagining the estrangement of awareness from its own content is to turn self-consciousness into self-*un*consciousness and thereby provisionally fulfill the "hopeless" project of "flight from self" (UN, 315, 367). The Unnamable's reference to his "creatures" (371) will clarify: "They never suffered my pains, their pains are nothing, compared to mine, the tittle I thought I could put from me, in order to witness it" (303–4). Here the purpose of devising fictional "mannikins" (306) is to enable their creator or "deviser" (COM, 34) to relate to his suffering as its witness rather than as its victim, and thus undergo his own pain vicariously. The same project to relate to suffering as its witness is taken one step further through "the matter of voices" (UN, 325). By identifying as the auditor-witness of a voice expressing self-consciousness that they repudiate, the Unnamable and his analogues extend "flight from self" to include repudiation of "the existence of self" (FL, 33). In alternate formulation, they transmute Mr. Endon's "immunity from seeing anything but himself" into immunity from ever seeing self: "It's not me, it can't be me" (TFN, 113).

&

The paradoxical function of the witness in Beckettian mimesis can be probed further. Conventionally, the function of a witness is to confirm that which is seen. Consider, for example, the first scene of

*Hamlet,* where Horatio is invited to the battlemented "platform" (1.2.213) of Elsinore Castle in order to verify the presence of the Ghost: "That if again this apparition come, / He may approve our eyes and speak with it" (1.1.31–32). In contrast, the function of the Beckettian witness is to confirm not presence but absence. But this task of confirming absence is undertaken in various ways. One way concerns the simple observation of another's interior oblivion, as when Watt watches Mr. Knott. Another way concerns the audition of a voice that is repudiated by the auditor to whom it belongs: "this voice which cannot be mine" (TFN, 94). We can now address a third way in which the witness sustains absence: one that concerns the eye of imagination construed as annihilating observer. Here, that which sees progressively diminishes what is seen, until nothing remains.

The annihilating witness operates in a manner contrary to that of the positive witness encountered in *Watt.* Whereas there the function of the positive witness is to enable what is seen to sustain the state of interior absence, the function of the annihilating witness is to eliminate what is seen so that the witness seeing might thereby enjoy the state of absence. The supreme example of the annihilating witness concerns *Ill Seen Ill Said*—a work whose very title foregrounds the role of witness. Here the ostensible object of narration involves an old woman, "already dead" (ISIS, 41), pursuing an existence of unremitting "monotony" (42). But the true subject is not the woman, but her witness, personified as "an eye having no need of light to see" (7–8). This "relentless eye" (29), which "[a]lone can cause to change" (53) that which it sees, maintains its "vigil" (19), until the object of its "intent gaze" (16) is "slowly dispelled . . . like the last wisps of day," leaving only "that void" (59). Through this process of "demolition" (9), which reduces place to the site "where no more [is] to be seen" (58), the annihilating witness eventually perceives "[a]bsence supreme good" (58) and thereby achieves "happiness" (59).

Hence, the annihilating witness is occupied not with "the agony of perceivedness" (the state of being seen—Berkeley's *percipi,* cited in MUR, 246), but with the agony of perception (Berkeley's *percipere*). Yet the perception in question concerns the contents of the "inner" world, not the "outer" one (COM, 62). For the project of the annihilating witness is to rid inwardness of disturbing content: "Nothing for it but to close the eye for good and see her. Her and the rest. Close it for good and all and *see her to death*" (ISIS, 30; my emphasis). The same project is expressed in *Eh Joe*: "Throttling the dead in his head" (EJ, 17). It is as if Watt and Mr. Knott were reconfigured as aspects of the same awareness, such that the state of absence (formerly associated with Mr. Knott) now depends on the annihilating function of his witness (formerly associated with Watt), who, through the "mental activity" (COM, 62) of *seeing to death*, renders awareness vacant.

⁂

On the level now under consideration, the great ambiguity in Beckettian mimesis concerns the axiological status of absence: that is, its nature and ranking as a value. On the one hand, absence is defined as the "supreme good" (ISIS, 58), but on the other, its achievement presupposes annihilation, negation, or "privation" (LO, 60)—the very operations associated in Thomistic metaphysics with evil: "Evil . . . is the privation of good, which chiefly and of itself consists in perfection and act" *(Summa Theologica,* 1, Q48, A5, resp.). Gilson reiterates: "Evil is a pure negation within a substance" (1956, 156). Indeed, as noted earlier, the function of the annihilating witness is described in brutally privative terms: "Throttling the dead" and "see her to death." The Beckettian doctrine of "Absence supreme good" (ISIS, 58) actually inverts the Thomistic paradigm, where good is defined in terms of plentitude (the perfection in which nothing necessary for self-realization is missing), and evil is defined in terms of privation or impairment of that plentitude. Whereas in the Thomistic paradigm "evil implies the absence of good" *(Summa Theologica,* 1, Q48, A3, resp.), in the Beckettian paradigm absence is itself the supreme good.

This dispensation has profound implications for "ethics" (LO, 58). For, as Gilson explains, "Morality consists in ordering all human acts in view of the true good, which is the true end" (1956, 715n. 118). Hence, if the true good is absence, then human acts ordered in view of that end will entail modes of privation, negation, or depletion—what Beckett terms "lessness": "minimally less. No more. Well on the way to inexistence" (ISIS, 54). Therefore, at bottom, the moral imperative in Beckettian mimesis entails the compulsion to empty: "[W]hen one fills, one seldom fills quite full, for that would not be convenient, whereas when one empties one empties completely, holding the vessel upside down, and rinsing it out with boiling water if necessary, with a kind of fury" (W, 95). Thus, the Beckettian mimesis of absence inverts the notion of the Absolute. As Bradley notes, "Anything is absolute when all its nature is contained within itself" (1930, 475). In the Thomistic paradigm, God is the supreme Absolute; for His Being is not only self-sufficient and self-caused, but it is the "superabundant" (Maritain's term) cause of all other being (1948, 42). In contrast, the Beckettian absolute entails not a Being whose plenitude and perfection, manifested as omniscience and omnipotence, overflow in the act of Creation, but "the famished one," "the all-impotent, all nescient," who "has nothing, is nothing" (UN, 346), "who could not be and gave up trying" (UN, 347). Whereas the Absolute is conventionally defined as that which contains all its nature within itself, the Beckettian absolute is that whose nature is to contain nothing. This is absence construed as supreme good.

In Beckettian mimesis, the aptitude to contain nothing is expressed in contrary spatial metaphors. One involves location in emptiness: "You'll be sitting there, a speck in the void, in the dark, for ever, like me" (END, 36). The other involves location in a confining "cocoon" (MAL, 282). The idea of *containing nothing* can be expressed by emphasizing vastness of vacancy or constriction of capacity. The latter alternative is exemplified by Winnie in *Happy Days*. At the opening of the first act, she is "[i]mbedded up to above her waist in exact centre of mound"; then, at the beginning of the second act, she is "imbedded up to [her] neck" (HD, 7, 49). Winnie is acutely aware of constriction, as she gazes into the empty "wilderness": "The earth is very tight today, can it be that I have put on flesh, I trust not" (HD, 21, 28). Ironically, as we can establish by reference to two passages from *Texts for Nothing*, that which contains Winnie is her own volubility—the "empty words" with which she attempts to absent herself from the reality of her predicament.

The linkage of words, engulfment, and absence is made explicit in *Texts for Nothing* (published, in French, three years before *Happy Days*): "Me, here, if they could open, *those little words, open and swallow me up*, perhaps that is what happened. If so let them open again and let me out, in the tumult of light that sealed my eyes, and of men, to try and be one again" (TFN, 112–13; my emphasis). The passage offers a lucid gloss on *Happy Days*—and, by extension, on the Beckettian notion of absence. For the "tumult of light" that absence seeks to escape by means of engulfment recurs in the play: "blaze of hellish light" (11); "With the sun blazing so much fiercer down, and hourly fiercer, is it not natural things should go on fire never known to do so, in this way I mean, spontaneously like" (38). The blazing "wilderness" from which Winnie seeks distraction by means of monologue is the world, the public or shared environment, which in essence is only glaring emptiness—what Clov in *Endgame* refers to as "Zero" (END, 29).

We reach now another ambiguity in the Beckettian mimesis of absence. In one sense, absence is construed as withdrawal, avoidance, or denial. In this mode, absence is epitomized by the phrase "not being there" (TFN, 125) because "there" is viewed as uninhabitable. In this context, absence entails a recoil from presence and can be maintained only by continuous distraction or preoccupation. A related passage from *Texts for Nothing* similarly links this kind of absence with volubility, in terms of an image concerning burial by words that anticipates Winnie's predicament in *Happy Days*: "That's right, wordshit, bury me, avalanche, and let there be no more talk of any creature, nor of a world to leave, nor of a world to reach, in order to have done with worlds, with creatures, with words, with misery,

misery" (TFN, 118). However, absence is associated not only with recoil by means of worded distraction but also with the project "to have done with worlds, with creatures, with words, with misery, misery." That is, the ultimate project of absence is not merely withdrawal from presence, but the "extinction" of presence (TFN, 139), so that absence alone remains. The first project entails *absence from presence*; the second seeks the *presence of absence*.

Perhaps the most relentless mimesis of the presence of absence is developed in *The Lost Ones,* where one after another those populating an enormous cylinder enter the ranks of "the vanquished," who remain "dead still where they stand or sit in abandonment beyond recall" (LO, 60). In its "last state," containing a multitude consecutively lapsed in oblivion, the cylinder becomes the container of absence: "So much roughly speaking for the last state of the cylinder and of this little people of searchers one first of whom if a man in some unthinkable past for the first time bowed his head if this notion is maintained" (LO, 62–63). The cylinder containing absence obviously recalls the mound containing Winnie. For eventually Winnie will be trapped inside the mound-cylinder, buried by her own "wordshit." The implications of this predicament can be clarified by careful analysis. To begin with, in virtue of the relation between volubility and progressive inhumation, Winnie exists in two modes: one concerns involvement in words spoken in the "wilderness"; the other concerns eventual enclosure in silence. The same duality applies to The Unnamable, who first identifies himself as something "in words, made of words," only then to identify himself as something elsewhere and "wordless": "I'm something quite different, a quite different thing, *a wordless thing in an empty place,* a hard shut dry cold black place, where nothing stirs, nothing speaks, and that I listen, and that I seek" (UN, 386; my emphasis).

The Beckettian self is an unstable compound of expression and silence, presence and absence, content and emptiness. It is animated by ambivalence. As represented by the annihilating witness, it seeks to rid awareness of content. But it seeks, with equal fervor (as Winnie will now illustrate), not to see its own emptiness. Earlier, we associated the wilderness surrounding Winnie with the outer or public world, reduced to its essential vacuity. But it is equally valid to associate the wilderness with her own interiority. For on one occasion Winnie actually refers to *herself* as the wilderness: "I say I used to think that I would learn to talk alone. (Pause.) By that I mean to *myself, the wilderness.* (Smile.) But no. (Smile broader.) No no. (Smile off.) Ergo you are there. (Pause.) Oh no doubt you are dead, like the others, no doubt you have died, or gone away and left me, like the others, it doesn't matter, you are there" (HD, 50; my italics in the dialogue, original italics in the stage directions).

Through speech, Winnie seeks to expunge awareness of her own interior vacancy. In order not to see that wilderness, she distracts her attention from it by producing words. Indeed, the unacknowledged purpose of her words is to enclose herself inside the mound they build, so that the wilderness of her own emptiness will no longer threaten her.

Willie, her companion-witness, corresponds to Winnie's refusal to confront her own emptiness, for she created him out of nothing: "Oh no doubt you are dead, like the others, no doubt you have died, or gone away and left me, like the others, it doesn't matter, you are there" (HD, 50). The narrator of *How It Is,* stranded without location in "perfect nothingness," also invokes a witness: "all alone and the witness bending over me" (HOW, 80). Valuable commentary on the invention of a witness for company occurs in *Company:* "Huddled thus you find yourself imagining you are not alone while knowing full well that nothing has occurred to make this possible. The process continues none the less lapped as it were in its meaninglessness" (COM, 86).

Thus, the Beckettian mimesis of absence depicts recourse to contrary witnesses: the annihilating witness, who, by ridding awareness of its content, enables "the blessedness of absence" *(MAL,* 222), and the preserving witness, who, though in reality absent, enables the illusion of presence: "always muttering, to lull me and keep me company" (TFN, 78).

The paradox of absence and presence, isolation and company, remains an irrational core in Beckettian mimesis, like the "Matrix of surds" (MUR, 112), "the square root of minus one" (TFN, 128), or "the true division . . . of twenty-two by seven" (MOL, 64). Ordinarily, the mind (and *a fortiori* the implied reader's mind) abhors irrationality and seeks to resolve it.[5] To forestall this temptation, Beckettian mimesis invokes yet another kind of witness—a hypothetical viewer whose orthodox rationality would misinterpret or misconstrue what is seen. Examples abound—*The Lost Ones*: "And the thinking being coldly intent on all these data and evidences could scarcely escape at the close of his analysis the mistaken conclusion" (LO, 39); *Endgame*: "Imagine if a rational being came back to earth, wouldn't he be liable to get ideas into his head if he observed us long enough" (END, 33); *How It Is*: "the ideal observer's lamps" (HOW, 95). These allusions to the hypothetical witness, whose conclusions are invalidated by their rationality, foreground the irrelevance of "logic" (LO, 19) in explaining Beckettian experience. Instead of logic, there are the contradictions of "preference" (HOW, 34).

Related symbols vividly express the irrelevance of reason. Brief consideration of two examples will clarify. The first concerns the umbrella, which, in *Watt*, is associated with the mind's recourse to "conceptions" by which to interpret or explain perplexing experience: "But it was a conception of which for the moment he had no need, and conceptions of which for the moment Watt had no need Watt did not for the moment unfurl, but left standing, as one does not unfurl, but leaves standing, in readiness for a rainy day, one's umbrella in one's umbrella stand" (W, 135). In *Molloy*, this conceptual umbrella is rendered useless, once Moran's "disintegrations" (MOL, 157) cause him to view as "wretched trifles" the intellectual practices "which had once been [his] delight" (161). Hence, the "canopy" of Moran's umbrella is reduced to "a few flitters of silk fluttering from the stays" (171).

A second symbol for the uselessness of reason concerns the open-

5. On the notion of the implied reader, see Iser (1974).

ing of tins, an action that in *Watt* represents the attempt to solve an intellectual problem: "So at first, in mind and body, Watt laboured at the ancient labour. And so Watt, having opened this tin with his blowlamp, found it empty" (W, 136). In the much later novel, *How It is,* the narrator frequently refers to tins and a tin-opener, but the reflex to resort to them is now merely vestigial, for he no longer requires that kind of nourishment: "[N]o appetite a crumb of tunny then mouldy eat mouldy no need to worry I won't die I'll never die of hunger" (HOW, 8). His compulsive recourse to "the old half-emptied tins" (39) invokes a passage from "The Calmative," where the narrator suddenly mentions tins in the context of posing a series of questions: "I see a kind of den littered with empty tins" (CAL, 27). The link between reaching for the tins and the vestigial habit to seek intellectual solution is reinforced in a passage in *How It Is,* which jumps suddenly from "the opener" to "minutiae" and "problems": "access to the sack that I have my left hand enters gropes for the opener here a parenthesis no minutiae no problems" (HOW, 65).

Thus, through the thwarting of reason, the Beckettian mimesis of absence is enabled to represent experience in terms that do not conform to logic. In other words, just as this mimesis blurs the distinction between the real and the imaginary ("Such confusion now between the real and—how say its contrary?" [ISIS, 40]), so it obscures the opposition between rational "necessity" and "absurdity" (W, 133). But the Beckettian mimesis of absence commingles another pair of contraries as well: "pathos" (LO, 39; ISIS, 47) and hubris. But before we can examine this commingling, we must clarify the terms involved. *Pathos* is the reaching out of pity or succoring emotion toward the victim of suffering or an unhappy predicament. Its ultimate motive is *unification* with the object, as the celebrated definition, formulated by Stephen Dedalus in James Joyce's *A Portrait of the Artist as a Young Man,* indicates: "Pity is the feeling which arrests the mind in the presence of whatsoever is grave and constant in human sufferings and unites it with the human sufferer" (1992a,

221). In contrast, *hubris*—defined by Dodds as "arrogance" or "self-assertion"—entails not unification, but separation (1951, 31, 48). That is, through hubris the individual elevates his or her importance above that of anyone else. Pozzo illustrates: "Yes, gentlemen, I cannot go for long without the society of my likes even when the likeness is an imperfect one" *(WFG,* 16).[6]

These distinctions between pathos and hubris often dissolve in Beckettian mimesis. For on many occasions, pathos concerns the vain wish to unify with absence, and hubris concerns the suffering evoking that wish. Consider Hamm, whose hubris concerns self-assertion through pain: "Can there be misery—loftier than mine?" (END, 2). In virtue of that pain he feels pathos for his inability to achieve absence from it: "If I could sleep I might make love. I'd go into the woods. My eyes would see . . . the sky, the earth. I'd run, run, they wouldn't catch me" (18). Perhaps the most striking linkage of pathos with the yearning for absence occurs in "Old Earth," where the narrator, gazing through a window, suddenly sees the past that he craves to rejoin: "[S]tanding before a window, one hand on the wall, the other clutching your shirt, and see the sky, a long gaze, but no, gasps and spasms, a childhood sea, other skies, another body" (OE, 54). The most concise fusion of pathos and hubris occurs at the end of *Company:* "And you as you always were. Alone" (COM, 89). Here aloneness evokes both pathos and hubris. It evokes pathos expressed in the mode of self-pity for isolation. But aloneness also expresses hubris—through signifying that nothing but self-pity is worthy of admittance to company.[7]

---

6. Critics frequently link Godot with the notion of absence on existential grounds. See Paul de Man: "Here the human self has experienced the void within itself and the invented fiction, far from filling the void, asserts itself in pure nothingness, *our* nothingness stated and restated by a subject that is the agent of its own instability" (1983, 19). Also see Lawrence Graver: "Godot has become a concept—an idea of promise and expectation—of that for which people aware of the absence of coherent meaning in their lives wait in the hope that it will restore significance to their existence" (1989, 43). For a reading counter to these positions, see E. Levy (1994a).

7. For a psychology of self-pity neurosis, with specific allusions to Beckett, see E. Levy (1994).

In *Ohio Impromptu,* the sympathetic Listener, whose sole function is to listen to "the sad tale" read by the Reader, personifies self-
pity.[8] Indeed, according to Beckett's stage directions, Reader and
Listener are "[a]s alike in appearance as possible" (OI, 11). That is,
they are the same character in different modes: preoccupation with
pain and self-pity for suffering it.[9] In *Krapp's Last Tape,* hubris and
pathos combine to plunge Krapp into absence, when at the end he
sits "motionless staring before him" (KLT, 28), contemplating a past
he cannot retrieve. Hubris appears in his habit of scorning his earlier
selves: "Just been listening to that stupid bastard I took myself for
thirty years ago, hard to believe I was ever as bad as that. Thank God
that's all done with anyway" (24). Pathos appears through his habit
of crying for the loss of love that his own hubris prevented him from
valuing properly when it was shared: "Scalded the eyes out of me
reading *Effie* again, a page a day, with tears again. Effie . . . (Pause.)
Could have been happy with her, up there on the Baltic, and the
pines, and the dunes" (25).[10]

The tragic dimension of Beckettian absence is that, through it,
suffering achieves no *anagnorisis* or recognition of its meaning:
"Then at last I can set about saying what I was, and where, during all
this long lost time" (UN, 331). The consequence of pain is not to
clarify, as in the Heraclitean doctrine, the role of character in determining fate, but to perpetuate "confusion of identities" (UN, 331):
"[P]erhaps it's not me perhaps it's another perhaps it's another voy-

8. Brater (1987, 126) cites the familiar view that the two figures represent Beckett and Joyce (with his Latin Quarter hat).

9. Bernard Beckerman relates *Ohio Impromptu* to No drama, in virtue of relation
between Reader and Listener: "they mirror the *waki* and *shite* of the No, the former
earthbound, the second the tormented soul of one dead, often unable to free himself
or herself from a long-lost love" (1986, 164). John Leeland Kundert-Gibbs claims
that "Metaphorically, *Ohio Impromptu* reaches the final stages of Zen training in
archery" (1999, 160).

10. Cf. Mercier: "[A]t the time when [Krapp] broke off relations with the girl in
the punt, he obviously valued his own future success more highly than her love"
(1977, 201).

age confusion with another" (HOW, 86).[11] Whereas in the classical tradition, as Werner Jaeger notes, "Suffering brings knowledge," in the Beckettian dispensation, the presence of "traumatic agents" (UN, 333) only perpetuates the need for absence: "But already I'm beginning to be there no more" (UN, 334; Jaeger 1945, 1. 257). Even death, the event that, by consummating fate, confirms and illumines the significance of the life it terminates, is reduced to just another opportunity for absence: "towards an even vainer death than no matter whose" (TFN, 115).

11. On the role of character in determining fate, see Heracleitus of Ephesus, fragment #119 (1966, 32).

# 4

## Living Without a Life

### The Disintegration of the Christian-Humanist Synthesis in *Molloy*

On the penultimate page of *Molloy,* after a circular journey has reduced to "wretched trifles" (MOL, 161) all the cherished certainties with which he began, Moran repudiates identification through the human species: "I have been a man long enough, I shall not put up with it anymore, I shall not try anymore. I shall never light this lamp again" (175). His renunciation foreshadows the Unnamable's allusion to "the little murmur of unconsenting man, to murmur what it is their humanity stifles" (UN, 325), and anticipates the narrator's comment in *How It Is:* "I was young I clung on to the species we're talking of the human" (HOW, 47). The Beckettian repugnance for humanity goes deeper than mere misanthropy, though Moran does apply that attitude to himself: "It's a strange thing, I don't like men and I don't like animals. As for God, he is beginning to disgust me" (MOL, 105). The "deep down" meaning of this repugnance (MOL, 14), as it is manifested in *Molloy,* can be introduced by a celebrated example of its opposite: Hamlet's praise of his dead father: "A was a man, take him for all in all: / I shall not look upon his like again" (1.2.186–87). Here, to have supreme distinction and value as a human individual is to constitute oneself as an incomparable instantiation of the human nature or "humanity" (3.2.35) common to all men. In this context, to be a great individual is not only to enhance one's own dignity but also to enlarge the scope of the dignity of man, and therefore elevate the meaning of human identity to a higher level: "What is a man" (4.4.33).

No such elevation occurs in *Molloy*. Instead, Molloy's "region" (MOL, 65), the condition of "being only human" (138), lies "somewhere between the mud and the scum" (14). Indeed, when traversing that region, Molloy abandons "erect motion, that of man" (89). Moreover, in the course of the "disintegrations" (157) punctuating his own trajectory across Molloy's region, Moran similarly abandons erect posture when "rolling over and over, like a great cylinder" (153) in order to retrieve his keys. In the novel, this method of locomotion has already been *twice* associated with repudiation of the dignity appropriate to "manhood" (169). Molloy sneers at the common need for examples of appropriate conduct: "[F]or the people, who so need to be encouraged, in their bitter toil, and to have before their eyes manifestations of strength only, of courage and of joy, without which they might collapse, at the end of the day, and roll on the ground" (24). Moreover, on being dragged from slumber, Moran's adolescent son succumbs to a tantrum whose primary symptom entails rolling on the ground: "[H]e broke from my hold, threw himself down on the floor and rolled about, screaming with anger and defiance" (126). But Moran is neither enraged nor despairing when he rolls to retrieve his keys. In fact, he methodically pauses to survey the territory from that debased perspective: "And from time to time I raised myself on my hands, to get a better view" (152).

Understanding the implications of this perspective is the project of this chapter. As already noted, the "view" pertains to having "been a man long enough" and, to reinvoke Hamlet's words, entails the refusal to identify oneself according to the conventional strictures of "[w]hat is a man." As such, it involves, as Moran indicates, extinguishing the "lamp" (MOL, 175) of reason by which humanity illumines its own meaning in order not to encounter the cognitive "disaster" (149) that Moran himself eventually confronts: "the kind of nothingness in the midst of which I stumbled" (123). Of course, Moran surmounts this crisis and registers a "growing resignation to being dispossessed of self" (149)—to no longer identifying himself, that is, as a man. In this process, he repudiates the "wretched trifles" (161) and "all those things at hand without which I could not bear being a man" (132).

Any critic interpreting *Molloy* and the "namelessness" that problematizes "the sense of identity" (MOL, 31) in the novel ironically confronts the same problem of incorrigibility (or the inability to verify correctness) that Molloy mentions when referring to his inner voice ("And perhaps I was understanding it all wrong" [59]), and which Moran acknowledges when interpreting the language of his bees: "I understood it, all wrong perhaps" (176). Moreover, no interpretation of Beckett, however bolstered by evidence, can completely escape the problem of intelligibility raised by Moran: "What all this was about I had not the slightest idea" (113). Nevertheless, since Beckett's fiction is founded on "Questions, hypotheses" (UN, 291), it is appropriate to develop an "agreeable hypothesis" (MOL, 169) regarding one stratum of meaning in *Molloy*.

The refusal to be a man ("I have been a man long enough" [MOL, 175]) is here to be explained not as an act of regression, but as a refusal or inability to take seriously the doctrine of Man, the rational animal, enunciated in the grand tradition of Christian-humanism: "Pupil Mahood, repeat after me, Man is a higher mammal" (UN, 337). More precisely, *Molloy*—and, by extension, the entire trilogy (comprising *Molloy, Malone Dies*, and *The Unnamable*) that it begins—constitutes a satirical critique of that tradition, and not merely a repudiation of it. Of course, to associate Beckett's art with the abandonment of earlier philosophical schools is not a new enterprise. Indeed, as Angela Moorjani notes, "One of the most pleasurable aspects of Beckett's writing is its force of reverberation with philosophical thought" (1992, 190). Many critics have illumined how Beckett's purpose in thus reverberating philosophical thought is to shatter the edifices of reason once built by that thought. For example, in his celebrated analysis of *Waiting for Godot* and the Theatre of the Absurd, Martin Esslin emphasizes the urgent need "to

express . . . the senselessness of the human condition and the inadequacy of the rational approach by the open abandonment of rational
devices and discursive thought" (1969, 6). Citing Esslin, William
Hutchings relates *Waiting for Godot* to "our inability in the modern
age to find a coherent system of meaning, order, or purpose by which
to understand our existence and by which to live" (1991, 28). In an
analysis of *The Unnamable,* Steven Connor foregrounds "the condition of ontological insufficiency consequent upon *the demotion of the
eye* and the values associated with it" (1997, 223; my emphasis).

That demoted eye ultimately symbolizes the faculty of reason,
for, in the tradition of classical rationalism that Beckett often invokes,
the respective operations of mind (reason) and eye (sight) are construed analogously. A. H. Armstrong and R. A. Markus elaborate:
"In the light which is in the mind, the mind's objects become intelligible to the mind just as sunlight renders material things visible"
(1960, 70–71). The Beckettian universe is ontologically challenged;
it comprises not plenitude, but impoverishment of "being and existing" (UN, 348). In that universe, as Theodore Adorno has noted,
"the Western pathos for the Universal and Permanent" is relentlessly
demolished (1969, 82). The result, to invoke Leslie Hill's phrase, is
an "ontological decay" (1990, 117) whereby, according to Thomas
Trezise, "humanist discourse" is called "radically into question"
(1990, 121). But as many critics have observed, this "disintegration
of metaphysical meaning" (Adorno's phrase) paradoxically enables a
new ontological orientation whereby that which is concealed by what
Esslin (above) terms "the rational approach" can at last emerge into
expression (Adorno 1969, 83). In this context, according to Richard
Begam (who invokes Foucault), "The question is no longer: How
can experience of nature give rise to necessary judgments? But rather:
How can man think what he does not think, inhabit as though by a
mute occupation something that eludes him [?]" (1996, 152). This
"something that eludes him" has itself been subjected to varying interpretations. For example, to Ruby Cohn it concerns "the infinite
void in which, against all possibility, life briefly stirs" (1973, 268).
But to J. D. O'Hara, the overcoming of "the Logos principle" and

the "discrimination of opposites" in *Molloy* enables expression of the archetypes of the Jungian collective unconscious (1997, 207).

Our own interpretive project will focus on the means by which *Molloy* ridicules and explodes central doctrines of the Christian-humanist synthesis (as manifested in both the Aristotelian-Thomist paradigm and Plato). The linking of Beckett's art with ontological satire has important precedents beyond those already indicated. In a study of *Endgame*, Sylvie Henning shows how Beckett deploys Menippean or "carnivalized" satire as "an alternative to the paralyzing despair so often detected at the heart of the modern situation" (1988, 87). In an earlier investigation, Stanley Cavell analyzes the same play as a philosophical satire of the rationalist tradition (1969, 115–62). It is worth noting that, according to James Knowlson, Beckett in 1932 read Aristotle and Plato extensively in the Reading Room of the British Museum (1996, 161). I have earlier shown how Beckett's *Mercier and Camier* satirizes the structure of Dante's *Divine Comedy*, the quintessential Aristotelian-Thomist literary text (Levy 1980, 39–53). But through that satire, Beckett's purpose is not to ridicule Dante's values, but to indicate their subsequent inaccessibility.

The relinquishing of Christian-humanism is alluded to by both the narrator in *How It is* ("the humanities I had my God") and Lucky in *Waiting for Godot*, whose reference to divinity ("Given the existence . . . of a personal God") establishes not certainty and perfection, but uncertainty and incompletion, "as a result of the labours unfinished" (HOW, 42; WFG, 28). The assault in *Molloy* on the doctrines of Christian-humanism centers on the definition of man as rational animal who inhabits a rational universe. The doctrines entrained by this definition are respectively debunked until, to interpolate the Unnamable, "Nothing will remain of all the lies they have glutted me with" (UN, 325).

The first of these premises is that the function of reason, the defining faculty of man, is to *know* or render intelligible. Indeed, according to the first sentence of Aristotle's *Metaphysics* (in W. D.

Ross's translation), "All men by nature desire to know"—or, in Richard Hope's alternate rendering, "All men naturally have an impulse to get knowledge" (1941a; 1952, 1.1.980a21). In the classical tradition propounded in Aristotle's *Metaphysics* (12.7.1072b20–23), "[T]he intellect finds fulfillment . . . in its exercise of knowledge." Moreover, "according to Aristotle, who knew everything" (TFN, 114), the mind has dignity, not intrinsically, but only through the achievement of knowledge: "For if this mind knows nothing, what dignity does it have? It is like one asleep . . . for it is because of its knowing that it [the mind] is honoured" *(Metaphysics,* 12.9.1074b17–22). These tenets are exploded in *Molloy,* where the supreme motive is no longer to know but *not* to know: "[T]o be beyond knowing anything, to know that you are beyond knowing anything, that is when peace enters in, to the soul of the incurious seeker" (MOL, 64). The "desire to know" by which, according to Aristotle, the mind achieves nobility is scorned as the "the falsetto of reason" (107). Whereas Aristotle compares the unknowing mind to "one asleep," Molloy compares his own awareness to endless sleep: "For my waking was a kind of sleeping" (53). Similarly, Malone compares his own state to unconsciousness: "I have lived in a kind of coma" (183). Moreover, whereas in the classical tradition knowledge and ignorance are contraries, to Molloy they are indistinguishable: "[O]ne knows already or will never know it's one or the other" (45). For Moran, the "effort of the intelligence" (50) only increases perplexity: "I felt a great confusion coming over me" (98). The function of the mind is no longer to illumine certainty, but to increase the scope of ignorance: "Unfathomable mind, now beacon, now sea" (106).

This disabling of reason applies not only to knowledge of reality outside the mind but also to self-knowledge: the defining concern of Platonic philosophy. According to Socrates, unlike conventional knowledge that involves knowing "something else," this other kind of knowledge entails the rigorous knowing or "science of a man's self" *(Charmides* 165e). Hence, the unexamined life is not worth living *(Apology* 38a), for in this context ignorance signifies "emptiness

. . . of soul" *(Republic* 9.585b) or sickness "for you will do me a much greater benefit if you cure my soul of ignorance than you would if you were to cure my body of disease" *(Lesser Hippias* 373a). Ernst Cassirer provides a superb summary of this Platonic doctrine of self-examination: "Man is declared to be that creature who is constantly in search of himself—a creature who in every moment of his existence must examine and scrutinize the conditions of his existence. In this scrutiny, in this critical attitude toward human life, consists the real value of human life" (1944, 6).

The reflex of self-examination persists in *Molloy*: "I thought much about myself" (MOL, 158). But instead of yielding certainty about the moral implications of identity, it leads only to the dismissal of them: "[A]ll these questions of worth and value have nothing to do with you" (46).[1]

Though, in the Beckettian universe, self-examination does not yield the results intended by Socrates, it nevertheless does engender novel clarity for Moran: "I not only knew who I was, but *I had a sharper and clearer sense of my identity than ever before,* in spite of its deep lesions and the wounds with which it was covered" (MOL, 170, my emphasis). But the sense of identity enabled through self-examination does not conform to the strictures of "the voice of reason" (165). Instead, it concerns awareness of an anonymous inner "voice" (91, 132) whose imperatives must be obeyed even though they might be incorrectly understood, as both Molloy and Moran register: "And perhaps I was understanding it all wrong" (59); "I understood it, all wrong perhaps" (176). At bottom, the commands of the voice are "hypothetical imperatives" (87) because, as seen later with the Unnamable, they reduce the sense of identity to "[q]uestions, hypotheses" (292) about its own nature—a condition anticipated by Malone: "I shall go on doing as I have always done, not knowing what it is I do, nor who I am, nor where I am, nor if I am" (226). Yet paradoxically, as Moran's claim about achieving "a sharper

1. For application of Plato's Allegory of the Cave to *The Unnamable,* see Duffy (1998).

and clearer sense of my identity than ever before" suggests, this state
is construed positively, for it replaces a false idea of "self" (149) with
an accurate one. From this perspective, to be a self according to the
discarded idea is to be a mere "contrivance" (114), a structure of values and strivings vainly superimposed on underlying "nothingness"
(123).[2]

In the trilogy, the inner voice directing Molloy and Moran culminates in ceaseless murmurs that disturb the Unnamable: "I shall
transmit the words as received, by the ear, or roared through a trum-
pet into the arsehole, in all their purity, and in the same order, as far as
possible" (UN, 349). But in *The Unnamable,* the voice that, in *Molloy,* seemed to be *internal* is provisionally registered as *external* utter-
ance(s) traversing emptiness: "[O]nly I and this black void have ever
been" (UN, 304). Awareness of the voice is the only factor preventing the Unnamable from himself becoming nothing: "Ah if only this
voice could stop, this meaningless voice which prevents you from
*being nothing*" (370; my emphasis). Yet paradoxically, awareness of
the voice is also the factor preventing the Unnamable from becoming
*something*—an entity, that is, with a separate and definite identity.
Since the awareness of the Unnamable is here imagined to be no
more than auditory experience, he has no way to establish the concept of his own selfhood ("It's not I . . . nothing but this voice and
the silence all round" [410]), no way to distinguish himself from that
which he hears: "a labouring whirl, you are in it somewhere, everywhere" (402).

The remarkably apt, antisolipsistic argument of P. F. Strawson
will explain: "Could a being whose experience was purely auditory,
make use of the distinction between himself and his states on the one
hand, and something not himself, or a state of himself, of which he
had the experience on the other?" (1959, 69). If the Unnamable is
only the experience of words that he hears—if, that is, he knows only

2. James Acheson attributes Malone's failure at introspection to the nature of
thought: "[T]he mind is imperceptible, it must be described indirectly, in metaphori-
cal language" (1997, 118).

sounds—how can he formulate the idea of himself as the *subject* of this experience and therefore something that is not a sound? Strawson explicates: "For how could . . . a sound be also what *had* all those experiences?" (1959, 89). We are here at the absolute contrary of the humanist notion of man. In that tradition, through proper adherence to the principle of reason, the self can maintain its inviolably determinate structure. Cassirer confirms: "Once the Self has won its inner form, this form remains unalterable and imperturbable" (1944, 7). Marcus Aurelius emphasizes this formative role of reason: "A sphere once formed continues round and true" (1961, bk. 8, par. 41).[3] In contrast, the Unnamable appears explicitly to parody this classical doctrine of the sphericity of selfhood: "I'm a big talking ball, talking about things that do not exist, or that exist perhaps, impossible to know, beside the point" (305).

From the perspective of the Christian-humanist tradition, "[i]t is difficult to speak of man, under such conditions" (MAL, 286) as those which Beckettian fiction imposes. For in the teleological view of that tradition, to be is to tend not toward nothingness or indeterminacy, but toward *entelechy* or the complete self-realization whereby each being fulfills its own intrinsic form: "Now everything seeks after its own perfection" *(Summa Theologica,* 1, Q6, A1, resp.).[4] That is, according to Aristotle, "[E]verything that changes, changes from what is potentially to what is actually" *(Metaphysics* 12.2.1069b14–15). But in *Molloy,* there is no longer a distinction between potency and actuality, and hence no more purpose for purpose. The only purpose is "finality without end" (MOL, 111): the endless elaboration of "formlessness" (197) instead of definite fulfillment of

3. The origin of the identification of Being with an "inviolate whole" or "well-rounded sphere" is Parmenides, frag. 8: "For, in all directions equal to itself, it reaches its limits uniformly" (1966, 44).

4. Compare with Pegis: "Every agent acts for an end, because all things seek the good which is their own perfection" (1939, 62).

inherent form: "And what I saw was more like a crumbling, a frenzied collapsing of all that had always protected me from all I was always condemned to be" (148).

The disintegration of *telos* or purpose in *Molloy* is rendered narratively through four related motifs: purposelessness, directionless movement, repetition compulsion, and circularity. The first of these, purposelessness, is illustrated by Molloy's comment (which slightly modifies the initial speech in *Waiting for Godot*): "Nothing or little to be done" (MOL, 54). The second anti-teleological motif, directionless movement, is formulated by Molloy: "Not knowing where I was nor consequently what way I ought to go" (60). Indeed, he comments explicitly on the relation between movement and purpose: "For how can you decide on the way of setting out if you do not first know where you are going, or at least with what purpose you are going there?" (98). The same idea informs Moran's description of the first intruder: "He walked with swift uncertain step, often changing his course, dragging the stick like a hindrance" (146–47). The third anti-teleological motif, repetition compulsion, is illustrated by Moran: "Whereas to see yourself doing the same thing endlessly over and over again fills you with satisfaction" (133). Of course, it is tempting to interpret Moran's repetition compulsion in terms of the Freudian theory of the anal personality, but a more specifically Beckettian implication concerns the reduction of *telos* to the meaningless reiteration of action.[5]

The fourth antiteleological motif, circularity, is the most complex. The entire plot of *Molloy* is founded on circularity. More precisely, it concerns concentric circles. As Moran undertakes a circular journey for Molloy, he feels his quarry (who also describes a circular journey, one involving return to his mother) "rise up within [him]" (MOL, 113). In Beckett's minimalist mimesis, this reiterated foregrounding of circularity represents or corresponds to "the customary cycle of birth, life and death" (52). The only intrinsic purpose re-

5. On the relation of Beckett's work to Freud, see O'Hara (1992). On repetition compulsion, see Meche (1995) and Baker (1997).

maining in life is completion of the circuit: "And the cycle continues, joltingly, of flight and bivouac, in an Egypt without bounds, without infant, without mother" (66). The *tour de force* regarding meaningless cycle concerns Molloy's celebrated problem of arranging the "circulation of the stones from pocket to pocket" (69), such that each of the sixteen stones "will have been sucked once in impeccable succession, not one sucked twice, not one left unsucked" (73). Significantly, Molloy describes this purposeless circulation in terms of the difficulty of fulfilling purpose: "I could never reach the goal I had set myself, short of an extraordinary hazard" (70).

The implications of the antiteleological reduction of life to "the customary cycle" (MOL, 52) can be clarified by considering Moran's alarm after receiving the imperative to find Molloy: "My life was running out, I knew not through what breach" (102). Moran here means not that his life, as a biological process, is ending, but that the interpretation of his existence in terms of "the inenarrable contraption I called my life" (114) has lost its relevance. To understand what Moran here means by life and why it eventually runs out though he himself lives on, we can turn first to Molloy's remark about his experience of the same situation: "My life, my life, now I speak of it as of something over, now as of a joke which still goes on, and it is neither, for *at the same time it is over and it goes on,* and is there any tense for that?" (36; my emphasis). The contradictory notion here of life as over yet continuing contradicts the humanist notion of "human life" (165), which must now be explained. Perhaps the most direct way to do that is to begin with Hamlet's definition: "And a man's life's no more than to say 'one' " (5.2.74; my emphasis).

Here Hamlet refers not so much to the brevity of life, as to the moral unity that temporal limitation confers on each life. Each lifetime constitutes a single temporal unit, construed as an integral process of becoming, by which the living individual tends toward his or her ultimate end. Just as, in Aristotle's theory of tragedy, an entire play concerns "the imitation of an action that is serious and also, as having magnitude, *complete in itself*" (*Poetics* 1449b24–25; my emphasis),[6] so all the particular actions performed by an individual in his or her lifetime sequentially express one underlying and "complete in itself" action: the teleological movement toward *entelechy*, which Ernst Auerbach defines as "the self-realization of the essence" (1961, 7). According to humanist principles, "This is life" (MOL, 57): a temporalized activity whose "true value," to interpolate Cassirer's words, is realized by exercising reason in accordance with "an eternal order that admits of no change" (1944, 8). Auerbach elaborates: "Man alone possesses freedom of choice, a power composed of intellect and will which, though closely connected with the natural disposition and hence always individual, reaches out beyond it; it is that power which enables him during his lifetime on earth, to love in the right or wrong way and so decide his own fate" (1961, 105).

But this is not life according to Molloy, for whom "[t]o decompose is to live too" (MOL, 25), nor it is the context in which he would ever seek "a meaning to my life" (19). As the Unnamable reveals, the Beckettian ideal is to live *"outside of life"* (UN, 346; my emphasis)—to live, that is, exempt from the rational process of self-actualization characteristic of the humanist notion of life: "But within, *motionless*, I can live" (UN, 325; my emphasis). In this way, the tending toward *telos* is discarded: "[T]he metamorphosis is accomplished, of unchanging future into unchangeable past" (367). In alternate formulation, the Unnamable endorses a life exempt from the responsibility for *telos* proper to living: "No, one can spend one's life thus, unable to live, unable to bring to life, and die in vain, having done nothing, been nothing" (358). In *Molloy*, which concerns an earlier stage of "decomposition" (MOL, 25) than does *The Unnamable, telos* succumbs to futility, with the consequence that striving toward a goal is hampered by "weariness" (14) and weakness: "And I grew gradually weaker and weaker and more and more content" (162). The only purpose left is to narrate the loss of purpose: "to obliterate texts than to blacken margins, to fill in the holes of words

---

6. On the relevance of Aristotle's *mimesis praxeos* (the imitation of an action) to Beckett's art, see Scanlon (1992).

till all is blank and flat and the whole ghastly business looks what it is, *senseless, speechless, issueless misery*" (13; my emphasis).

The reduction of living to "senseless, speechless, issueless misery" overthrows another humanist doctrine: *eudaemonia*. According to that doctrine, the fruit of *entelechy* or self-realization is happiness that, as Aristotle claims in the *Nichomachean Ethics*, "is always desirable in itself and never for the sake of something else" (1097a35–36). In this schema, happiness is construed as the appropriate use of the highest faculty (in the case of man, reason), such that its enjoyment is both intrinsic to the subject concerned and supreme among the goods he or she can achieve. Hence, the root of *eudaemonia* is "self-sufficiency" (1097b8): "the self-sufficient we now define as that which when isolated makes life desirable and lacking in nothing; and such we think happiness to be" (1097b14–16).[7] In *Molloy*, there are frequent references to happiness or contentment, but they do not pertain to the Aristotelian schema. Unlike Aristotle, Moran finds happiness not in "an activity or actions of the soul implying a rational principle" *(Nichomachean Ethics* 1098a13–14), but in frustration of the rational principle: "And I said with *rapture*, Here is something I can study all my life, and never understand" (MOL, 169; my emphasis). Similarly, Molloy associates happiness with mental oblivion: "And just enough brain intact to allow you to exult!" (140). Whereas for Aristotle, *eudaemonia* enables the achievement of "a complete life" (1098a17), to Molloy happiness in this sense is meaningless. For life offers not completeness, but pointless continuity: "the slow and painful progress . . . to a veritable cavalry, with no limit to its stations and no hope of crucifixion" (MOL, 78). Striving toward completeness is futile in a life where "all the muck is the same muck" (41). In these circumstances, *eudaemonia* is reduced to "the eudemonistic slop" (55).

---

7. For more detailed discussion of *eudaemonia,* see E. Levy (1998, 95–99). For unelaborated linkage of "the eudemonistic slop" to Schopenhauer, see O'Hara (1997, 147).

❧

In concluding this chapter on *Molloy*, it is appropriate to empha-size that the disintegration of the Christian-humanist synthesis in the novel does not necessarily entail an endorsement of existentialism. Of course, it is a commonplace of contemporary criticism to link Beckett's works with that philosophical movement. For example, Michael Collins relates *Waiting for Godot* "to existentialism (and par-ticularly to Sartre's essay 'Existentialism Is a Humanism'): God is dead, life is absurd, existence precedes essence, ennui is endemic to the human condition" (1991, 33).[8] But though, as we have seen, the problem of meaninglessness or "absurdity" is raised in *Molloy* (MOL, 142), it does not provoke an existentialist solution. Far from seeking to make meaning where none is present, the Beckettian project is to confirm meaninglessness or, more precisely, "senseless, speechless, is-sueless misery" (13) *ad infinitum*: "[W]hatever I do, that is to say whatever I say, it will always as it were be the same thing" (45–46). Or *ad nauseam*: "[K]eep your mouth open and your stomach turned, perhaps you'll come out with it one of these days" (UN, 336).

We can clarify this matter by brief consideration of the notion of freedom in Sartre's philosophy. Sartre explicitly opposes his own no-tion of freedom to the teleology of Aristotle, which he interprets as a form of determinism driven by the exigencies of inherent and defin-ing essence: "Indeed, for him . . . man's freedom lies less in the con-tingency of his evolution than in the exact realization of his essence" (1955, 57). To overcome this perceived impediment to freedom, Sartre replaces the notion of *essence* in man with the notion of *noth-ingness*: "Thus, liberty is not *a* being: it is the being of man, that is to say his lack of being" (qtd. in Blackham 1952, 129). I. M. Bochenski

---

8. Other existentialist interpretations appear in McCandless (1988) and Butler (1984), drawing on Heidegger and Sartre. Vivian Mercer associates the Unnamable's plight with the failure to engage in choice as prescribed in Sartrean doctrine (1977, 170). In contrast, Milton Rickels highlights existential themes in the novel (1962, 134–47).

explicates: "First, man as such has no nature, no fixed essence. His essence is simply his freedom, his indeterminateness" (1965, 177). In this context, as H. J. Blackham indicates, freedom is the striving of finite non-being (the *pour-soi*) toward the being *(en-soi)* it wishes to become: "My consciousness of myself thus already implies a projection of myself towards my possibility, what I lack in order to be myself identified with myself; and this is the structure of desire and the movement of fulfillment" (Blackham 1952, 113).

The problem of freedom is indeed raised in *Molloy* by both Molloy ("Can it be we are not free?" [MOL, 36]) and Moran ("Does this mean I am freer now than I was?" [176]). But insofar as Sartrean freedom means "projection into the new" (Blackham 1952, 129), there is not freedom in *Molloy* but determinism—what Molloy terms "the pre-established harmony" (MOL, 62) and what Moran terms "a frenzied collapsing of all that had always protected me from all I was always condemned to be" (148). Yet it is a determinism driven not by essence or pre-existing structure, but by their perpetual lack: "[T]he voice is of a world collapsing endlessly, a frozen world" (40). Paradoxically, the fundamental principle of this deterministic process of disintegration is not determinism at all, but the relapse into chaos: "the indestructible chaos of timeless things" (39).[9]

The refutation of determinism in *Molloy* can be explained by another route. For Sartre, the hallmark of determinism is its reliance on *a priori* concepts: "Its sole purpose is to force the events, the persons, or the acts considered into pre-fabricated moulds" (1963, 37). The same reference to prefabricated conceptual moulds occurs in *Molloy* (in a passage that seems an apt gloss on Lucky's celebrated speech in *Waiting for Godot*): "You invent nothing, you think you are inventing . . . and all you do is stammer out your lesson, the remnants of a pensum one day got by heart and long forgotten" (MOL, 32). But the

---

9. For the application of the modern chaos theory of James Gleik (1987) to Beckett's fiction, see Meriwether (1994) and S. Levy (1996). For more traditional discussions of Beckettian chaos, see Dearlove (1982) and Federman (1965).

prefabricated moulds determining thought have disintegrated, and thinking can only repeat the futility of either reconstructing or transcending them: "Whereas to see yourself doing the same thing endlessly over and over again fills you with satisfaction" (133).

Hence, the ontological dispensation in *Molloy* pertains neither to freedom nor to determinism. On the one hand, freedom implies self-directedness, and in *Molloy* that faculty is surrendered to the inner voice: "And I feel I shall follow it from this day forth no matter what it commands" (MOL, 132). On the other hand, determinism implies a stable and definite principle whose efficacy engenders the complete determination or self-realization of the process or entity it influences. But in *Molloy* the first principle is "chaos" (39), and its efficacy leads not to determination or self-realization, but to indetermination or "namelessness" (31) and the "growing resignation to being dispossessed of self" (149). In place of freedom and determinism, there is only reiteration of the inability either to be or not to be. The preeminent expression of this state in *Molloy* is provided by Molloy: "To be literally incapable of motion at last, that must be something! My mind swoons when I think of it. And mute into the bargain! And perhaps as deaf as a post! And who knows as blind as a bat! And as likely as not your memory a blank! And just enough brain intact to allow you to exult! And to dread death like a regeneration" (140). Its analogue is the Unnamable's plight, wherein he can neither be nor not be, neither narrate nor go silent: "[Y]ou must go on, I can't go one, I'll go on" (UN, 414).

This brings us to a final paradox involving freedom and determinism in Beckett's fiction. On the one hand, there is the determinism of narrative repetition: "[T]here's nothing new there, it's all a part of the same old irresistible baloney" (UN, 377). On the other hand, the narrator (in this case, Molloy) claims the freedom to produce novelty: "Saying is inventing" (MOL, 32). At bottom, this situation can be construed as a *parody* of the humanist ontology that posits a reality in which each being repeats, in its own unique way, the same teleological process of tending toward complete *actualization*. In the Beckettian universe, however, as Molloy insists, the only end to achieve is lessness or *de-actualization*: "[T]he most you can hope for is to be a little less, in the end, the creature you were in the beginning, and middle" (32). *Entelechy* now concerns not full realization of individual being, but asymptotic simulation of primordial nonbeing.

# 5

# *Malone Dies* and the Beckettian Mimesis of Inexistence

In his study of narrative, Peter Brooks derives the convention of plot from "the problem of temporality: man's time-boundedness, his consciousness of existence within the limits of mortality" (1984, xi). As its title suggests, perhaps no novel is more unremittingly concerned with "existence within the limits of mortality" than *Malone Dies*. From his first sentence, Malone, the eponymous first-person narrator, foregrounds the inevitability of death: "I shall soon be quite dead at last in spite of all." But in narrating his own elapsation, Malone replaces the convention of plot (which concerns a temporal sequence of events tending toward some terminus or end) with the convention of "programme" (MAL, 269) whose function, unlike that of plot, is not causal but diversionary: "While waiting I shall tell myself stories, if I can" (180).[1] This shift from plot to programme has profound implications. For human temporality or, in Brooks's phrase, "existence within the limits of mortality," is now "freed from all responsibility" (231) concerning action and consequence or "cause and effect" (240) in life. In the Beckettian universe, as formulated in *Malone Dies,* the only valid or relevant concern is "[t]o be dead . . . and never have to die any more, from among the living" (264). Here existence

1. Leslie Hill interprets Malone's notion of "play" as "a regressive activity having for him the same function it has perhaps for children [i.e.,] a means of exploring the limits between the fictional and the real, self and other, order and disorder, identity and difference" (1990, 102).

is construed as the state of "mortal tedium" (217) endured while the subject "wait[s], before he die[s], for his body to be dead" (198).

But the great paradox of Beckettian mimesis is that the obverse of its reduction of life to the waiting for death is the reduction of death to the continuation of life: "There is naturally another possibility . . . and that is that I am dead already and that all continues more or less as when I was not" (MAL, 219). Like the maxima and minima in Beckett's analysis of Giordano Bruno ("The maxima and minima of particular contraries are one and indifferent"), life and death ultimately coincide: "till you begin to wonder if you have not died without knowing and gone to hell or been born again into an even worse place than before" (MAL, 227; DBVJ, 6). Like Molloy's different "regions" that "gradually merge into one another" (MOL, 65), life and death, for Malone, lose their respective distinctness: "The truth is, if I did not feel myself dying, I could well believe myself dead" (MAL, 183). As Leslie Hill observes, "Living and dying, like extremes, converge to erase all that may have taken place between their confines" (1990, 101). Angela Moorjani concurs: "Throughout the novel . . . it is uncertain whether Malone awaits death or birth" (1982, 120). Hence, "existence within the limits of mortality" (Brooks's phrase again) becomes existence without the limits of mortality: "And there comes a time when nothing more can happen and nobody can come and *all is ended but the waiting that knows itself in vain*" (MAL, 241; my emphasis).

The result of this predicament is a detemporalizing of time, wherein time continues but without the succession of before and after, which is its defining property: "And perhaps he has come to that last stage of his instant when to live is to wander the last of the living in the depths of an instant without bounds, where the light never changes and the wrecks look all alike" (MAL, 233). Here, to invoke formulations in *How It Is,* it is "the same instant always everywhere" (HOW, 112), an undifferentiated duration where "all the various times before during after" merge in the same "vast tracts of time" (HOW, 107) bereft of "subdivisions" (HOW, 95). Similarly, the Unnamable, who can "understand nothing about duration"

(UN, 407), observes that "the seconds must all be alike and each one is infernal" (UN, 395). Malone expands this notion of the relentless continuity of time to include the idea of time continuing beyond the possibility of change proper to temporality: "And the ticking of an invisible alarm-clock was as the voice of that silence which, like the dark, would one day triumph too. And then all would be still and dark and all things at rest for ever at last" (MAL, 203). Here time itself becomes timeless, as if, to invoke Vladimir's *mot* in *Waiting for Godot,* "Time has stopped" (WFG, 24). For there can be no more change in it, only a static flux. In his reference to "the indestructible chaos of timeless things," Molloy posits a kinetic version of the same condition (MOL, 39).

As Malone observes, there are indeed deaths in Beckettian fiction: "How many have I killed, hitting them on the head or setting fire to them?" (MAL, 236).[2] However, their result is not to end temporal existence but simply to change the context of its interminable continuity: "Then it will be all over with the Murphys, Merciers, Molloys, Morans and Malones, *unless it goes on beyond the grave*" (236; my emphasis). Yet, as the narrator of *Texts For Nothing* suggests, in the Beckettian universe posthumous existence ultimately signifies not the realm of the afterlife, but the death already in life: "dead like the living" (TFN, 91). On passing a "graveyard," Moran makes a similar observation: "If only that were the only perpetuity" (MOL, 174). At bottom, this death already in life pertains not to lack of life, but either to lack of desire for life (as in Molloy's "daily longing for the earth to swallow me up" [80]), or to lack of clarity concerning why life must be endured, as in Macmann's quandary: "And without knowing exactly what his sin was he felt full well that living was not a sufficient atonement for it or that this atonement was in itself a sin, calling for more atonement, and so on, as if there could be anything but life for the living" (239). But because of what Molloy calls "the well-known mechanism of association" (48), life under

2. For an early and cogent relating of Malone to previous Beckettian narrators, see Hesla (1971, 105–6).

these conditions cannot be distinguished from posthumous punishment, as the Unnamable suggests: "I was given a pensum, at birth perhaps, as a punishment for having been born perhaps" (UN, 310).[3]

## Existence as Inexistence

This confusing of life and death is aggravated by the construing of death as birth, as when Malone describes himself as "an old foetus" (MAL, 225), straining toward "birth into death" (283). But the difficulty of achieving birth into death derives from the prior failure to achieve birth into life, as the Unnamable indicates: "I alone am immortal, what can you expect, I can't get born" (UN, 383). Malone concurs: "I shall never get born and therefore never get dead" (MAL, 225). Hence, at bottom, existence in the Beckettian universe entails a state of "inexistence" exempt from both birth and death: "I exist, in the pit of my inexistence" (TFN, 91). Thus, *Malone Dies* unfolds a dual project. The first is to bring Malone's life to an end through eventual death: "if I succeed in my breathing my last" (MAL, 235). The second is to debunk, through the narration of his dying, the "ballsaching poppycock about life and death" (225) and replace it with the notion of that third mode of existence: "inexistence."[4]

In the novel, it is not so much that Malone dies as that a mimetic convention concerning the representation of life is terminated or, more precisely, terminally minimalized.[5] Through this reduction of life, Beckettian mimesis is enabled to represent a mode of existence

3. For a relating of *Malone Dies* to "the legacy left by *Pilgrim's Progress* to the tradition of the English novel" with respect to "the inescapable inheritance of a death that is figured in literary terms as the 'end of the line,' " see Thomas (1989, 385).

4. For a poststructuralist interpretation of Malone's mode of being as "haecceity" or immanent existent (a term borrowed from the contemporary philosophers Deleuze and Guattari), see Uhlmann (1999, 120–24).

5. On the Beckettian tendency to undermine mimetic conventions, see Moorjani: "Beckett's novels from *Watt* onward . . . undermine the classic project of the novel to mirror outer and inner reality, the fiction of transparency" (1982, 45). In *Malone Dies*, on the tendency to "end the tradition of meticulous fictional editing that begins with Richardson," see Abbott (1988, 126).

unencumbered by antecedent associations or presuppositions. Hence, the purpose of Malone's stories is not merely, as noted earlier, to provide distraction "while waiting" (MAL, 180) for death: "That's the style, as if I still had time to kill" (248). Their deeper purpose is not to kill time but to kill or dispose of the "axioms" (187) regarding purpose and appropriate procedure entrained in conventional notions of life and how to live it.[6]

Malone deploys a variety of devices by which to evacuate the notion of life and thus to render accessible the "stratum" (MAL, 226) of inexistence. In narrating his own decline toward death, Malone emphasizes the lifelessness of the period preceding it—"I have lived in a kind of coma" (183)— and then applies that same condition to everyone—"Coma is for the living" (194). He also undermines the notion of life by obscuring the transition from living to dying: "As to the events that led up to my fainting and to which I can hardly have been oblivious at the time, they have left no discernible trace, on my mind" (183). Malone further obliterates the significance of individual life by indicating that the only distinguishing factor in any life is the time required to end it: "Here lies Malone at last, with the dates to give a faint idea of the time he took to be excused and then to distinguish him from his namesakes, numerous in the island and beyond the grave" (271).

In Malone's stories of the Saposcats, the Lamberts, and Macmann, the same depletion of life occurs. The adult Lamberts are "grown men and women *embedded deep in life*" (MAL, 199; my emphasis).[7] But the life in which they are ensconced is founded on futility: "At the same time angry unanswerable questions, such as, What's the use? fell from her lips" (202). Similarly, the conventions of life pursued by the Saposcats succumb readily to a *reductio ad absurdum*: "The life of the Saposcats was full of axioms, of which one at least es-

6. For a relating of *Malone Dies* to a critique of the Western notion of "the progress of history," see Uhlmann (1999, 125).

7. Ruby Cohn observes that the name "Lambert" was rendered as "les Louis" in *Malone Meurt*, and refers to Balzac's Louis Lambert (1973, 94).

tablished the criminal absurdity of a garden without roses and with its paths and lawns uncared for" (187). The result is another fore-grounding of futility: "It was as though the Saposcats drew the strength to live from the prospect of their impotence" (188). The in-tervals of movement punctuating Macmann's habitual torpor com-plete the reduction of life to rudimentary movement with merely functional value: "Because in order not to die you must come and go, come and go, unless you happen to have someone who brings you food wherever you happen to be, like myself" (232). The same no-tion is later expressed in anal terms: "only rose again when the elan vital or struggle for life began to prod him in the arse again" (243). In *How It Is,* the spasmodic and exhausting movement of Bom and Pim across the vast tracts of mud—"right leg right arm push pull"—is provoked by the identical stimulus—"stab him simply in the arse" (HOW, 27, 71).

## Transcendentals and the Mimesis of Inexistence

As the axioms and conventions regarding the significance of life are debunked or decomposed, the mimesis of inexistence emerges. But as this state of inexistence is riddled with paradoxes, an intellectual device is required to facilitate our analysis of it. The device in ques-tion concerns what metaphysics terms *transcendentals.* As Calvin Schrag indicates (with reference to Heidegger), these are defined as a priori and necessary conditions of human experience: "The primary structures or universal determinants of existence" (1967, 286). As "ontological structures of existence," transcendentals "are present in the concrete existent, providing its very condition for being" (Schrag 1967, 287, 289). As Ernst Cassirer indicates (with reference to Kant), transcendentals are not of "empirical origin" (1981, 51). That is, they are not derived from experience; instead, as Wilhelm Windel-band explains, "lying at the basis of all empirical perceptions," they determine how we experience what we experience and thus constrain the boundaries and possibilities of subjectivity (1958, 2.539). Ac-cording to Schrag, since the transcendentals, by definition, concern "universal structures of human being as they show themselves in the actualization of existence," each existent is thus, to invoke Paul Tillich, "the door to the deeper levels of reality," which determine the essential form of human "existence itself" (Schrag 1967, 284; Tillich 1963, 1:62).

There are many indications in *Malone Dies* of the universality of the experience depicted: "for he was no more than human, than the son and grandson and greatgrandson of humans" (MAL, 240–41). But that experience is founded on and discloses distinctly Beckettian transcendentals or "essentially necessary structures of experience" that redefine the meaning of human being (Blackham 1952, 87). The transcendental emphasis in *Malone Dies*—and indeed in the entire trilogy—is evident in the frequent references to the irrelevance and interchangeability of *particular* experience. That is, all particular experiences merge into and express the same unchanging and fundamental condition whose representation is the ultimate task of Beckettian mimesis: "The noises of nature, of mankind and even my own, were all jumbled together in one and the same unbridled gibberish" (207). Molloy affirms the same idea: "And wheresoever you wander, within its distant limits, things will always be the same, precisely" (MOL, 66). Through the representation of particular experiences, the Beckettian narrator intends to disclose the primary structures or "laws of the mind" (MOL, 13) ordering—or disordering—all experience. In other words, the mimetic aim here in representing distinct experiences is, to interpolate James Edie's words from a different context, to "search for the ultimate, constitutive foundations of experience" in Beckettian terms (1967, 241).

Many critics have noted the similarity between Beckettian fiction and Husserl's phenomenology, founded on the principle of transcendental reduction by which empirical or sensory experience is reduced to its eidetic or formally structuring components: "Everything . . . is essentially prefigured" (Husserl 1931, sect. 135).[8] But our own concern here is not to offer another phenomenological analysis of Beck-

---

8. For an application of Husserl to Beckett's *Company,* see Locatelli (1990, 162–66). For an application of the Husserlian device of "bracketting" to Beckett's fic-

ett, but to use the concept of transcendentals as a lens allowing us (if we may transpose Remy Kwant's phrase from a different context) "to disengage the essential core from the accidental" in the Beckettian mimesis of experience (1967, 381). In this regard, one is reminded of Malone's attempt to describe "the Stick, shorn of all its accidents" (MAL, 254).

Perhaps the quintessential statement in *Malone Dies* concerning the transcendental project to disengage the essential core from the accidental appears in Malone's dictum: "The forms are many in which the unchanging seeks relief from its formlessness" (MAL, 197). In an alternate formulation of the same project, Malone emphasizes the relation between the variant experiences narrated in his stories and the unchanging condition of their narrator: "Shall I be incapable, to the end, of lying on any other subject? I feel the old dark gathering, the solitude preparing, by which I know myself" (189). The transcendental project to disengage the essential core from the accidental is further suggested by Malone's ultimate enclosure of the external world inside a head that is not his own: "You may say it is all in my head . . . and that these eight, no, six, these six planes that enclose me are of solid bone. But thence to conclude the head is mine, no, never" (221). That is, the basic concern of Beckettian mimesis, at the level now under consideration, is to represent neither particular objects nor the particular subjects perceiving them, but instead the impersonal and primordial function by which their very conception is constituted.

So far this sounds remarkably close to Paul Ricoeur's formulation of "transcendental" as that which pertains to "any attempt at relating the conditions of the appearance of things to the structure of human subjectivity" (1978, 76). It also recalls Husserl's characterization of the transcendental standpoint as that which addresses "how objective unities of every region and category 'are consciously constituted' " by noetic or psychical processes whose operation is governed by uni-

---

tion, see Butler (1984, 78). Regarding Derrida's critique of Husserl, see Trezise (1990, 10–13) and Uhlmann (1999, 166–69).

versal principles (1931, sect. 86). But far from mimicking the method of transcendental phenomenology to uncover the functions by which structure is constituted or filled in, Beckettian mimesis, as exemplified in *Malone Dies*, seeks instead to represent the "peculiar logic" (MAL, 276) by which structure and order are drained and evacuated. The result of these "gurgles of outflow" (287) is a drainage of certainty, not a constitution of it. Whereas, according to Husserl, the phenomenological method begins "in absolute poverty, with an absolute lack of knowledge," and then proceeds "to genuine knowing," Beckettian mimesis represents unremitting "incomprehension" (UN, 325), as evident, for example, in Malone's "inability to grasp what order is meant" (210; Husserl 1960, 2).

Further reference to phenomenology will enable us to clarify the implications of inexistence in *Malone Dies* and elsewhere in Beckettian fiction, but in a way that contradicts the very principles by which phenomenology defines that mode of being. Husserl developed phenomenology as the science or logical study of the intrinsic and a priori structures of consciousness. The first principle in this regard is that consciousness *intends* or is directed toward an object—something to be conscious of. As Joseph Kockelmans explains, "[A]ll consciousness is consciousness-of-something" (1967, 32). Husserl elaborates: "Conscious processes are also called *intentional*; but then the word intentionality signifies nothing else than this universal fundamental property of consciousness: to be consciousness *of* something; as a *cogito* to bear within itself its *cogitatum*" (1960, 33). For example, to invoke Franz Brentano, "in judgment something is affirmed or denied, in love something is loved, in hate something hated, in desire something desired, etc." (1960, 50). Now, the mental being that an object has in the mind or consciousness intending it is called *inexistence*, a term which Husserl derived from Scholastic philosophy.[9] Thus, according to the phenomenological paradigm, consciousness *exists* only if objects *inexist* in it.

Beckettian narration develops a spectacular *reductio ad absur-*

9. See Brentano (1960, 50) and Kockelmans (1967, 32).

*dum* of this phenomenological paradigm where, according to Quentin Lauer, "[t]o be is to be given to consciousness" or "to be present in consciousness" (1967, 151). For in the Beckettian dispensation, the supreme object inexisting in consciousness concerns the *lack* of objects: the "void" (MAL, 234), "absence" (222), or "nothing" (192). But if, as Malone claims, "Nothing is more real than nothing" (192) and the preeminent object of consciousness is therefore nothing, then consciousness itself cannot be distinguished from a vacuum: "[I]n my head I suppose all was streaming and emptying away as though through a sluice, to my great joy, until finally nothing remained, either of Malone or of the other" (224). That is, consciousness is no more than the site where nothingness inexists. But without relation to objects through intentionality or directedness toward them, consciousness itself loses its defining function. For in phenomenological terms, as Edie notes, in virtue of "the strict correlativity of subject and object in experience," consciousness is defined through its relation to the objects toward which it is directed: "[T]he subject is constituted as subject only through its active involvement with the world" (1967, 245). A consciousness in which nothing inexists cannot itself exist as consciousness.

Malone dismisses the assumption regarding "the strict correlativity of subject and object in experience": "[T]he subject falls from the verb, and the object lands somewhere in the void" (Edie 1967, 234). This dissociation of the terms (subject and object) on whose relation the phenomenological notion of consciousness depends is the indispensible first step by which Beckettian mimesis eventually represents a consciousness in which nothing inexists. The project to convert conscious existence into the inexistence of nothing underpins the unrelenting self-consciousness displayed by Malone: "All my senses are trained full on me, me" (MAL, 186). Here, Malone becomes the object of his own attention and hence inexists in it. Consistent with phenomenological practice, Malone plans to define himself, through his long-delayed "reckoning" (181), as a consciousness *of*—that is, in terms of his relation to the complete "inventory" (251) of objects in his possession: "For only those things are mine the whereabouts of which I know well enough to be able to lay hold of them, if necessary, that is the definition I have adopted, to define my possessions" (249). But in the course of his narrative, Malone loses many of the objects in his possession and the stick with which he brings himself in relation to them. In becoming the object of his own attention and thus inexisting in that attention, Malone progressively evacuates himself of all content. Hence, his inexistence in his own attention becomes the inexistence of nothing: "never anything there any more" (288).

Brief investigation of Malone's exercise-book will clarify the implications of this predicament.[10] At first, the book records the object of consciousness (that which inexists in Malone's mind). But then Malone's thinking undergoes a regress such that the object of thought becomes the *fact* that he has recorded his thought: "I have just written, I fear I must have fallen, etc." (MAL, 208). The writing records the object of consciousness, but then itself becomes a secondary object of consciousness, while the original object of consciousness becomes irretrievable: "That is not what I said, I could swear to it, that is what I wrote" (209). This situation anticipates that in *The Unnamable*, where consciousness exists as the awareness of a voice or articulating consciousness that it repudiates but with which it is exclusively concerned: "Ah if only this voice could stop, this meaningless voice which prevents you from being nothing" *(UN,* 370). That is, consciousness exists through the inexistence in it of a prior consciousness that is not its own but through awareness of which it sustains a minimal being. In alternate formulation, the existence of a primary consciousness becomes inexistence in a secondary

10. For the relation between Malone's exercise-book and the exercise book (now in the Humanities Research Center at Austin) in which Beckett wrote the last pages of *Watt* and the first pages of *L'Absent* (the original title of *Malone Meurt*), see Connor (1988, 70). The reference is to Malone's comments about beginning his entry near the bottom of a page already written on: "The first pages are covered with ciphers and other symbols and diagrams, with here and there a brief phrase" (MAL, 209). For a seminal discussion of Beckett's self-conscious art, see Copeland (1975).

consciousness, which is conscious only of "incomprehension" (UN, 325) concerning it.

## Provenance of the Mimesis of Inexistence

It is impossible to derive the Beckettian mimesis of inexistence from any single factor or precursor. But insofar as Beckettian inexistence concerns the absolute isolation of the object of consciousness from the subject in which it inheres or inexists, one source involves Beckett's own early emphasis, in "Three Dialogues with Georges Duthuit," on the breakdown of the relation between subject and object, or "representer and representee" (BVV, 125). The same idea is expressed in a miscellaneous piece republished in *Disjecta* and applied to Eliot's 1922 work "The Waste Land": "The artist who is aware of this may state the space that intervenes between him and the world of objects; he may state it as a no-man's land, Hellespont or vacuum, according as he happens to be feeling resentful, nostalgic or merely depressed. A picture by Mr Jack Yeats, Mr Eliot's 'Waste Land', are notable statements of this kind" (D, 70).

Significantly, *Malone Dies* does contain a passage that almost certainly alludes to the situation described in "The Fire Sermon" section of "The Waste Land," concerning the "violet hour, when the eyes and back / Turn upward from the desk, when the human engine waits / Like a taxi throbbing waiting" (Eliot 1963, 71). Malone's account emphasizes the sudden spasm of release when office workers, "their long day ended" (MAL, 229), pour into the streets where "[f]or an instant they cluster in a daze, huddled on the sidewalk or in the gutter, then set off singly on their appointed ways" (229–30). Eliot's comparison, in the typist seduction passage, of lustful expectancy to "a taxi throbbing waiting" is echoed—perhaps even parodied—by Malone: "Some even take a cab to get more quickly to the rendez-vous or, when the fun is over, home or to the hotel, where their comfortable bed is waiting for them" (230). Moreover, the frequent testicular references in the trilogy, epitomized by Malone's allusion to "this ballsaching poppycock about life and death" (225), can also—with some discrete stretching—relate to "The Waste

Land." For one of the myths underpinning that work concerns the Fisher King, Anfortas, whose land is blighted because of the wound in one of his testicles.

Unlike "The Waste Land," whose mimetic project, according to Beckett, is to "state the space that intervenes between [the perceiver] and the world of objects" (D, 70), *Malone Dies* withdraws entirely from that world of objects. Ultimately, in a manner recalling the phenomenological *epoche* (abstention or refraining from judgment), that outer world of objects is bracketed and left out of consideration, while the focus instead is trained on inner experience and imagination: "You may say it is all in my head" (MAL, 221). Hence, the intervening space between subject and object no longer matters. For concern with objective space has been replaced by concern for the subjective experience of time: "What tedium" (187). In alternate formulation, concern with objective space is replaced by preoccupation with "all that inner space one never sees . . . where thought and feeling dance their sabbath" (MOL, 10). The Unnamable elaborates: "How all becomes clear and simple when one opens an eye on the within, having of course previously exposed it to the without, in order to benefit by the contrast" (UN, 342–43). But inner experience—what the Unnamable here terms "the within"—is itself problematized by the condition of Beckettian inexistence whereby consciousness is estranged from its own content, which then improvises its own existence by obsessively repudiating the consciousness in which it inexists or inheres.

## Inexistence and Kenosis

The hallmark of Beckettian mimesis is the representation of the "psychological commotion" (UN, 323) by which consciousness is emptied of the content that inexists in it. The deeper implications of this remarkable evacuation can be explored by reference to the doctrine of the *kenosis* or *evacuatio* (self-emptying), whereby, according to W. H. C. Frend, Christ "voluntarily divested himself of power in submitting to incarnation for the purpose of conquering death and saving man" (1972, 210). The doctrine, derived from 2 Cor. 8.9, is epitomized by Aquinas (here quoting Augustine): " 'He emptied Himself, taking the form of a servant, that he might become a servant; yet did He not lose the fulness of the form of God' " (qtd. in Frend 1972, 210). Through kenosis, as Aloys Grillmeier notes, Christ chose "a mode of existence which is a concealment of his proper being" (1975, 1.21). The purpose of Christ's kenosis is to enable the salvation of man through awakening faith in the redemptive power of divine love.

Eventually, the Christological concept of kenosis was transposed to the human dimension in order to define religious morality in higher terms. Here the supreme moral project of the individual, in achieving relationship with God, is to evacuate everything within that springs from or expresses the "[h]uman nature" (MOL, 35) shared by all members of the species. As Vladimir Lossky explains, "the perfection of the person consists in self-abandonment [kenosis]" by which everything within that pertains to the common human nature is expunged, with the result that "[t]he person is free from its nature, is not determined by it" (1957, 144, 122). In this liberated state, as Lossky observes, "the person expresses itself most truly in that it renounces to exist for itself," in terms of the drives imposed by human nature, and instead exists for God (1957, 144).

Precisely this kind of evacuation of human nature in the individual occurs in *Molloy*, when Moran repudiates his humanity ("I have been a man long enough, I shall not put up with it any more") and devotes his existence to heeding the inner voice that now addresses him: "I was getting to know it better now, to understand what it wanted" (MOL, 175, 176). By the time the trilogy reaches *The Unnamable*, the kenotic evacuation of human nature associated with the audition of the voice includes the evacuation of the object of consciousness from the consciousness in which it inexists or resides. At this point, we reach an undiscovered stratum of signification in Beckettian fiction. In some way, in virtue of its kenotic associations, the celebrated disjunction of voice and narrator or consciousness and content has redemptive properties, just as did the kenosis of Christ. Indeed, *Malone Dies*, the fiction with which we are principally concerned, abounds in allusions to Christ: (a) Macmann's question, "Why two Christs?" (MAL, 263); (b) Moll's sole-remaining tooth carved "to represent the celebrated sacrifice" (264); (c) the "stations" of Sapo's early suffering in life (206); (d) the "crucifix" affixed to the chimney-piece in the Lamberts's home; and (e) Macmann's cruciform posture in the rainstorm: "His hands at the ends of the long-outstretched arms clutched the grass, each hand a tuft, with as much energy as if he had been spread-eagled against the face of a cliff" (239).

There is no intention here of linking the notion of kenosis with a devoutly Christian interpretation of *Malone Dies* in particular or Beckettian fiction in general.[11] Indeed, Malone repudiates "the consolations of some religion or other" (248), and the Unnamable mocks "belief in God" (UN, 343). Moreover, the blasphemous strain in Beckett's art very early achieved notoriety, beginning with the attempt of the defense attorney in the 1937 Gogarty-Sinclair libel trial to discredit Samuel Beckett (witness for the plaintiff) by citing, according to James Knowlson, a passage from *More Pricks Than Kicks* (published in 1934) as a "blasphemous caricature of Jesus Christ" (Knowlson 1996, 279). A far more vulgarly blasphemous example occurs in the defecation scene in "First Love," where Beckett boldly oversteps the decorum displayed by the Joycean narrator when describing Leopold Bloom's bowel movement in the "Calypso" chapter of *Ulysses*: "At such times I never read, any more than at other times, never gave way to revery or meditation, just gazed dully at the almanac hanging from a nail before my eyes, with its chromo of a bearded stripling in the midst of sheep, Jesus no doubt, parted the cheeks with both hands and strained, heave! ho!, with the motions of one tugging at an oar, and only one thought in my mind, to be back in my room and flat on my back again" (FL, 15).

11. Compare with Hill on the topos of crucifixion in Beckett's fiction: "the sign of an unsolved conundrum, as a paradigm for the strange impossibility of joining word and flesh together in such a way as to give birth to a speaking human subject in whom name and body share a common bond of identity" (1990, 104).

As this passage suggests, Beckettian fiction offers a scatological interpretation of kenosis or "evacuation" (UN, 349), not a Christian one. There's only "shit" (UN, 365) in the head: "fucking awful business this" (UN, 282). The thoughts and feelings that inexist in consciousness are to be evacuated like a "hard stool" (to borrow a phrase from *Watt* [251]). That is perhaps the psychological origin of the mimetic kenosis we have examined, wherein the Beckettian narrator (whether named or anonymous) is represented in terms of inexistence: in terms, that is, of an object of consciousness, a swarm of thoughts, dissociated from the consciousness in which it inexists or resides. The primary Beckettian analogue of this predicament is that of words or voice dissociated from the mouth from which they issue. The kenotic function of this "wordshit" (TFN, 118) is to enable the Beckettian narrator to empty himself of himself, to be himself through the negation of himself, so that his pain will be suffered at one remove. Such is the purpose of Beckettian inexistence. An alternate image for the process of evacuation is vomiting: "I vomit, someone vomits, someone starts vomiting again, that must be how it happens" (UN, 409). But this interpretation of kenosis in Beckett's fiction contradicts the deconstructionist view, well epitomized by Daniel Katz, that "Beckett's characters don't 'produce' thought as much as interpret, translate, and repeat the 'thought' to which they are subject" (1999, 91). According to that view, "The moment of originary expression is always an echo" (92).

## The Discrepant Aspects of Beckettian Mimesis

We are ready now to reconcile the discrepant aspects of awareness represented in Beckettian fiction and, more specifically, in *Malone Dies*. On the one hand, there is the consciousness of silence or nothing. On the other hand, there is the consciousness of noise or distraction attributed to the object of consciousness that, through kenosis or evacuation, has been dissociated from the consciousness in which it properly inexists or inheres: "Somewhere in this turmoil thought struggles on, it too wide of the mark. It too seeks me, as it always has, where I am not to be found" (MAL, 186). These two poles, consciousness of nothing (or silence) and consciousness of distraction (or noise) can be construed as correlative aspects of the same condition. Viewed in terms of the evacuating agent, the consciousness of nothing pertains to the emptiness in consciousness that results from the kenosis by which consciousness evacuates its own content. Viewed in terms of the evacuated product, the consciousness of distraction pertains to the subjectivity attributed to the nexus of thought that, through kenosis, has been expelled from the consciousness whose object it is and of which it remains vestigially aware.

Beckettian narration tends to oscillate between these two poles: the void resulting from evacuation and the perplexed subjectivity attributed to the evacuated content. But this mimetic paradigm is complicated by a third factor, the ceaseless effort of the evacuating consciousness to reestablish contact with its evacuated content: "a voice like this, who can check it, it tries everything, it's blind, it seeks me blindly, in the dark" (UN, 410). Beckettian mimesis represents an almost Manichean struggle in consciousness between the need to evacuate and the need to accumulate, the need for awareness and the need for oblivion—a conflict localized in Malone's celebrated exercise-book, which records both consciousness and the gaps in consciousness: "I have spent two unforgettable days of which nothing will ever be known" (MAL, 222).[12] As Malone suggests, it is the struggle between "the blessedness of absence" (222) and the need to grasp "at last the true nature of absurd tribulations" (224).

12. For applications of "Manichean dualism" to Beckett, see Knowlson (1996, 445); Moorjani (1982, 124); and Uhlmann (1999, 117–19).

# 6

## *The Unnamable*
### The Metaphysics of Beckettian Introspection

The novel begins with an identity crisis more fundamental—and, for the reader, perhaps more bewildering—than any occurring elsewhere in literature: "Where now? Who now? When now? Unquestioning. I, say I. Unbelieving. Questions, hypotheses, call them that." Here personal existence, stripped of the fundamental certainties of time ("When now") and place ("Where now"), is reduced to one obsessive action: introspection—the act by which the very concept of selfhood ("Who now") is to be constituted. But it is a strangely passive introspection whose questions remain "[u]nquestioning" and whose imperative to affirm selfhood achieves only lack of conviction in it: "I, say I. *Unbelieving.*" Many critics argue that *The Unnamble* expresses the fundamental motive or principle of all introspection. According to Ruby Cohn, "The Unnamable seeks himself, and by extension the essence of all selfhood" (1973, 108).[1] Livio Dobrez interprets the Unnamable as "the eternal fretting of consciousness" (1976, 221). To Paul Foster, "Beckett suggests that the nature of 'I' is ineffable" (1989, 211). Considering the Unnamable under the heading, "Subjectivity as the Autogenous Cancellation of Its Own Manifestations," Wolfgang Iser concludes that "the self can only experience its own reality through an unending sequence of unintegrated and unintegratable images" (1974, 164, 175). More conventionally, David Hesla

1. For related views, see Garzilli (1986, 91) and Saint-Martin (1976, 207).

insists that the Unnamble's introspection, by splitting his identity between the nominative and objective cases, remains problematic: "It is impossible . . . that I should speak of 'I', for I can speak only of 'me' " (1971, 118).[2] In contrast, Thomas Cousineau offers a Lacanian analysis of the Unnamable's introspection: "[L]anguage allows a corrupt culture to seduce the individual with a distorted conception of himself" (1979, 2).[3] Other critics treat the Unnamable's introspection as an expression of the artistic process of creation (Blanchot 1979, 119; Copeland 1975, 111–12). To C. J. Ackerley, the "autograph text" of *The Unnamable* "reflects in itself the immediate circumstances of its very composition" (1993, 58n. 4).[4]

These interpretations have made a notoriously difficult novel more accessible by attempting to universalize the experience it concerns. But at a more profound stratum of signification, the Unnamable's project is not to achieve or express selfhood, but to repudiate it. More precisely, he seeks to fabricate an identity at once more unique and less onerous than selfhood—a property that all persons, insofar as they *are* determinately constituted as persons, share. In the course of this enterprise, he disintegrates the notions of identity enunciated respectively by three celebrated metaphysical systems: the Aristotelian, the Plotinian, and the Cartesian.

It is convenient to begin with his assault on the Cartesian *cogito*. The Unnamable's reduction of thought to the search for intro-

2. For an extensive discussion of this dichotomy between the two cases of selfhood, see Ilie (1967, 28–47).

3. For attempts to link the Unnamable with the Heideggerean notion of *das Man,* see Thiher (1983, 82).

4. Another group of critics considers the introspection in exclusively linguistic terms. Dina Sherzer views *The Unnamable* as "a text about language" (1998, 89); Dearlove studies the "dual processes of fragmentation and tessellation" (1982, 61); Moorjani examines patterns of "narrative repetition" (1982, 56); Morot-Sir interprets the novel as "language destructing bound variables and reducing grammatical deictics to anaphoric relations" (1984, 239); Connor offers a Derridean reading wherein the Unnamable is reduced to the "hymeneal suture between cessation and continuance" (1988, 75).

spected certainty invokes, as many critics have noted, a renowned precedent: the methodological doubt by which Descartes in his *Meditations* ultimately recovers metaphysical truth. There Descartes, by questioning the validity of everything in his awareness, uncovers a primary and apodictic certainty: his own act of doubting, or, more precisely, thinking—hence, the famous deduction: "I think, therefore I am." But the certainty about self ("I am") so readily proved by the Cartesian *cogito* ("I think") is unavailable to the Unnamable for whom thinking, instead of confirming existent selfhood, merely increases doubt about it. For him, "I think, therefore I am" is better rendered "I think, therefore I am a mere state of confusion about identity," or more precisely, "There is a thinking going on but whose is it, where is it, and when is it?" A closer look at the Cartesian deduction will clarify the Unnamable's predicament. In its full form, the deduction runs, "I think therefore I am a thinking thing" *(sum res cogitans)*. For Descartes, the proof of existence is simultaneously a proof of essence.[5] His metaphysics assumes that to be is to be *something*, i.e., an entity with determinate boundaries of identity. As the Second Meditation states, "[I]t could not happen that, when I see, or what amounts to the same thing, when I think I see, I who think am not *something*" (1964b, 90).[6]

But unlike his Cartesian ancestor who, by thinking on his thinking, proves his own unitary identity as an existent thinking thing, the Beckettian *cogito* (as improvised by the Unnamable) confirms only his utter "confusion" (UN, 330, 404) about his identity: "At no moment do I know what I'm talking about, nor of whom, nor of where, nor how, nor why" (338). The attempt to answer his inaugural questions, "Where now? Who now? When now?" (291), becomes a labor worthy of "Sisyphus" (MOL, 133), an exercise in futility. The Un-

---

5. Compare with Gilson's observation concerning Descartes: "[W]hen confronted with the problem of existence, he flatly denied its distinction from essence" (Gilson 1952, 109).

6. For the first linking of *The Unnamable* to this aspect of the Cartesian argument, see E. Levy (1976).

namable cannot achieve certainty about his own existence because he moots or problematizes the "substantiality" (UN, 343, 390) of the selfhood supposed to be existing: "I doubted my own existence, and even still today, I have no faith in it, none" (390–91). Instead of simply positing his own selfhood, the Unnamable attempts to *theorize* it, to convert selfhood into a series of "Questions, hypotheses" (291) about its own identity: "[A]t your age, to have no identity, it's a scandal" (377). The hypotheses follow each other in a self-consuming series, each undermining its predecessor: "affirmations and negations invalidated as soon as uttered, or sooner or later" (291). In this way, the hypotheses enable not understanding, but continuation of the "perplexity" (294) from which they spring: "[H]ypotheses are like everything else, they help you on" (404).

Hence, the unitary identity available to the Cartesian *cogito* is denied to the Unnamable, whose attempts at self-definition merely explode the identity to be defined into hypothetical fragments or fragmentary hypotheses. In fact, this relentless fission attacks even his awareness of his own thinking, which is described as the hearing of words articulating the silence of a "black void" (UN, 304). Since his experience of his thinking involves this polarity of "noise" (388) and silence, he cannot found his identity exclusively on either pole: "[I]t has not yet been our good fortune to establish with any degree of accuracy what I am, where I am, whether I am words among words, or silence in the midst of silence" (388). A provisional solution is to define himself as "the partition" between them—or as "the tympanum" whose vibrations, caused by the noise impinging on one side, allow the silent awareness or "mind" on the other side to hear (383). But he proposes this solution only to repudiate identification with *both* poles: "I don't belong to either" (383).

Thus, the Cartesian *cogito* and the Unnamable are rationalist contraries. Both begin in absolute doubt, and both begin with introspection. But each uses doubt and introspection in a way opposite to that of the other. Whereas the Cartesian *cogito* doubts now in order to know or affirm apodictic and indubitable truth later, the Unnamable doubts now in order to go on doubting in the future. For motives we shall soon clarify, he prefers to remain unknowing: "I always liked not knowing" (309). As a strict rationalist with only his doubt to guide him, Descartes knows he can never be deceived, for thinking, properly conducted, is validated by the rules of reason: "I can already establish as a general principle that everything which we conceive very clearly and very distinctly is wholly true" (1964b, 92). The Unnamable, though equally subject to "the laws of the mind" (MOL, 13), ensures that thinking will only continue incertitude. By enfeebling his own thought ("[A]s far as thinking is concerned I do just enough to preserve me from going silent" [UN, 307]), and by obfuscating his own knowledge ("I know without knowing what it means" [338]), the Unnamable guarantees that his quest for self-knowledge merely confirms self-doubt: "[Y]ou're there, you don't know who, you don't know where" (370).

For the *cogito*, introspection (thinking about its thinking) yields the first truth on which all others are founded. According to Descartes, only after formulating clearly and distinctly the idea "which represents myself to myself" can the *cogito* move on to other ideas and so fulfill the goal of perfecting its knowledge (1964b, 99). Unlike the Unnamable, the Cartesian *cogito* is instantaneously reflective: It both thinks and knows it thinks in the same instant. As Sartre has pointed out: "The *cogito* is only the manifestation of consciousness. In knowing I am conscious of knowing" (1967, 114). The same observation occurs in Gilbert Ryle's especially apt description of Cartesian privacy: "[M]ental processes are 'overheard' by the mind whose processes they are, somewhat as a speaker overhears the words he is himself uttering" (1949, 159). In contrast, the Unnamable's introspection remains an inconclusive and problematic act, baffled by the polarity of noise and silence. It is as if a sudden amnesia always intervened between the act of thinking and awareness of having thought—"I think I must have blackouts" (UN, 368)—with the result that the Unnamable, though overhearing an act of thinking, cannot claim it as his own—"[A]s if I were speaking, to myself, out loud, in the end you don't know any more, a voice that never stops, where it's coming from" (369).

His quandary can be formulated more precisely. Imagine the *cog-ito* or "I think" suddenly separated from its own *cogitatum* or thought while in the act of reflecting on it. In this case, that which is thought (the *cogitatum*) concerns the very act of thinking, for to prove its own existence the *cogito* thinks on its thinking. Now imag-ine this *cogitatum* (that which is thought) endowed with its own rudimentary *cogito* with which to reflect on its own thinking, just as did the original *cogito* whose *cogitatum* it is. We are now on the "threshold" (414) of the Unnamable's elusive identity. He is the *cog-ito* at one remove from itself, a thought *(cogitatum)* sundered from the act of thinking *(cogito)* that produced it and forced it to exist on its own in the only way possible—through thinking on the act of thinking or *cogito,* whose thought or *cogitatum* it is and on which its existence therefore depends.[7] Yet, through identifying as a *cogitatum* estranged from its *cogito,* the Unnamable reduces his existence to in-voluntary introspection—the interminable awareness of a thinking that is not his own and which he can neither stop nor understand.

Before proceeding with our analysis, we must remember that the Unnamable's predicament is pure fantasy, as he himself admits: "It's I who am doing this to me, *I who am talking to me about me*" (UN, 394; my emphasis). The project to negate the "substantiality" (343, 390) of his own selfhood by repudiating the act of introspection that formulates it has a profound and unexpected motive, but under-standing it requires refocusing the two poles defining the Unnam-able's experience: noise and silence, *cogito* and *cogitatum,* thinking (as subjective act or process) and thought (as resultant mental ob-

7. Since here the Unnamable attempts to identify with the idea of himself as sus-tained by the act of introspection which he then repudiates, his reference to his "inex-istence" (UN, 344) recalls (perhaps inadvertently) Franz Brentano's use of the term to indicate the purely intentional or mental being that an object has in the mind that thinks it: "Every mental phenomenon is characterized by what the scholastics of the Middle Ages called the intentional (and also mental) *inexistence* of an object" (Brentano 1960, 50; my emphasis). The term occurs again in Samuel Beckett: "I exist, in the pit of my inexistence" (TFN, 91). To put this in Cartesian terms, as *cogitatum* the Unnamable *inexists* in the mind or *cogito* thinking him.

ject), the introspecting self and the self introspected. In a crucial section, the Unnamable deepens the meaning of this dichotomy by *four times* linking the phrase "sign(s) of life" with the irrepressible utterance of the voice and, consequently, associating the craving for "silence" and "peace" with the paradoxical wish to live undisturbed by life:

> Ah this blind voice, and these moments of held breath, when all listen wildly, and the voice begins to fumble again, without knowing what it's looking for, and again the tiny silence, and the listening again, for what, no one knows, a sign of life perhaps, that must be it, a sign of life escaping someone . . . if only all that could stop, there'd be peace, no, too good to be believed, the listening would go on, for the voice to begin again, for a sign of life . . . what else can there be but signs of life . . . one could multiply examples. (UN, 372)

In this context, the Unnamable's purpose in elaborately imagining his predicament at last becomes clear. Life means change, and the defining wish of the Unnamable is to remain immutable: "all change to be feared, incomprehensible uneasiness" (UN, 295). Through his fiction of the vain act of introspection, he sustains the fantasy of immunity to change: "[I]t's too soon, to return, to where I am, emptyhanded, in triumph, to where I'm waiting, calm . . . knowing, thinking I know, that nothing has befallen me, nothing will befall me" (363). To ward off change, he withdraws into an unchanging confusion where nothing happens but his own experience of uncertainty: "[S]upposing nothing, asking yourself nothing, you can't, you're there, you don't know who, you don't know where, the thing stays where it is, nothing changes, within it, outside it, apparently, apparently" (370). In this state, perpetuating preoccupation with indeterminate introspection, the Unnamable will always remain what he already is. Thus, he lives but without the encumbrance of life: "But within, motionless, I can live, and utter me for no ears but my own" (325). Or, in reverse formulation, he describes himself as having a life but without the developmental potential proper to living: "No, one can spend one's life thus, unable to live, unable to bring to life, and die in vain, having done nothing, been nothing" (358). The attempt to forestall change entails the effort to stop time: "[T]he question may be asked . . . why time doesn't pass . . . why it piles up all about you, instant on instant, on all sides, deeper and deeper . . . why it buries you grain by grain neither dead nor alive, with no memory of anything, no hope of anything, no knowledge of anything, no history and no prospects, buried under the seconds, saying any old thing, your mouth full of sand" (UN, 389). Through perseverating the same futility, the Unnamable renders all moments identical and nullifies the succession that time involves: "another instant of my old instant" (400). By never ceasing the same "lamentation" (393), the Unnamable secures the illusion that time does not move, until ultimately the pain lamented concerns this very absence of change: "[T]he nuisance of doing over, and of being, same thing, for one who could never do, never be" (370).

It is important to understand the Unnamable's strategy. By denying time or, more precisely, the mutability it entails, he replaces one kind of pain (vulnerability to change) with another: the "impossible sorrow . . . as of one buried before his time" (UN, 393). He arrests change by prolonging the excruciating experience of sameness: "No one asks him to think, simply to suffer, always in the same way, without hope of diminution, without hope of dissolution. . . . Agreed then on *monotony*" (367; my emphasis). According to this strategy, unremitting repetition of "the same old litany" (374) is the only means of eventual release from the pain of uttering it: "The search for the means to put an end to things, an end to speech, is what enables the discourse to continue" (299).[8] His tactic is to continue the tedium of utterance until his identity is wholly defined by the need for utterance to stop: "I'll speak of me when I speak no more" (392). Hence, the paradoxical purpose of his introspection is not to

---

8. Compare with Moran: "Whereas to see yourself doing the same thing endlessly over and over again fills you with satisfaction" *(MOL, 133).*

determine selfhood, but to forsake it and thus achieve the state of "being nothing" (370).

The condition of "being nothing" is the Unnamable's goal, but one that does not imply physical extinction.[9] Instead, it concerns an awareness that persists not after life is over, but when the change and development characteristic of life have been refused. The Unnamable pursues his own way of resolving Hamlet's dilemma, "To be, or not to be." His solution is to reduce being to the act of self-denial by turning self-denial into an affirmation. In other words, he turns "it's not I" (UN, 370, 402, 409) into "it will be I" (414). By now we have become well acquainted with his method of doing so. Through reducing life to an "anguish" (395) of frustrated confusion, he identifies with the inability to establish certainty. Yet the admission of futility ultimately becomes an affirmation of purpose, for the Unnamable's aim is to remain isolated from change by conviction of his own "unchanging" (346) ignorance. By obsessively confirming this conviction, the Unnamable seeks to approximate the vacuous identity attributed to Worm, the last persona he creates: "The one outside of life we always were in the end, all our long vain life long. . . . The one ignorant of himself and silent, ignorant of his silence and silent, who could not be and gave up trying" (346–47).

A tremendous ambiguity between giving up and trying complicates the Unnamable's predicament, for the purpose of his struggle is to encourage capitulation, to prove that only failure should be desired. Hence, giving up requires unflagging effort; surrender demands indomitable endurance. To lapse into the silent vacancy he craves, the Unnamable must prolong the "voluable" (UN, 374) introspection he detests until that impossible point where struggle and rest coincide, as his celebrated conclusion reveals: "[P]erhaps they [i.e., his words] have carried me to the threshold of my story, before the door that opens on my story, that would surprise me, if it opens, it will be I, it will be the silence, where I am, I don't know, I'll never

---

9. Compare with *Molloy*: "But the thought of suicide had little hold on me" (MOL, 79).

know, in the silence you don't know, *you must go on, I can't go on, I'll go on*" (414; my emphasis). In his very last words (which I have italicized) the Unnamable, though unbearably exhausted, vows to persevere in his exertions. But this supreme commitment is immediately contradicted by silence, for the end of the novel intervenes.

The contradiction dissolves when we remember the circumstances of its appearance. As he himself suggests, the Unnamable has indeed been carried by the words into the "silence" of his completed "story" (UN, 414) and by implication persists there, "outside of life" (346) but living, not with his awareness but with ours. For, as readers of the story, we are now the awareness of his silence, while he himself has fulfilled the wish for total oblivion. In fact, we are now in the position that he occupied before this consummation—aware of an oblivion from which we are separated by our very awareness of it: "One alone turned toward the all-impotent, all-nescient, that haunts him, then others" (346). This "all-impotent, all-nescient" that "could not be and gave up trying" (347) is the Beckettian ideal: "Who seems the truest possession, because the most unchanging" (346). As such, it is remarkably similar to the One that, in the metaphysics of Plotinus, also transcends Being and knowledge. Just as a brief consideration of Descartes helped begin our inquiry, so some treatment of Plotinus will help continue it.

Plotinus posited the One as the first cause of reality in order to found his metaphysics on an absolutely simple principle. As Etienne Gilson observes, the One "ultimately causes being [or that which is really real] by giving it unity" (1952, 21). According to Plotinus, being must be derived from a principle beyond being, for in itself being lacks unity and only that which is one can properly be said to be. Being is not one because, through its very intelligibility, it is split in two. Gilson explicates: "[T]he One transcends all conceivable intelligibility, for the simple reason that, as soon as the relation of knower to known appears, unity steps out of the picture to make room for duality" (1952, 27). The same division applies to introspection, when the knower and the known coincide in the same act. Again Gilson elucidates: "Yet, even then, for one and the same thing to be both knowing and known means for it to be no longer one, but two.

Now how could the absolutely one possibly be two?" (1952, 23). For this reason, the first principle of reality from which all being emanates must itself remain unreal (that is, above being) and hence unknowable—even to itself, as Plotinus explicitly states: "If there is a reality that is the simplest of all, it would have no self-knowledge. Had it such knowledge, it would be a multiple being. Consequently, it does not think itself, nor does one think it" *(Enneads,* 5.3.13, qtd. in Gilson 1952, 23). As first principle, the supreme purpose of the Plotinean One is to enable being to be. Its own perfect unity, beyond reality and intelligibility, is both the source of being and the state of ineffable simplicity with which rational beings can aspire to unite through that ecstatic vision Plotinus calls "a flight of the alone to the Alone" (1964, *Enneads,* 6.9.11). The same aspiration to return to a first principle lacking both being and intelligibility, but nevertheless preceding life and determining its ultimate meaning, motivates the Unnamable, as a crucial passage quoted earlier confirms: "One alone turned toward the all-impotent, all-nescient, that haunts him, then others. . . . The one outside of life we always were in the end, all our long vain life long" (UN, 346). Yet, though similarly beyond being and knowledge, the Beckettian first principle functions very differently from its Plotinean counterpart. Instead of *conserving* being by guaranteeing the unity necessary to it, the Beckettian first principle fosters an *abdication* of being by representing the impossible act of existential capitulation: "who could not be and gave up trying" (347). As such, the Beckettian ideal concerns the utter resignation of selfhood, not the transcendence of it.[10]

※

We come now to perhaps the greatest paradox in the novel. Though confined to introspection, the Unnamable frequently posits the universality of his situation: "[T]here must be others in other

10. John Pilling also describes Worm as an ideal but with no elaboration: "Worm . . . represents an ideal, a much lower ideal than most thinkers would allow, but an ideal none the less" (1976, 60).

elsewheres, each one in his little elsewhere" (UN, 403). Of course, because of what the Unnamable terms "the fault of the pronouns" (404), there is tremendous ambiguity here concerning reference. The pronoun *they*, which seems obviously to signify other selves, instead refers to the words heard by the Unnamable: "He knows they are words, he is not sure they are not his . . . one day he'll make them his" (354). The others who share the void with the Unnamable merely personify the words from which he is alienated by the act of utterance.[11] Moreover, on many occasions the Unnamable extends pity to these words despite their tormenting behavior: "[T]hey are doing the best they can, with the miserable means at their disposal, a voice, a little light, poor devils" (368).

This ambiguity between words and selves has profound implications. In this context, words are indeed like selves, because a self is here defined as "a labouring whirl" of words (UN, 402), circulating vainly around an emptiness it can never express. But "if this notion is maintained" (to borrow a recurrent phrase from *The Lost Ones*), it follows that truly intimate communication between selves can never occur. For the words used communicate only their own irrelevance: "Is there a single word of mine in all I say?" (347). Hence, the void or emptiness that words cannot communicate ultimately signifies the conviction that self-expression and the self-knowledge enabling it are futile: "[N]one will ever know what I am, none will ever hear me say it" (325). This predicament is not inevitable but willed; its origin is not the nature of selfhood but the wish to avoid it. As we have seen, obsessive uncertainty about identity derives from the need to avoid the more fearsome uncertainty threatened by change. Endlessly perplexed self-preoccupation perpetuates a state perfectly resistant to change. Fixation prevents maturation.[12]

11. Enrica Garzilli also notes that *they* refers to the Unnamable's words (1986, 90). But Allen Thiher relates *they* to Heidegger's *"das Man,* the anonymous 'they' that speak, through inauthentic speech, the fallen logos of everyday existence" (1983, 82).

12. Compare with Dewey: "Maturation and fixation are polar opposites" (1934, 41).

Hence we glimpse the deeper meaning of the Unnamable's fantasy of universality: "each one in his little elsewhere" (UN, 403). According to this hypothesis, all selves inhabit the same void where the fundamental experience of each concerns estrangement—not just from others, but also from his or her own identity. But the preoccupation of each never leads to the collective awareness of all. The only function of community in the Beckettian universe is to multiply the experience of isolation. The most elaborate image of such contradictory community occurs in *The Lost Ones*, where the inhabitants of a cylindrical world lapse consecutively into a state of "vanquished" torpor in which each, if aware of anything, knows only the inanity of movement. Obviously, the purpose of Beckettian community is not to dispel isolation, but to alter its meaning. No longer a singular anomaly, isolation becomes the common state. This illusion of universality is intended to lessen the pain caused by isolation. For there is now no distinction between isolation and company, as the Unnamable himself suggests: "[L]et us go on as if I were the only one in the world, whereas I'm the only one absent from it, or with others, *what difference does it make*" (401; my emphasis).

The fantasy of universality has additional consequences that can be highlighted by brief reference to other Beckettian works. If all selves share the same frustrated need to communicate, then life is reduced to a "senseless, speechless, issueless misery" (MOL, 13) where each, to borrow a phrase from *Company*, is "[b]uried in who knows what profounds of mind" (COM, 34). As the Unnamable indicates, this withdrawal seethes with implacable rage at life for inflicting such torment: "The head is there, glued to the ear, and in it nothing but rage" (UN, 356). Sometimes the fury erupts as obscenity: "[F]uck all that" (399). Similarly vulgar objurgations occur in *Mercier and Camier* ("Bugger life!") and *Rockaby* ("[F]uck life") (MC, 114; ROCK, 20). The only relief from this impotent anger is to focus even more obsessively on its cause: futility. Preoccupation with futility ultimately leads beyond rage to sadness at everything that can never be and never was, until the only connection with life is the desire to become oblivious to it: "Regretting, that's what helps you on . . . regretting what is, regretting what was . . . that's what transports you, towards the end of regretting" (UN, 371). The combination of rage and grief is prominently emphasized by the Unnamable: "Tears gush from it practically without ceasing, why is not known . . . whether it's with rage, or whether it's with grief" (359–60).

But near the outset of his narration, the Unnamable contradicts this admission of dual passion by claiming that he is "devoid of feeling" (UN, 293). In fact, in doing so he uses the same image of tearing eyes: "The tears stream down my cheeks from my unblinking eyes. What makes me weep so?" (293). His question underscores the Unnamable's preference not to know his own feelings. Indeed, this very passage includes more evidence of emotional ignorance: "Nothing ever troubles me. And yet I am troubled" (293). Feelings entail involvement and unpredictability, whereas the Unnamable prefers detachment and regularity: "All has proceeded, all this time, in the utmost calm, the most perfect order, apart from one or two manifestations the meaning of which escapes me" (293–94). Moreover, emotions prove his own reality, whereas the Unnamable refuses to take his selfhood seriously: "To make me believe I have an ego all my own, and can speak of it, as they of theirs. Another trap to snap me up among the living" (345). Hence, he substitutes a fantasy world for the real one: a mental world in which emotion is subordinate to thought or, more precisely, in which emotion is eventually dissipated through the sheer monotony of thinking about frustration.

The extreme pathos of the Unnamable's predicament is exceeded only by its irony. The suffering that defines his existence derives from the same need for ordered perfection that inspires metaphysics. Just as the metaphysician by the power of thought seeks to abstract from the complexity of experience the apodictic principle(s) on which all meaning and purpose ultimately depend, so the Unnamable, through his introspective torment, satisfies the need to purify life of all inconsistency until only one invariable mode of being remains: utter impotence and ignorance. In fact, on the first page of his narration, the Unnamable foregrounds the metaphysical nature of his quest by twice using the term *aporia*: "What am I to do, what shall I do, what should I do, in my situation, how proceed? By aporia pure and simple?" (UN, 291). A few lines later he adds: "I should mention before going any further, any further on, that I say aporia without knowing what it means" (291).

This coy reference to *aporia* at the outset of a dissertation on "being and existing" (348) inevitably recalls the method of Aristotle in Book B of the *Metaphysics* concerning the aporematic treatment of causes. Joseph Owens provides an etymology of the term: "The vocabulary of the Aristotelian aporia is based on the Greek 'poros,' meaning 'passage.' The privative alpha gives the signification 'lack of passage.' In an aporia the intellect has no passage. It can make no headway. Something is holding it back" (1951, 214). According to Aristotle, in a passage quoted by Owens, the success of any rational inquiry depends on "drawing up the aporiae," for without a clear understanding of the obstacles to be encountered the deliberation will lack direction: "Hence one should have surveyed all the difficulties beforehand . . . because people who inquire without first drawing up the aporiae are like those who do not know where they have to go; besides a man does not otherwise know even whether he has at any given time found what he is looking for or not; for the end is not clear to such a man, while to him who has first drawn up the aporiae it is clear" (1951, 218). [13]

The significance of the Unnamable's reference to aporia is clarified by this excerpt. By not drawing up the aporiae, he dooms his inquiry to failure and becomes, to repeat Aristotle's words, "like those who do not know where they have to go"—or who, having got there, do not know that they have arrived.[14] But sustaining uncertainty is

13. More generally, Leslie Hill defines *aporia* as a "rhetorical impasse" (1990, 63). Alan Astro erroneously defines it as "a logical difficulty to which there is no solution" (1990, 81).

14. Another famous foregrounding of *aporia* occurs in Plato's *Meno*, but *The Unnamable* bears no internal evidence of alluding to it. Werner Jaeger summarizes:

the Unnamable's purpose.[15] His incessant "Questions, hypotheses" (UN, 291) merely extend the dominion of ignorance to the point where he cannot even determine whether he wakes or sleeps: "[P]erhaps it's a dream, all a dream" (414). Indeed, in the first novel of the trilogy, Molloy recommends this strategy: "[Y]ou have to be careful, ask yourself questions, as for example whether you still are, and if no when it stopped, and if yes how long it will go on, *anything at all to keep you from losing the thread of the dream*" (MOL, 49; my emphasis). In his dream, the Unnamable knows only an immediate succession of experience where the distinction between truth and falsehood does not yet apply, as we see in the rapid oscillation from affirmation to negation back to affirmation: "[Y]ou wait, in anguish, have they forgotten me, no, yes, no, someone calls me, I crawl out again, what is it, a little hole, in the wilderness" (395). In this context, selfhood is no more than the unrestrained expression of perplexity.

Thus the Unnamable is essentially an *anti*-metaphysician, pursuing the opposite of Wisdom or the science of being. He seeks the supreme principle by which meaning is reduced to "babble" (UN, 354) and order to self-stultifying repetition. Yet the original question of his identity still remains: Who is the Unnamable? Following his own use of the *via negativa*, we can best determine who he is by first clarifying who he isn't. The Unnamable is *not* the literary representation of a person, for he lacks a body ("I am the absentee again . . .

---

"[Meno says that] Socrates possesses the dangerous art of leading people into an impasse, from which they can go neither forward nor back. He compares him with the electric eel, which numbs the hand that touches it. But Socrates turns the edge of the metaphor by saying that the eel must electrify itself too, for he himself is the victim of his *aporia*, his helplessness." Further: *"aporein,* to be helpless . . . is the first stage on the way towards the positive knowledge of truth" (1945, 2:169).

15. Compare with Molloy and Moran on ignorance. First Molloy: "For to know nothing is nothing, not to want to know anything likewise, but to be beyond knowing anything, to know you are beyond knowing anything, that is when peace enters in, to the soul of the incurious seeker" (MOL, 64). Then Moran on observing the dance of the bees: "And I said with rapture, Here is something I can study all my life, and never understand" (MOL, 169).

who has neither body nor soul" [413]) and the world he inhabits has no reality apart from his own way of formulating it. As such, he is no more than a mentality or way of thinking about life—and one that, in less extreme form, can influence any person susceptible to it. To understand the Unnamable in these terms is to grasp the ironic implications of the universality that he tentatively claims.

Through the elaborate fiction of his own narrative project, the Unnamable progressively distances himself not only from reality, but even from its mimesis in order ultimately to emerge as a mere perspective on life—or a way of thinking about it. A brief review of the evidence will clarify this process. To begin with, the Unnamable obviously represents what might be called the Beckettian consciousness as manifested in fiction, aware of the long sequence of personae (or "ponderous chronicle of moribunds" [UN, 308]) its own expression has created: "To tell the truth I believe they are all here, at least from Murphy on . . . but so far I have seen only Malone" (293).[16] When describing himself as this Beckettian consciousness, the Unnamable uses the paradigm of ventriloquist and puppet to suggest that the verisimilitude of creatures was subservient to his own need for expression: "I think Murphy spoke now and then, the others too perhaps, I don't remember, but it was clumsily done, you could see the ventriloquist" (348). Moreover, early in *Molloy* (the first novel in the trilogy), this creative consciousness, just before fusing with Molloy and long before emerging in its own right in the third novel as the Unnamable, twice foregrounds its own creative act from which the three texts will emanate: "Yes, let me cry out, this time, then another time perhaps, then perhaps a last time" (MOL, 25); "And this enables me, what is more, to know when that unreal journey began, the second last but one of a form fading among fading forms" (16–17).[17]

16. According to Rubin Rabinovitz, the Unnamable "claims that Molloy, Moran, Malone and Mahood are unrealistic versions of himself created in his many attempts to define himself" (1992, 96).

17. Steven Connor notes that the phrase, "then perhaps a last time," does not occur in the French version (1988, 78).

In the course of this process of emanation, the conventional function of fiction as the imitation of life slowly drains away, as Moran himself intuits: "My life was running out, I knew not through what breach" (MOL, 102). With Malone's dying "gurgles of outflow" (MAL, 287), which conclude the second novel of the trilogy, the drainage is complete. Once *The Unnamable* begins, mimesis now exclusively concerns an experience of "credible perplexity" (UN, 294) where the conventional distinctions between subjective and objective, mental and physical no longer apply. Having discarded his puppets, the "ventriloquist" (348) has also abandoned the illusion of selfhood attending them. The Unnamable is not dead, but he refuses to identify with the living—despite the futility of intransigence: "[L]ittle by little the old problem will raise its horrid head, how to live, with their kind of life, for a single second" (334). As we have seen, his ideal is the inaccessible singularity of "The one outside of life" (346), whose "all-impotent, all-nescient" exclusion can never be violated.

Yet at the same time that he scorns life, the Unnamable desperately craves it: "my longing to have floundered in *the great life torrent* streaming from the earliest protozoa to the very latest humans" (UN, 322; my emphasis). Paradoxically, this yearning for life clarifies the reason for detesting it. According to the passage just quoted, the essence of life is evolutionary community—immersion, that is, in the magnificent "torrent" (322) of evolution that sweeps all along. But to live in these circumstances is to lose unique identity; it is to have that uniqueness subsumed by the larger developmental process that it serves.

The problem here is crucial to the Unnamable. The only way to be uniquely oneself is to be different from everyone else.[18] But how

---

18. Gilson provides a very terse definition of the individual: "undivided in himself and divided from all else" (1936, 200). Compare with the Hegelian notion of self-consciousness in *Phenomenology of Spirit*, as rendered by Kojève with bracketed commentary: "[I]t is identical-to-itself by excluding from *itself* everything *other* [than itself]" (Kojève 1969, 10). For a reduction of the Unnamable to the Hegelian notion of consciousness, see Butler (1984, 126–27).

can one be different from everyone else if life always entails being a member of a certain species, which in turn is only one among innumerable other species? In the Beckettian universe, to be an individual in the human species is to suffer estrangement from one's own unique identity: "Ah but the little murmur of unconsenting man, to murmur what it is their humanity stifles, the little gasp of the condemned to life, rotting in his dungeon garrotted and racked, to gasp what it is to have to celebrate banishment, beware" (UN, 325). The same complaint is made by Moran, who feels "exiled in his manhood" (MOL, 169). Similarly in *How It Is*, the narrator refers to his eventual alienation from species: "I was young I clung on to the species we're talking of the human" (HOW, 47).

Yet loss of species entails loss of identity, for an individual owes its identity *as* an individual to the species to which it belongs. To be an individual is to individualize a form or essence, and it is species that provides this necessary designation.[19] For example, as Gilson explains: "the essence of man is *humanitas* [i.e., the "humanity" that the Unnamable mentioned above], which notion covers everything by which man is man—a reasoning animal composed of body and soul" (1956, 88). Without membership in species, the individual would lack any form defining what type of individual it is.[20] As such it would be literally unintelligible. In this context, the Unnamable's motive for identifying with his lack of identity, and for explicitly denying possession of either body or soul, becomes clearer. One way to repudiate species and reclaim individuality is to identify, not with form, but with its opposite—unintelligibility: "Dear incomprehension, it's thanks to you I'll be myself in the end. Nothing will remain of all the

19. Gilson elaborates: "[P]recisely because the form is *specific* it is of the same nature in all of the individuals of the same species" (1936, 193–94). Compare with Woods: "It is the species-form *man* which supplies us with a principle for individuation for man; it is only in virtue of possessing the form *man* that bits of matter which constitute men are marked off from one another" (1967, 237).

20. Ernst Cassirer formulates this "[f]undamental principle of cognition" in its most general terms: "[T]he universal can be perceived only in the particular, while the particular can be thought only in reference to the universal" (1957, 1:86).

lies they have glutted me with" (UN, 325).[21] Thus, the Unnamable overcomes what Gilson calls "the famous Aristotelian principle that the individual exists for the sake of the species" (1936, 202).[22]

The repudiation of form in favor of uncomprehending "formlessness" (Malone's term [MAL, 197]) has further implications. By ceaselessly narrating the experience of confusion through the sequence of personae, the Unnamable or the Beckettian consciousness that he localizes ultimately identifies not with individuality, but with species or, more precisely, with the principle of generation whereby species secures its own perpetuation. Thus, in order to escape the uniformity of one species, the Unnamable associates himself with another of his own devising, but in doing so condemns himself to "this hell of stories" (UN, 380).

But the Unnamable also adopts the contrary of this tactic in order to defect from species. While identifying with the principle of generation by which species multiplies its members, he simultaneously identifies as a mere unit in the series thus generated. The following passage illustrates: "like a caged beast born of caged beasts born of caged beasts born of caged beasts born in a cage and dead in a cage, born and then dead, born in a cage and then dead in a cage, in a word like a beast . . . *with nothing of its species left but fear and fury*" (UN, 386–87; my emphasis). Here, by exaggerating the primacy of species, the Unnamable almost overcomes it. For in his exasperation he is identified not through the form imposed by the species, but through his emotional reaction to imprisonment in it.[23] The rational-

21. In contrast, Iser argues that this passage refers to "the incomprehensibility of reality, and indeed of the ego itself, that gives rise to the creation of fiction" (1974, 268).

22. A different account of the primacy of species appears in Freud's essay, "On Narcissism: An Introduction," where the ultimate end of sexuality is "to provide for the extension of individual life into that of the species" (1984, 11:71). According to Freud, "The individual does actually carry on a twofold existence: one to serve his own purposes and the other as a link in a chain, which he serves against his will, or at least involuntarily" (1984, 11:70).

23. For the first sustained discussion of "species" in the trilogy, see E. Levy

ity that is the form of the species, man (the *rational* animal, "in the jargon of the schools" [MOL, 51]), is here reduced to fear and fury. The fury results from frustration with captivity, and the fear results from acquired anxiety about freedom.[24]

A strange inversion of the doctrine of metempsychosis or reincarnation occurs here—one that epitomizes the predicament of individuality in *The Unnamable*. According to the doctrine of metempsychosis, the cycle of life and death involves a transmigration of the same soul through a series of different bodies such that the form assumed in each new incarnation results from the moral quality of the life preceding it. But in the Unnamable's account, individuality loses all responsibility for the cycle in which it is caught. For now the purpose of the cycle is not to enable the individual eventually to earn release from reincarnation, but simply to allow a species to perpetuate itself through the generations of individuals whose identity *as* individuals it defines. Consequently, far from confirming moral responsibility, awareness of one's own suffering *exempts* from all responsibility.[25] Pain signifies not expiation of guilt incurred in the past, but the irreproachable innocence of the sufferer in the present. His only sin is the necessity of living (as an individual in a species): "I was given a pensum, at birth perhaps, as a punishment for having been born perhaps" (UN, 310). Meaningless suffering or, more precisely, the suffering of meaninglessness is all that the Unnamable asks for

---

(1980, 62–71).

24. Astro dismisses this section as "a compulsively repetitious passage, where the rhythm drowns out the sense" (1990, 91). Barker interprets it as an allusion to Freud's "Return of the Repressed" (1990, 135).

25. From different perspectives, many critics have noted the Unnamable's renunciation of responsibility. To P. J. Murphy, *"The Unnamable* reveals how a being (whether fictional or human) who does not accept the possibility of his own freedom needs to create fictions of guilt and punishment" (1990, 29). To Vivian Mercier, "The reason why The Unnamable cannot achieve true being is surely his inability to make any of those conscious choices through which authenticity is attained according to Sartre's doctrine" (1977, 170). In contrast, Milton Rickels (1962) highlights existential themes in the novel.

and all that can be asked of him: "Let them scourge me without ceasing and evermore . . . in the end I might begin to look as if I had grasped the meaning of life" (353). The reduction of life to the protest of uncomprehending innocence against the injustice of "an incomprehensible damnation" (308) is the essence of the Beckettian metaphysic, as formulated in *The Unnamable.*

This incomprehension has profound implications. As noted, the Unnamable's emphasis on the subordination of individuals to the species they sustain recalls the Aristotelean metaphysics where, according to Gilson, "[I]ndividuals do not matter in themselves; their species uses them in order to endure" (1952, 72). But the Unnamable invokes that metaphysic only to contradict the very principle on which its meaning and purpose depend: *entelechy,* or what Erich Auerbach calls "[t]he doctrine of the self-realization of the essence," according to which individual beings tend toward the full actualization of their respective forms (1961, 7). Werner Jaeger elucidates: "In them form appears as an orderliness and determinateness building from within and unfolding itself from the matter as from a seed" (1962, 384). For each individual human being, the species-form to be progressively realized is, of course, *reason* or, in Wilhelm Windelband's more extensive phrase, "the practice of rational activity" (1958, 1:151). Now, "according to Aristotle, who knew everything," the highest and most perfect thinking the human individual can achieve concerns the intellection of eternal certainties (TFN, 114). As Sir David Ross elaborates, "The happy life is not one of search for truth, but one of contemplation of truth already attained" (1949, 234).

The Unnamable adopts this Aristotelian framework only to invert its principles. Instead of using thought to achieve self-realization, he forces thought to endure its own frustration—in the sense of never completing what in *Company* is called "a successful act of intellection," whereby the passage from ignorance to knowledge unfolds (COM, 63). The same tactic appears in *Waiting for Godot,* where Vladimir and Estragon exploit dialogue as the means of thwarting any deliberation by which a solution to their predicament might be attained: "In the meantime let us try and converse calmly, since we are incapable of keeping silent. It's so we won't think" (WFG, 40). A similar hampering of reason appears in *Play* ("If only I could think" [PL, 56]), in "I Gave Up Before Birth" ("impossible I should have thoughts, and I speak and think, I do the impossible" [IGUBB, 45]), and, most emphatically, in *Watt,* where "the need to think," to render experience intelligible, is repeatedly frustrated: "Then Watt did not know what to think" (W, 74, 64). For the Unnamable in this predicament, reason thinks only of its own impotence. There is nothing to know but the certainty of ignorance. The only entelechy to fulfill is the sense of purposelessness: "No need to think in order to despair" (UN, 367).[26]

---

26. It is hoped that the foregoing analysis rescues the novel from the judgment of Alvarez: *"The Unnamable* gets perilously close to being the Unreadable" (1973, 63).

# 7

## False Innocence in *Waiting for Godot*

Perhaps the most enigmatic play of this century is *Waiting for Godot.* The act of waiting for Godot, a figure whose identity is notoriously difficult to determine, has given rise to myriad interpretations. In a recent study, Andrew Kennedy provides a brief bibliography of four persistent readings: existentialist, Marxist, Freudian, and Christian (where Vladimir and Estragon are seen as waiting in vain for the Savior) (1989, 31).[1] His findings are by no means exhaustive. For example, some politically oriented critics regard the play not in Marxist terms, but as an anticipation of the passive resistance movement dominating the early sixties.[2] In contrast, Robert Zaller invokes the political vision of Hobbes.[3] To many philosophically inclined critics, Descartes is a more compelling antecedent than the existentialists (Rabillard 1992, 114n. 2). Literary theory has also been applied to the play in remarkable variety. Among the many contributions in this area, one might note those pertaining to semiotics (Alter 1987, 42–56), speech-act theory (Corfariu 1984, 119–33), and reader-response theory (Iser 1989, 152–93). The text has even been sub-

---

1. Similar to the existentialist interpretation, the absurdist reading, pioneered by Martin Esslin (1961, 18–19), has won many adherents. See Webb (1972, 26) and Alvarez (1973, 6). However, Vivian Mercier (1977, 84) argues against this view. For more recent existentialist interpretations, see McCandless (1988), drawing on Tillich; and Butler (1984, 74–113), drawing on Heidegger and Sartre.

2. See Blau (1991, 9) and Lamont (1975, 217).

3. See Zaller (1986, 160–73).

jected to biographical analysis with intriguing results (Gontarski 1985, 35–36; Bair 1978, 386).

While all these approaches have illumined or at least emphasized some important aspect of the text, they tend to subordinate the work to extraneous principles or facts. This tendency is not necessarily a shortcoming, for the complex interplay of ideas in the play has often been clarified through careful juxtaposition with ideas from another framework. But there remains the possibility of studying the play from within in order to learn how a unique attitude toward life, distinctly Beckettian but not formulated with the same intensity in any other of his works, gains expression. Allusions to other authors can then be pursued once the internal evidence is seen to point incontrovertibly toward them.

Repeatedly, Vladimir and Estragon voice their inability to continue or to succeed: "But I can't go on like this!" (WFG, 44); "I can't go on!" (58); "The best thing would be kill me" (40); "Nothing we can do about it" (16); "There's nothing to do" (48); and the recurrent pronouncement, "Nothing to be done." On the one hand, these statements express a defeatist or suicidal mentality that views life as an exercise in futility impossible to endure. Indeed, in both acts Vladimir and Estragon laboriously consider the possibility of hanging themselves. Moreover, at one point Vladimir even rebukes Estragon for his persistent negativity: "Will you stop whining! I've had my bellyful of your lamentations!" (46). But on the other hand, these are not so much complaints about failure as enunciations of task. The purpose of Vladimir and Estragon *is* to do nothing: to prove redundantly that theirs is an existence in which "nothing happens" (26, 27). The "void" (42), "nothingness" (52), or "abysmal depths" (51) in which they languish derives from their own refusal to seek fulfillment. Godot is no more than an excuse for waiting, as Vladimir unwittingly implies after the return of Pozzo and Lucky: "We are no longer alone, waiting for night, waiting for Godot, waiting for . . . waiting (50). More precisely, their waiting is itself the savior they await, for in this condition (to adapt a phrase from *Texts For Nothing,* the only Beckettian work containing a direct reference to *Waiting for*

*Godot*), life can require nothing of them but to go on giving up: "I'll have gone on giving up, having had nothing, not being there" (TFN, 125).[4]

Futility is the guiding principle of Vladimir and Estragon. Their goal in life is to perpetuate the reassurance of frustration: "That's been going on now for half a century" (WFG, 42). In this regard, dialogue plays a vital role: The purpose of communication is not to resolve difficulty but to inhibit the possibility of doing so. As Estragon observes, "In the meantime let us try and converse calmly, since we are incapable of keeping silent. It's so we won't think" (40). When words fail, desperate demand for them results: "Say anything at all!" (41). This compulsive use of words to thwart deliberation is clarified by a passage in *Texts for Nothing*: "It's an unbroken flow of words and tears. With no pause for reflection" (TFN, 111). In fact, both Vladimir and Estragon applaud their success in preventing reflection. When one affirms, "We're in no danger of ever thinking any more," the other responds, "But at least there's that" (WFG, 41).

But what exactly do Vladimir and Estragon mean by "thinking," and why are they so eager to avoid it? The defining function of thought is to render its object *intelligible* or (to use the Cartesian terms) clear and distinct to the understanding.[5] If the two stragglers were to clarify their predicament by means of thought, they would, in principle at least, render it susceptible to solution. But Vladimir and Estragon prefer confusion to clarity, for as long as they remain bewildered, they are protected from responsibility and change. There is "nothing to be done" but to sustain the same state of frustrated perplexity. The play abounds with references to confusion and uncertainty; a small sample here will suffice: "Nothing is certain when

---

4. For the allusion to Pozzo, see *Texts for Nothing*: "Why did Pozzo leave home, he had a castle and retainers?" (TFN, 96).

5. The famous phrase appears frequently in the Cartesian canon. See, for example, Descartes (1964a, 29). Molloy also refers to "notions clear and distinct" (MOL, 82). For a bibliography of opinions concerning "Beckett's Cartesian comedy," see Rabillard (1992, 114n. 2).

you're about" (WFG, 10); "It's not certain" (35); "No, nothing is certain" (35). Estragon's contemptuous remark, "People are bloody ignorant apes" (9), applies ironically to himself and Vladimir—but in their case ignorance is a deliberate choice, since it excuses them from breaking their dependence on passivity: "Yes, in this immense confusion one thing alone is clear. We are waiting for Godot to come" (51). Indeed, resistance to clarifying thought motivates Estragon's notorious reflex to turn the dialogue into a game whose sole purpose is to trivialize the matter it treats: "That's the idea, let's contradict each other" (41).

The deeper significance of the refusal to think emerges in connection with the solitary tree, conspicuous in the stark landscape of the setting. As Beckett's stage directions introducing act 2 indicate, the formerly bare tree has somehow sprouted "four or five leaves" (WFG, 37). Of course, such prominent change demands explanation, and the play does indeed provide one. At precisely the point when Vladimir and Estragon reaffirm their determination to continue conversing in order not to think, the motif of "leaves" (40) enters the dialogue. In terse stichomythia, the two sustain a brief account of their need to avoid silence. For the sake of brevity, the dialogue will be quoted here in continuous format, but the speakers alternate antiphonally with each new sentence. The emphasis on words involving leaves is mine: "It's so we won't think." "We have that excuse." "It's so we won't hear." "We have our reasons." "All the dead voices." "They make a noise like wings." "Like *leaves*." "Like sand." "Like *leaves*." "They speak at once." "Each one to itself." "Rather they whisper." "They *rustle*." "They murmur." "They *rustle*." "What do they say?" "They talk about their lives." "To have lived is not enough for them." "They have to talk about it." "To be dead is not enough for them." "It is not sufficient." "They make a noise like feathers." "Like *leaves*." "Like ashes." "Like *leaves*" (40; my emphasis).

In this context, the leaves on the tree, far from suggesting renewal of life, explicitly signify a posthumous existence whose consuming need is to "talk about" the life already ended. This kind of loquacious afterlife is a recurrent motif in Beckett's fiction. Its *locus classicus* appears in *Molloy*: "My life, my life, now I speak of it as of something over, now as of a joke which still goes on, and it is neither, for at the same time it is over and it goes on, and is there any tense for that?" (MOL, 36).[6] The predicament of Vladimir and Estragon is clarified by this peculiar eschatology. Their present state reiterates the emptiness of their past. Their suffering seems determined by the life they lived in the past, as if their present were a static afterlife or "habit" (WFG, 51, 58) whose nature has been fixed by the pattern of the life preceding it. As Estragon complains: "All my lousy life I've crawled about in the mud. . . ! Look at this muckheap! I've never stirred from it!" (39).

But the motif of the afterlife has deeper implications: Vladimir and Estragon *refuse* the challenge of life. They exhaust themselves in the vain attempt to avoid definition. Indeed, Estragon boasts: "We always find something, eh Didi, to give us the impression we exist?" (WFG, 44). The unintended irony here is startling. All Vladimir and Estragon want is the "impression" of existing—the illusion that their lives have no substance beyond the distractions or anxieties of the moment. In this way each lives, but without responsibility for giving significance to his life. At bottom, Vladimir's comment, "This is becoming really insignificant" (44), is not so much a complaint as an unwitting expression of triumph. Their outlook might be termed anti-existential.

This attitude can be clarified by the tree, whose leaves have already advanced our analysis. The Edenic implications of this central plant are unavoidable, especially given the prominent references to Adam (WFG, 25), Cain (53), and Abel (53). But whereas eating the forbidden fruit of the biblical tree led to the *felix culpa* and the gaining of moral knowledge, Vladimir and Estragon remain, to borrow a phrase from *Molloy*, "greatly innocent" (10). In place of the disobedience precipitating the biblical Fall, Vladimir and Estragon are rooted in obedience to Godot, and the tree is the measure of their fi-

---

6. Another example occurs in *Texts for Nothing*: "I'm dead and getting born, without having ended, helpless to begin, that's my life" (TFN, 119).

delity: "He said by the tree" (10). Through this obedience, their waiting simulates a false innocence by which responsibility to live life by their own decisions is denied. The inadequacy of this attitude emerges vividly when Estragon, allowing his alarm at the approach of strangers to obscure all other options, obeys Vladimir's frantic appeal to hide behind the spindly tree, only to discover that his bulk remains prominently exposed: "Decidedly this tree will not have been the slightest use to us" (48). Despite this admission, the couple continue to exploit their relation to the tree as a means of hiding from moral freedom and the choices it requires, as shown by the recurrent refrain: "Let's go." "We can't." "Why not?" "We're waiting for Godot." Here, it is as if Adam and Eve, after brief consultation, refused to leave the garden and relinquish the protection of innocence.

Vladimir and Estragon repudiate the knowledge of good and evil. They don't want to know what decisions other than the prolongation of helplessness are possible. Their ignorance extends even to the identity of Godot, whom they would be unable to recognize, as Estragon observes: "Personally I wouldn't even know him if I saw him" (WFG, 16). Ironically, Godot closely resembles the couple in his avoidance of moral clarity, for he is as vague and noncommittal as they are. When Estragon asks, "What exactly did we ask him for?" Vladimir answers: "Oh . . . Nothing very definite." Estragon adds: "A kind of prayer. A vague supplication" (13). Similarly, in response to the question, "And what did he reply?" Vladimir and Estragon construct an antiphonal reply: "That he'd have to think it over." "That he couldn't promise anything." "Before taking a decision" (13).

The deferral of decision characteristic of both the couple and Godot serves as a postlapsarian simulacrum of innocence. For the couple, habit is the indispensible means of postponing decision, for it discourages them from doing anything different from that which has already been done. As Molloy states, "I knew how difficult it was not to do what you have done before" (MOL, 85). But by fostering repetition, habit generates an enduring sameness where memory cannot operate, for nothing distinct stands out from the unremitting tedium. Life collapses into "one enormous second," to use a phrase from *Texts for Nothing* (TFN, 82), a fused series of indistinguishable redundancies where decisiveness or change becomes meaningless because life itself seems meaningless.

Nowhere is the deadening influence of habit more subtly suggested than in Estragon's praise of a carrot, one of the innumerable on which he munches: "I'll always remember this carrot" (WFG, 14). The irony of his remark is illuminating. In the first place, his notoriously unretentive memory will obviously have no more success remembering this particular carrot (so similar to all the others he has consumed) than it has remembering anything else: "Is it possible you've forgotten already?" (39) Vladimir asks when Estragon does not recognize the tree. As a result of habit, "[Estragon's] memory is uniform" (to adapt an observation in Beckett's *Proust* [29]). Each new experience simply repeats its predecesors and thus effaces their distinctness. But the significance of the carrot deepens when we relate it to the forbidden fruit in the Garden myth. In Eden, by conferring moral knowledge, eating ends innocence. But in the play, eating signifies dependence on the habits that vitiate the power to discriminate and hence to choose.

The deeper significance of false innocence in *Waiting for Godot* will emerge once we understand that the barren landscape, dominated by the scraggly tree to which the couple return night after night, is associated not only with a superannuated Eden, but also with the proscenium or stage on which actors, in virtue of their profession, discharge the duty of performance. But in this case, the performance must be improvised night after night without benefit of a script. Though many critics have highlighted the theatrical metaphor in the play, a review of its more obvious instances will provide a basis for further analysis.[7] Direct reference to location in a theater occurs in

7. For examples, see Connor (1988, 116); Homan (1984, 42); and B. Fletcher (1978, 50–51). In addition, Mercier emphasizes the importance of improvisation in the actions of Vladimir and Estragon (1977, 85), while several other critics stress the vaudeville elements. See Kenner (1968, 135) and J. Fletcher (1972, 63–68).

act 2. When Estragon "recoils in horror" from his only direction of escape—namely, "towards auditorium"—Vladimir is sympathetic: "Well I can understand that" (WFG, 47). A few moments later, their flyting or contest of insult culminates with the coup de grâce delivered by Estragon: "Crritic!"—a word clearly reinforcing reference to the audience or, more precisely, to its spokesperson or representative.[8] Further reference to Vladimir and Estragon as actors struggling to perform in a play with no script appears in Vladimir's joy at the arrival of Pozzo and Lucky: "Reinforcements at last! . . . We were beginning to weaken. Now we're sure to see the evening out" (WFG, 49). Conversely, in act 1, the couple is momentarily identified not as two actors but as members of the audience. When Vladimir departs hastily to urinate, Estragon provides directions: "End of the corridor, on the left." Vladimir responds: "Keep my seat" (23).

It is convenient to consider the lattermost reference first. Vladimir and Estragon *are* spectators of their own lives. In fact, this attitude epitomizes their false innocence. Their primary action is to focus upon the impossibility of action, so that the problems of decision and choice can never arise. But a more profound motive of their false innocence is suggested by the passages where the couple is identified not as spectators, but as actors whose performance inevitably implies the presence of an audience or group of spectators. The most obvious example of this implied audience occurs in act 2 when Estragon, trying unsuccessfully to "do the tree, for the balance," suddenly cries out in frustration: "Do you think God sees me?" (WFG, 49). Vladimir tells him he "must close [his] eyes" in order to imitate the tree properly (49). But after following this instruction Estragon "staggers worse," and "at the top of his voice" shouts with brandished fists: "God have pity on me!" (49).

In his voluntary blindness, Estragon's habitual sense of helplessness so intensifies that all he can see is his own need for pity. God becomes no more than a reification of the pitying awareness that his helplessness requires. It is no accident that the tree with Edenic asso-

8. For a discussion of flyting in the play, see Kern (1986, 146–47).

ciations is the occasion of this crisis, for insistence on pity is the direct result of false innocence. Instead of acknowledging responsibility for the choices precipitating his impotence, Estragon prefers to suffer the agony of his predicament until a higher power recognizes *its* responsibility to help. In the "futile anxious life" pursued by the couple (here we have borrowed a phrase from MOL, 122), the will must will to fail, it must always will to fail, in order to exploit the pathos of its plight.

Yet there is a striking conflict in the play between the need for pity and the resentment of it. The earliest example of this opposition appears on the first page, when in response to Vladimir's solicitous inquiry, "It hurts?", Estragon "angrily" retorts: "Hurts! He wants to know if it hurts!" (WFG, 7). Vladimir instantly criticizes Estragon's preoccupation with his own pain: "No one ever suffers but you. I don't count. I'd like to hear what you'd say if you had what I have" (7). But it soon turns out that Vladimir is as preoccupied with his own pain as his companion, for in response to Estragon's repentant offer of sympathy, Vladimir replies "angrily" with the same words as those he has just faulted: "He wants to know if it hurts!" (7). The circularity of this dialogue is obvious. Instead of relieving or consoling suffering, pity only heightens the victim's awareness of his own pain.

This paradox can be explained by remembering the origin of the pain pitied. In the case just examined, the pain concerns Estragon's boots. Superficially, the discomfort involves cramping or pinching of the foot but, as the opening lines of the play suggest, the more profound pain signified by Estragon's vain effort to remove his boots concerns belief in helplessness: "Nothing to be done"—a futility whose pervasiveness, as already noted, is indicated by the recurrence of this phrase in different contexts throughout the play. This faith in helplessness is the protector of false innocence. As long as Vladimir and Estragon suffer as helpless victims or, more precisely, as the victims of helplessness, they will never be forced to admit responsibility for the meaning of their own lives. Thus, at the same time that the two seek pity for helplessness ("Help me!" [WFG, 7]), pity is the last thing they will accept. For to reduce their helplessness is to undermine the protection it affords. Hence, their only security is to remain beyond rescue: Pity must be refused even as it is implored.

An analogue of this attitude is presented by Lucky, Pozzo's exhausted porter. Though his misery evokes Estragon's pity and the compassionate attempt to wipe away the sufferer's tears, Lucky's response is to kick Estragon "violently in the shins" (WFG, 21). This brutal reaction is clarified by Pozzo's explanation of Lucky's reason for never putting down his burden despite overwhelming fatigue: "He imagines that when I see how well he carries I'll be tempted to keep him on in that capacity" (21). As Pozzo's comment indicates, Lucky increases his suffering not to evoke pity, but to ensure his own security. In their own way, Vladimir and Estragon are doing exactly the same thing. Like Lucky, the only salvation they seek is the continuation of suffering (which in their case involves the futility of waiting for a figure who never comes), so that they will not be forced to live life without the master on whom they are accustomed to depend. Ultimately, that master is not Godot (whom they never meet) but their own belief in the need for him—their belief that security depends on obedience to habit, which decrees that they can do only what they have already done and must go on doing forever.

The role of the second couple (Pozzo and Lucky) as an illuminating analogue of the primary couple (Vladimir and Estragon) becomes clearer when we examine the relevant details one by one. The analogy is first suggested when Estragon, wanting to clarify the nature of their relationship to Godot, asks: "We're not *tied*?" (WFG, 13; my emphasis). Vladimir replies: "To Godot? *Tied* to Godot! What an idea! No question of it. For the moment" (14; my emphasis). When Pozzo and Lucky suddenly appear a few moments later with the latter conspicuously *tied* by a rope to the former, it is as if we were presented with a vivid symbol of the primary couple's attachment to Godot, as Vladimir has just defined it. The analogy gains force when Estragon mistakes Pozzo for Godot: "You're not Mr. Godot, Sir?" (15). The pain inflicted on them by their attachment to Godot—and, more profoundly, to the reliance on habit that he represents—is suggested by the "running sore" (17) on Lucky's neck, caused by the chafing of the rope against his skin.

A closer look at this rope will clarify the nature of the primary couple's pain. The cord is "passed round" (WFG, 15) Lucky's neck in a manner obviously suggestive of the rope by which Vladimir and Estragon plan to hang themselves in order to end their futile waiting: "Remind me to bring a bit of rope to-morrow" (35); "You haven't got a bit of rope?" (60). But the suicide they contemplate is not so much a decisive action designed to end pain as both a metaphor and extension of the indecisive state causing that pain. Indeed, the very intention to commit suicide exemplifies this indecision, since they never go through with their plan. The habitual indecision whereby independent action is interminably deferred turns life into an imitation of the inertness characteristic of death. As Vladimir observes in perhaps the most ironic utterance in the play, "[H]abit is a great deadener" (58). The suicidally deadening effects of habit are implied by Vladimir's and Estragon's sudden noticing of the mortuary environment in which they are located: "Where are all these corpses from?" "These skeletons." "A charnel-house! A charnel-house!" (41). This is what habit has done to their lives: conferred on them a deathlike "changelessness" amid inevitable "vicissitudes," to adapt a phrase from *Texts for Nothing*: "what vicissitudes within what changelessness" (TFN, 118). Indeed, the couple has its own way of expressing the deathlike immobility imposed on life by habit: "One is what one is." "No use wriggling." "The essential doesn't change." "Nothing to be done" (WFG, 14).

The suffering induced by this self-immobilizing attitude can be better understood if we consider Lucky again. As porter, his most prominent function is to carry a large and ponderous bag. But when Vladimir asks, "What is there in the bag?" Pozzo replies, "Sand" (WFG, 57). Apparently, there is no purpose to Lucky's burden except to be burdened by it. Similarly, the only purpose of Vladimir's and Estragon's waiting is to prolong their own frustration, for by that means they are freed from responsibility for decision. To apply a phrase from *Malone Dies,* theirs is "the waiting that knows itself in vain" (MAL, 241). The suicidal implications of this commitment to futility emerge more forcefully when we juxtapose Lucky's bag of sand with the only other mention of sand in the play: Vladimir's and Estragon's dialogue (quoted earlier) concerning the voices that recall lives once lived: "They make a noise like wings." "Like leaves." "Like *sand*." "Like leaves" (WFG, 40; my emphasis). Here sand is associated with the same idea discussed in connection with leaves—namely the need of false innocence, as displayed by the couple, to treat life itself as a kind of afterlife, filled with compulsive repetition of regrets about the experience of living. Indeed, in his celebrated tirade, as if giving words to the voices of which Vladimir and Estragon speak and which in turn are associated with the sand in his bag, Lucky expresses the excruciating futility wherein man "wastes and pines" (29).

Lucky thus represents in grotesque, physical form the mental anguish endured by Vladimir and Estragon through their false innocence and the indecision sustaining it. But they are not as passive as they seem. Unlike Lucky's suffering, their suffering results not from external duress, but from their own active contribution to it. The boredom oppressing them is the direct consequence of an obsessive adherence to habit that ensures security from change and from new decisions that change would require. The tedious waiting that appears submissive on the surface derives from a tyrannical insistence that nothing will happen but the same experience of futility, for that is the only means by which responsibility for themselves can be avoided. This tyrannical imperative is represented by Pozzo. Just as Lucky embodies or represents the piteous misery of Vladimir and Estragon, so Pozzo incarnates the pitiless demands of habit behind that misery. In other words, while Lucky clarifies the effect, Pozzo clarifies the cause of the primary couple's plight. But analysis of his character must proceed cautiously. At the same time that Pozzo represents the rule of habit, he also represents the motive for submitting to it.

Pozzo's role as the personification of habit is prominently suggested by his tendency to define himself in terms of *decorum* or the observance of established routines, schedules, and social rituals.[9]

9. For a discussion of ritual in the play, see Clausius (1987, 124–43).

Even the simplest action must be justified by his code of formalities: "But how am I to sit down now, without affectation, now that I have risen? Without appearing to—how shall I say—without appearing to falter" (WFG, 19). The power of habit is further emphasized through its contrast with Pozzo's social arrogance. He is presented as a compulsive extrovert requiring the company of others for his meaning to be completed: "I cannot go for long without the society of my likes . . . even when the likeness is an imperfect one" (16). The most peremptory expression of this attitude is his exhortation prior to formal address: "Is everybody looking at me?" "Is everybody listening?" "I don't like talking in a vacuum" (20). But his imperiousness is a sham, for at bottom Pozzo is the slave of his own habits and can do nothing that would compromise them. His ultimate master is time, which dictates the order and duration of each activity or modulation of appearance: "But I really must be getting along, if I am to observe my schedule" (24). Indeed, as this quotation suggests, Pozzo lets time dominate him as he dominates Lucky: "Up pig!" (30). Moreover, his subservience has the same motive as Lucky's: the need for security.

As we saw, the purpose of Lucky's subservience to Pozzo is preserve himself from dismissal. Similarly, the purpose of Pozzo's subservience to time is to ensure that it does not go on without him: He does not want to *lose* time. This concern is manifested in the precipitous haste with which he departs whenever his period of rest is over. It is also manifested in his reply to Vladimir's statement that "Time has stopped": "Whatever you like, but not that" (WFG, 24). But what security offered by time can be worth such zealous devotion? This question can be answered by considering the very different one asked by Pozzo: "Do I look like a man that can be made to suffer?" (23). The deepest motive for Pozzo's observance of time is the need for the most fundamental security of all—invulnerability. By maintaining his awareness of time, Pozzo gains the illusion of protection not just against the loss of time, but against something even more threatening: the pain of loss that time inevitably causes. As long as Pozzo sustains his preoccupation with time and defines himself through it, what he loses to time cannot ultimately matter. For he still retains the basic principle on which his identity is founded.

It is as if, in his need for invulnerability, Pozzo tries to turn his heart—the organ of feeling—into a timepiece so that he will never suffer the pain time causes. The play itself suggests this image. After losing his watch, Pozzo tries vainly "to apply his ear to his stomach" (WFG, 30) in order to determine if the missing item is ticking somewhere on his person. Bending close to assist in the search, Estragon soon detects a noise but identifies its source as "the heart." Ironically, of course, this tendency to care only for time is Pozzo's tragic fault. In the course of the play, he loses one possession after another: his pipe, his watch, and finally his eyesight: "I used to have wonderful sight" (54). But even in his blindness, time continues to define Pozzo's life with its inexorable movement, which forces him from one ordained action to the next, just as he does to Lucky: "On!" (57). The only difference in Pozzo's attitude is that he now hates the temporal master on whom he formerly fawned: "Have you not done tormenting me with your accursed time! It's abominable!" (57). His reduction of life to a succession of movements ordered by time has robbed life of its meaning. Life becomes a fleeting duration with no purpose but its own expiry: "[O]ne day we were born, one day we shall die, the same day, the same second, is that not enough for you? They give birth astride a grave, the light gleams an instant, then it's night once more" (57).

Pozzo's vision of life as no more than the blank passage of time is the essence of his tragic blindness. But however dramatic it seems, at bottom this blindness is as frivolous and unnecessary as that which Estragon, in his false innocence, momentarily adopts while imitating the tree with his eyes closed. The connection between Pozzo and Estragon's blindness is emphasized by a crucial juxtaposition. The blind Pozzo enters precisely when the staggering Estragon, frustrated in his attempt to "do the tree" (WFG, 49), cries out in his assumed helplessness for divine pity: "On me! On me! Pity! On me!" A few moments later, Pozzo falls and calls out repeatedly for help: "Pity! Pity!" (53), just as Estragon did until interrupted by the sudden entry of Pozzo. As befits a play subtitled *A Tragicomedy in Two Acts,* here the same blindness is portrayed in two different modes: comic and tragic. In both cases its cause is preoccupation with time. In the first case, there is too much time, and the ensuing boredom emphasizes the need for "diversion" (WFG, 52)—hence the comic mode. In the second, there is too little time, and the consequent sense of doom invokes the tragic mode. But each pole is interfused with the characteristics of its opposite. Vladimir early in the play intuits his doom: "The last moment. . . . Sometimes I feel it coming all the same. Then I go all queer. How shall I say? Relieved and at the same time . . . appalled. AP-PALLED" (8). Moreover, near the end of the play he paraphrases Pozzo's great enunciation of doom: "Astride of a grave and a difficult birth" (58). Conversely Pozzo, the tragic figure, exploits Lucky as a means of comic diversion: "What do you prefer? Shall we have him dance, or sing, or recite, or think, or" (26).

The intermingling of tragic and comic modes has profound implications.[10] It involves the fundamental ambiguity of the play: Is the plight of Vladimir and Estragon serious or trivial? Does their waiting signify a crass diversion or an inexorable fate? Thus far, our analysis has shown that refusal of purpose is responsible for their relentless futility. But Lucky's speech can help us grasp their predicament at a deeper level.

The best introduction to Lucky's thinking, "quaquaquaqua" (WFG, 28), is provided by a later Beckettian work, *How It Is*: "[T]hat voice quaqua the voice of us all . . . the last scraps to have come down to us and in what a state" (HOW, 138). And further: "[T]his anonymous voice self-styled quaqua . . . tells us what we are as best he can" (139).[11] These two passages explicitly identify the "voice quaqua" as

10. For a conventional discussion of tragicomedy in *Waiting for Godot,* see Berlin (1986, 54–56).

11. Lucky's "quaquaquaqua" has puzzled critics. Rosette Lamont (1975, 209) suggests that it derives from "Quoi? Quoi? Quoi?" Claudia Clausius (1991, 76) identifies "quaquaquaqua" as "duck nonsense."

"the last scraps" of a once vigorous deliberation whose purpose is to define the nature and meaning of humanity. Lucky's utterance obviously displays these characteristics of decrepitude and explication, for in stammered fragments it describes the current condition of our species: "man in short . . . man in brief" (WFG, 29). But the results of his analysis become more intelligible if we probe further into the tradition of humanist explication, which his expression sputteringly prolongs.

One source of this "voice quaqua," now at its last gasp, is Aristotle, "who knew everything" (TFN, 114).[12] In the *Metaphysics*, he enunciated the nature of "being *qua* being" (or "being as being") and man *qua* man through formulating the metaphysical order extending from mere potency or matter through the hierarchy of forms to pure act (i.e., the "personal God" to whom Lucky refers [WFG, 28]) (*Metaphysics* 1941a, 731). In fact, the use of *qua* as a formula for precise definition is echoed in Pozzo's commentary on the sky: "What is there so extraordinary about it? Qua sky" (25).

In the first sentence of his *Metaphysics*, Aristotle states (in W. D. Ross's translation), "All men by nature desire to know," (1941a, 1.980a 21). In Lucky's speech, reason ("Think!") or the desire to know can no longer find the absolute truth it seeks despite exhausting efforts to do so: "the labors unfinished of Testew and Cunard," "the labors of Fartov and Belcher left unfinished," "the labors lost of Steinweg and Peterman" (WFG, 28–29). As a result, the desire to know—to deduce, that is, metaphysical certainties—succumbs to the sense of futility. The need for truth is disappointed even as it is affirmed: "[I]t is established beyond all doubt all other doubt than that which clings to the labours of men that . . . man in short than man in brief . . . wastes and pines wastes and pines" (28–29).[13] Lucky's

12. Beckett here recalls the phrase uttered by Dante in *Divine Comedy*, when Aristotle, "Master of those who know," is encountered in Limbo, on the margins of Hell (Alighieri 1970, 1.4.131).

13. According to Lance St. John Butler, Lucky renders *esse* and *posse*, two central terms in scholastic philosophy, as "Essy" and "Possy" (1991, 52).

speech thus represents what Charles Cochrane in a different context calls "the final effort of classical reason to attain to a correct picture of the universe and of man's place in it" (1940, 172).

But this failure to satisfy the need to know has devastating consequences. When reason cannot find the truth, it succumbs to the moral sorrow called *acedia* or sloth, "in the jargon of the schools" (MOL, 51). *Acedia* is defined by St. Thomas Aquinas as "sorrow for spiritual good," " 'an oppressive sorrow,' which, namely, so weighs upon man's mind, that he wants to do nothing" (*Summa Theologica*, 2, Q35, A1, resp). The wasting and pining to which Lucky refers are clear expressions of that sorrow. Estragon's sadness ("I'm unhappy" [WFG, 33]) falls into the same category. Aquinas further characterizes *acedia* as "a kind of weariness" (*Summa Theologica*, 2, Q35, A2, obj. 3). The torpor of Estragon ("I'm tired" [WFG, 45]) is ultimately an expression of sloth. Moreover, the waiting of both Vladimir and Estragon, sustained by the conviction, "Nothing to be done," seems literally to enact Aquinas's description of sloth as the desire "to do nothing." Indeed, the following passage from Beckett's *Words and Music* provides an excellent gloss on *Waiting for Godot*: "Sloth is of all the passions the most powerful passion and indeed no passion is more powerful than the passion of sloth, this is the mode in which the mind is most affected" (WM, 23).

For corroboration, we should note that numerous references to sloth occur in the Beckettian canon. Belacqua Shuah in *More Pricks Than Kicks* is named after Belacqua, the slothful soul whom Dante encounters in *Purgatorio* 4. An explicit allusion to this very scene appears in *The Lost Ones*, where the narrator compares the dejected posture of one figure to that of Belacqua, whose attitude "wrung from Dante one of his rare wan smiles" (LO, 14). A clinching reference occurs in *How It Is*: "Belacqua fallen over on his side *tired of waiting*" (HOW, 24; my emphasis).[14]

A closer look at Pozzo and Lucky will reveal the deeper implica-

---

14. The role of sloth in *Waiting for Godot* was first noted by Strauss (1959). Hoffman (1964, 15) links Beckettian sloth with Goncharov's hero, Oblomov.

tions of slothful waiting in the play. On the one hand, the secondary couple clarifies the predicament of the primary one by incarnating the reliance on habit that protects from change and from the decisions that change demands. But on the other hand, Pozzo and Lucky also incarnate the two faculties of the rational soul, reason and will, posited by humanism. Lucky's connection with reason is clear from his one stupendous action: thinking. Pozzo is just as vividly connected with will by his reduction to the blind imperative of movement: "On!" This characteristic represents the defining tendency of the will to tend toward its proper end or that in which it finds satisfaction. In this case, however, the notion of end has been removed; all that remains is the reflex of tending toward it. Similarly, in Lucky's thinking, the proper object of thought, truth, has been erased, leaving only the intellectual need to clarify it. Thus, Pozzo and Lucky are a composite representation of the rational soul, retaining its functions but unable to fulfill them. In fact, a striking description of the soul in this plight appears in *Malone Dies*: "the soul that must be veiled, that soul denied in vain, vigilant, anxious, turning in its cage as in a lantern, in the night without haven or craft or matter or understanding" (MAL, 222). An explicit reference to the dwindling of will and reason occurs in *The Unnamable*: "I don't yet now how to move. . . . I don't know how to want to. . . . Similarly, my understanding is not yet sufficiently well-oiled to function without the pressure of some critical circumstance" (UN, 350).

Further analysis of the rational soul will deepen our understanding of false innocence, for that condition denies free will—a capacity that, as Etienne Gilson explains, "is constituted in its very essence by the agreement of intellect and will" (1938, 407). To understand how the collaboration of reason and will engenders free will, we must note the reciprocal relation between these two faculties. Again Gilson explicates:

> If the soul possessed reason alone it would be capable of reflecting upon its act . . . but it would not be capable of setting itself in motion or deciding its own activity. If on the other hand it possessed

only desire, without reason, it would be able to set itself in motion
. . . but since it would be incapable of reflecting upon and judging
its own act, it would be incapable likewise of self-restraint, and
would therefore not possess self-mastery. (1938, 407)

Pozzo's compulsion to move, even when there is nowhere in particular he must go, is a perfect example of this lack of self-mastery. In
combination, however, reason and will enable the individual to deliberate about choices *and* to enact his decision.

But reason and will, as represented by Lucky and Pozzo, are denied their normal relation. Instead of accomplishing what reason
proposes, will abuses reason: "Think, pig!" (WFG, 28). But without
the guidance of reason, the will cannot know what it wants. More
precisely, under such conditions, it wants only the continuation of its
own vain movement: "I really must be getting along" (24). Yet as
Cochrane points out, St. Augustine in the *Confessions*—a book cited
by Beckett as an influence on *Waiting for Godot*—disclosed the consequences of separating will from reason: "For ultimately there is no
satisfaction to be discovered merely in motion, apart from an intelligible and worthy goal [which only reason can determine]" (1940,
391).[15] This situation illumines that of Vladimir and Estragon. They
too abuse reason: "It's so we won't think" (WFG, 40). They too reduce the will to a tendency with no purpose but its own perpetuation.
The only difference is that, with the secondary couple, the tendency
is to remain in motion, whereas with the primary couple it is to remain at rest.

The allusion to Augustine's *Confessions* leads inevitably to a reinterpretation of the "heavy bag" (WFG, 15) filled with "sand" (57),
which Lucky carries. In Book 13, Augustine describes the inner principle of the will in analogical terms as a weight that causes the will to
move toward its proper place just as, according to classical physics,
each of the four elements (fire, air, earth, and water) tends toward its
proper level if left unimpeded. Gilson elaborates: "In every soul, as in

15. For Beckett's reference to St. Augustine, see Hobson (1956, 154).

every body, there is a weight drawing it constantly, moving it always to find its natural place of rest; and this weight we call love. 'My weight,' says Augustine, 'is my love *(pondus meum amor meus)*; *eo feror quocumque feror* (by it am I borne whithersoever I am borne)' " (Gilson 1960, 134).[16] For Augustine, the proper resting place of the will is the love of God, the ultimate good. From this perspective, Lucky's burden constitutes a grotesque pun on Augustine's famous dictum. The "weight" that in the *Confessions* signifies the tendency of the will to move toward its proper fulfillment assumes a very different meaning in *Waiting for Godot*. There, "weight" signifies the burden of futility carried by reason so that the only purpose left for the will to tend toward is the continuation of its frustration. This condition is the essence of sloth and the means of sustaining false innocence or the refusal to know what choices are available.

The nemesis of sloth is that it will do nothing to help itself, as we see hilariously demonstrated when both Pozzo and Vladimir, each preoccupied with his own inability "to get up," call out, "Help!" one after the other (WFG, 52). Such helplessness puts its need for pity above everything else, even the pain of another, as Vladimir ironically observes: "He can think of nothing but himself!" (53). In fact, as noted in the primary couple's treatment of both Pozzo and Lucky, sloth can exploit the pain of others to gain "diversion" from its suffering (52). Moreover, the importunity of another's appeal for pity tends only to arouse indifference in the slothful, for it demands the definite motivation that sloth prefers to avoid. The finest example of this is Estragon's response to Pozzo's appeals for pity: "Don't mind him. Sleep" (53). Here indifference and sloth are combined in one utterance.

In this context, Pozzo's tragic *anagnorisis*, or recognition after becoming blind, recapitulated by Vladimir as he stands above the sleeping Estragon, can be more completely understood: "They give birth astride of a grave, the light gleams an instant, then it's night once more" (WFG, 57). As Vladimir himself implies after paraphras-

16. See also Augustine *(Confessions, 273)*.

ing Pozzo's oration, this is not a waking vision of truth but an illusion sustained by sleep: "At me too someone is looking, of me too someone is saying, He is sleeping, *he knows nothing*, let him sleep on" (58; my emphasis).[17] Ironically, Vladimir's recognition of the meaningless brevity of life does indeed pertain to sleep—in this case the sleep of knowing nothing or false innocence. The lack of purpose lies not in life itself, but in the will of the slothful, a will that blames ignorance of alternatives for its own inertia.[18]

We are left now with the event that occurs near the end of both acts: the sudden arrival of the Boy who announces that Godot will not "come this evening but surely to-morrow" (WFG, 33). On the literal level, the Boy functions as an emissary whose task is to announce the absence of his master, Godot. But the Boy reveals a truth about Vladimir and Estragon as well. As a child, he is the very type of obedient innocence, for he obeys a master about whom he knows nothing. Five times in the course of his two encounters with the couple he expresses this ignorance: "I don't know, Sir." As a child, the Boy *is* still innocent and not yet responsible for determining the choices in his life. But Vladimir and Estragon are adults—and rather senior ones at that: "That's been going on now for half a century" (42). They long ago outgrew the innocence appropriate to the Boy. In fact, the childishness of their attitude is prominently implied in the play. When Pozzo asks, in reference to Vladimir, "What age would you say he was?" Estragon replies: "Eleven" (19).

17. Compare with Molloy's observation: "For my waking was a kind of sleeping" (MOL, 53).

18. However, Esslin takes Pozzo and Vladimir's *anagnorisis* at face value as an indication of "the full horror of the human condition" (1961, 44). See also Broer (1987, 11–19).

# 8

# To Be Is to Be Deceived

## The Relation of Berkeley and Plato
## to *Waiting for Godot*

*Waiting for Godot* has provoked a wide range of interpretations, respectively emphasizing Christian, existentialist, Marxist, Freudian, Hobbesian, political, Cartesian, semiotic, and biographical factors (to cite only some better-known approaches).[1] But perhaps the most recurrent—if not consensual—assumption made by critics regarding the play is that it concerns the universal plight of man, unprotected by earlier cultural assurances or belief systems. A seminal critic in this regard is Martin Esslin, according to whom the play reveals "the full horror of the human condition" (1961, 37–38). Indeed, the play itself suggests its own universality, as when Vladimir identifies Pozzo's fallen state with "all humanity" (54), or attributes Everyman status to himself and Estragon: "But at this place, at this moment of time, all mankind is us, whether we like it or not" (51). In "Berkeley Inside

---

1. For a summary of critics treating the first four categories, see Kennedy (1989, 31). For more recent existentialist interpretations, see McCandless (1988, 48–57), drawing on Tillich; and Butler (1984, 74–113), drawing on Heidegger and Sartre. For a Hobbesian reading, see Zaller (1986, 160–73). For relation to the later passive resistance movement of the early sixties, see Blau (1991, 9) and Lamont (1975, 217). For Cartesian commentary, see Rabillard (1992, 114n. 2). For semiotic and linguistic interpretations, see Alter (1987, 42–56); Corfariu and Roventa-Frumusana (1984, 119–33); and Iser (1989, 152–93). For biographical analysis, see Gontarski (1985, 35–36); Bair (1978, 386); and Knowlson (1996, 378–82).

Out: Existence and Destiny in Waiting for Godot," Norma Kroll offers a valuable reinterpretation of the play as an inversion of the extreme nominalism of Bishop Berkeley. According to Kroll, Beckett "inverts [Berkeley's] trust in God's unwavering regard of his creation" such that God's perception (represented by the absent Godot) is withdrawn "from the human predicament," forcing humanity to contend with the resultant metaphysical "discontinuities" (1995, 530, 535).[2] In Kroll's view, the play illumines the problematics of human existence in terms of metaphysical factors beyond the control of living individuals, who are to be construed as "particular manifestations of the general fortune of mankind" (1995, 552).

This chapter will pursue a contrary analysis of the play, replacing the notion of universality or irremediable human condition with the idea of deliberately sustained self-deception. In this context, the plight of Vladimir and Estragon is neither inherent nor inevitable, but doggedly devised. Underpinning this interpretation is an uncovering of heretofore unnoticed allusions to or invocations of the works of both Berkeley and Plato. The opposition between constructions of reality respectively pertaining to each of these philosophers is crucial to a deeper understanding of *Waiting for Godot*. Moreover, the relation that we shall find of Berkeley to Beckett is completely different from the one adduced by Kroll. For example, whereas, according to Kroll, Godot symbolizes the absence of God who, in Berkeley's system, is the sole guarantor of certainty, we shall discover that Godot justifies or excuses the perpetuation of uncertainty.

### The Relevance of Berkeley to *Waiting for Godot*

Lance St. John Butler (1991, 52) notes without commentary that the play invokes, in the course of Lucky's stupendous speech, the name of "Bishop Berkeley" (WFG, 29). But it has never before been observed that Lucky is also explicitly associated with Berkeley's celebrated description of the intellectual confusion resulting from

2. For a Berkelean interpretation of Beckett's later work, *Film*, see Henning (1982, 89–99).

improper philosophical concepts. According to Berkeley, the uncertainty that arrests the mind in its progress toward certainty about the nature of reality stems not from the unintelligibility of reality, but from the erroneous intellectual principles employed to understand "the nature of things" (Berkeley 1957, 5). Speculative reason stymies its own philosophical investigations by the mistaken ideas with which it thinks: "that fine and subtle *net of abstract ideas,* which has so miserably perplexed and entangled the minds of men" (21). The image of the intellectual net, which "stay[s] and embarrass[es] the mind in its search after truth," explicitly recurs in the figure of Lucky who, just before the stupendously inconclusive act of thinking ("unfinished for reasons unknown" [29]) in which he mentions Bishop Berkeley and does a dance depicting entanglement in a net: "The Net. He thinks he's entangled in a net" (WFG, 27; Berkeley 1957, 6). Both this phrase describing Lucky's and Berkeley's phrase describing intellectual perplexity deploy the words *net* and *entangled.* Indeed, Lucky's declamation concerning the quandary in which man—or, more precisely, his philosophical search for meaning— "wastes and pines wastes and pines" (WFG, 29) constitutes an unrivaled example of what Berkeley, in the famous inaugural paragraph of *A Treatise Concerning the Principles of Human Understanding,* terms "forlorn skepticism" (Berkeley 1957, 5).

In fact, on closer inspection, that paragraph provides a remarkably penetrating gloss on the inaugural situation in *Waiting for Godot,* where Estragon is seen "sitting on a low mound" by the side of a "country road" (WFG, 7). After a prolonged and futile struggle to "take off his boot," he lapses, "giving up again," and declares his frustration: "Nothing to be done" (7). Berkeley's paragraph displays the same imagery—a figure seated by a road in a state of dejected futility as that found at the beginning of Beckett's play. But in Berkeley's passage, that sense of futility is caused by *intellectual,* not physical, frustration. For the seated figure, perplexed by the efforts of reason to illumine "the nature of things," has given up the attempt to ascertain truth by philosophic "speculation" and has succumbed to "a forlorn skepticism":

Yet so it is, we see the illiterate bulk of mankind that walk the *high road of plain common sense,* and are governed by the dictates of nature, for the most part easy and undisturbed. To them nothing that is familiar appears unaccountable or difficult to comprehend. They complain not of any want of evidence in their senses, and are out of all danger of becoming skeptics. But no sooner do we depart from sense and instinct to follow the light of a superior principle, to reason, meditate, and reflect on the nature of things, but a thousand scruples spring up in our minds concerning those things which before we seemed fully to comprehend. Prejudices and errors of sense do from all parts discover themselves to our view; and, endeavouring to correct these by reason, we are insensibly drawn into uncouth paradoxes, difficulties, and inconsistencies, which multiply and grow upon us as we advance in speculation, till at length, having wandered through many intricate mazes, we find ourselves just where we were, or, which is worse, *sit down in a forlorn skepticism.* (Berkeley 1957, 5; my emphasis)

To clarify the perplexity and frustration that encumber life in *Waiting for Godot* is the goal of the present analysis. We can take our first step toward that end by clarifying Berkeley's solution to the problem of speculative reason perplexing itself by its own thinking. According to Berkeley, the mind knows reality only through the ideas of it formed by sense perception: "[W]e hold indeed the objects of sense to be nothing else but ideas which cannot exist unperceived" (1957, 45). In this context, the term *ideas* includes sensory qualities such as color, size, smell, taste, etc. Just as pain exists only in the awareness suffering it, so external objects exist only as ideas in the mind perceiving them: "All things that exist, exist only in the mind, that is, they are purely notional" (Berkeley 1957, 38). To Berkeley, as Cassirer notes, "The reality of perception is the only certain and utterly unproblematical—the only primary—datum of all knowledge" (Cassirer 1957, 3:23). Hence, to be is to be perceived *(esse est percipi)*; that is, to be is to be an idea or complex of ideas in the mind. By this reasoning, Berkeley "demolished the conception of corporeal substances" (Windelband 1958, 2:469). Cassirer elaborates: "Thus

Berkeley summons inner experience to battle against outward experience, psychology against physics" (1957, 3:24).

Unlike Berkeley, who seeks to overcome "forlorn skepticism," Vladimir and Estragon devote their lives to sustaining it. But whereas, for Berkeley, the skepticism to be overcome concerns the nature of reality, for Vladimir and Estragon the skepticism to be prolonged concerns the meaning and purpose of life. The primary ideas they entertain concern their own thwarted state of uncertainty: "Nothing is certain when you're about" (WFG, 10); "No, nothing is certain" (35). By prolonging perplexity regarding purpose ("What do we do now?" [49]), they ultimately render purpose irrelevant. The only certainty they know is the necessity of waiting: "Yes, in this immense confusion one thing alone is clear. We are waiting for Godot to come" (51). But, at bottom, that waiting awaits the arrival of purposelessness so that there will be no need for purpose ever again to disturb them or make them suffer boredom in its absence: "You'd rather be stuck there doing nothing?" "Yes" (45). To transpose Vladimir's words from a different context, they wait "[i]n anticipation of some tangible return" (51), which in this case concerns the shelter of their own perplexity. By this means, they are absolved of the responsibility to fulfill their own freedom ("We've lost our rights?" "We got rid of them" [13]) and determine their own meaning—a project similarly rejected by Hamm and Clov in *Endgame*: "Mean something! You and I, mean something! Ah! that's a good one!" (END, 33).

In this regard, the relation between Godot and the primary couple (Vladimir and Estragon) is especially instructive. Conventionally, Godot is interpreted as a reification of the ideal plenitude or sufficiency of being which "humanity" (WFG, 54) lacks but inconsolably yearns for. To Alan Knight, for example, the play concerns "the dilemma of man who, having projected his best qualities onto an external and abstract being, is rendered impotent when that abstraction does not come to save him from his self-induced anxieties" (1971, 186). Though critics tend to regard Godot as an ideal exempt from the failings of his adherents, this figure whose function is to explain purpose is himself explicitly associated with *postponement* of purpose, for he is expected to delay response to "supplication": "[H]e'd have to think it over" (13).

The function of Godot can be clarified by reference to the function of God in Berkeley's metaphysics. For Berkeley, to be is to be perceived: "[T]he objects of sense [are] nothing else but ideas which cannot exist unperceived" (Berkeley 1957, 45). But there is an obvious distinction between (a) ideas that belong to the internal world of imagination only and are susceptible to instantaneous change or disappearance, and (b) ideas that pertain to the external world of things that do not change or disappear according to the vagaries of the mind perceiving them. For Berkeley, the greater constancy and clarity of ideas pertaining to real things (as opposed to imaginary ones) is a result of the action of God: "The ideas imprinted on the senses by the Author of Nature are called *real things*; and those excited in the imagination, being less regular, vivid, and constant, are more properly termed *ideas* or *images of things* which they copy and represent" (Berkeley 1957, 38). Windelband elaborates: "The reality of bodies consists, therefore, in this, that their ideas are communicated by God to finite spirits, and the order of succession in which God habitually does this we call *laws of Nature*" (1958, 2:470).

Unlike Berkeley's God, whose function is to guarantee the distinction between reality and illusion, Godot is an agency of indeterminacy. Indeed, his emissary, the Boy, repeats the statement, "I don't know, Sir," five times in the course of the play. Just as Berkeley's God sustains ideas of real things in human minds, so Godot sustains the idea of waiting in the minds of Vladimir and Estragon. Through this waiting, Vladimir and Estragon are relieved of the need to determine their own reality independently. For them existence is no more than an illusion, not to be taken seriously: "We always find something, eh Didi, to give us the impression we exist?" (WFG, 44). More precisely, they construe their existence as the suffering of excruciating futility, which can never mean more than enforced endurance: "I can't go on like this." "That's what you think" (60). In this context, the significance of the recurrent inability to confirm experience emerges: "Do you not remember?" "You dreamt it" (39); "I tell you we weren't here yesterday. Another of your nightmares" (42). Whereas Berkeley's God assures the distinction between reality and illusion, waiting for Godot assures that nothing has more reality than the need to avoid the disturbance of recognizing the truth: "At me too someone is looking, of me too someone is saying, He is sleeping, he knows nothing, let him sleep on" (58).

Despite appearances to the contrary, for Vladimir and Estragon avoidance of truth and perpetuation of "forlorn skepticism" is a demanding exercise requiring exhausting intellectual effort: "Use your intelligence, can't you?" (WFG, 12). In this case, reason must labor to conceive distractions that hamper its own activity:

> In the meantime let us try to converse calmly, since we are incapable of keeping silent.
>     You're right, we're inexhaustible.
>     It's so we won't think. (WFG, 40)

To hamper thought and ensure its inability to move forward, Vladimir and Estragon engage in interminably inconclusive dialogue. The use of dialogue to avoid truth parodies the Socratic use of dialogue to achieve truth. In fact, in addition to invoking Berkeley's *Treatise Concerning the Principles of Human Knowledge*, *Waiting for Godot* also refers frequently to the Platonic dialogues. Later we shall examine the implications of Beckett's fusion of Berkeley and Plato. But first we must identify and interpret the Platonic allusions, which on their own—whether or not we can confirm Beckett's direct citation in each case—function as lenses on which to focus our thoughts and illumine an important stratum of meaning in the play.

### The Relevance of the Platonic Dialogues to *Waiting for Godot*

Before embarking on this phase of our inquiry, it important to follow Aristotle's advice (in Book B of *Metaphysics*) and draw up the aporia:

that is, anticipate the intellectual obstacles or, more literally, obstructions of passage we might encounter. Unlike our earlier discussion of Berkeley, our enterprise now cannot always rely on direct internal evidence in order to demonstrate that a given utterance or dramatic situation explicitly invokes an external, philosophical text. Though we shall, in at least one instance, be able to confirm Beckett's deliberateness of citation, and though in other cases the evidence will at least be preponderant, there are other cases where the relevance of a particular section of a Platonic dialogue to *Waiting for Godot* cannot be confirmed or supported on purely textual grounds. But by the time we conclude our consideration of the Platonic dialogues, we shall have established that they contain striking metaphors and situations that can deepen the signification of the play, whether through Beckett's deliberate intention or simply through fortuitous correspondence.

It can be confirmed that the dramatic emphasis in *Waiting for Godot* on removing boots ("Estragon, on a low mound, is trying to take off his boot" [WFG, 7]) or putting them on ("Come on, give me your foot" [44R]) refers directly to a section of the *Theaetetus* (193cd). In that Platonic dialogue, the problem of true and false judgment of objects is analyzed in terms of correct and incorrect matching of present perception with the corresponding memory impression or "imprint" obtained by past identification of that object (*Theaetetus* 193c). Correct identification of the perceived object is compared to the action of putting one's foot into the correct boot (or memory impression). Mistaken identification of the object is analogous to putting one's foot in the wrong boot:

> It remains, then, that false judgment should occur in a case like this—when I, who know you and Theodorus and possess imprints of you both like seal impressions in the waxen block, see you both at a distance indistinctly and am in a hurry to assign the proper imprint of each to the proper visual perception, *like fitting a foot into its own footmark to effect a recognition,* and then make the mistake of interchanging them, like a man who thrusts his feet into the wrong shoes, and apply the perception of each to the imprint of the other. (*Theaetetus* 193c; my emphasis)

There appears to be no question that the references in Beckett's play to removing or donning boots do indeed invoke this passage, for in *Watt* (an earlier Beckettian text), an explicit linking of problematic perception with mismatching footwear occurs. After describing Watt's mismatched footwear ("a boot, brown in colour, and a shoe, happily of a brownish colour also"), the narrator addresses Watt's futile attempt to identify a perceived object: "So Watt waited with impatience, for the figure to draw very near indeed" (W, 218, 227). However, Watt is no more concerned with objective identification of the object than he is with correct matching of foot with footwear. He simply wants to clarify what the object *appears* to be, not what it actually is: "For Watt's concern, deep as it appeared, was not after all with what the figure was, in reality, but with what the figure appeared to be, in reality" (227).

Watt's indifference to reality and his concern with mere appearance inverts the Platonic metaphysics, where the goal of knowledge is to ascend from the shifting illusions of opinion to the unchanging truth of the Ideas or Pure Forms. In the Beckettian universe, the only truth is knowledge of its irrelevance. The paradoxical Beckettian answer to the problem of distinguishing appearance from reality is that nothing is real because, as Malone writes in his paraphrase of Democritus of Abdera, the pre-Socratic philosopher, *"Nothing is more real than nothing"* (MAL, 192).[3] There are many analogues of this claim in *Waiting for Godot*: "In an instant all will vanish and we'll be alone once more, in the midst of nothingness!" (WFG, 52); "There's no lack of void" (42). In psychological and moral terms, the primacy of nothingness means that life is reduced to awareness of triviality ("This is becoming really insignificant" [44]), boredom ("We wait. We are bored" [52]), and futility ("Nothing to be done" [7]). For Vladimir and Estragon, life is a verbalized version of "the soundless tumult of the inner lamentation" expressed in *Watt* (W, 217), a reiterative complaint about the pointlessness of living: "I can't go on!"

3. Compare with Democritus of Abdera: "Naught exists just as much as Aught" (1966, frag. 156). An echo also occurs in Samuel Beckett's *Murphy*: "the Nothing, than which in the guffaw of the Abderite naught is more real" (246).

(WFG, 58). There is "[n]othing to be done" (7) because there is only the absence of purpose in which to do it.

Whereas the celebrated purpose of Platonic dialogue is to clarify truth by disclosing error, the Beckettian dialogue in *Waiting for Godot* cannot distinguish truth from falsehood because it has lingered so long in doubt: "You think so?" "I don't know." "You may be right" (WFG, 51). The situation in the play is exactly opposite to that described in the Allegory of the Cave—the most famous Platonic myth in the *Republic* and one that Brian Duffy has already linked to *The Unnamable* (1998, 51–71). In that allegory, the requisite intellectual movement is from the flickering shadows of illusion inside the cave, toward the radiantly constant light of truth shining outside. Through this movement, as Werner Jaeger indicates, the soul turns "away from the realm of becoming, until it can bear to look at the brightest pinnacle of reality" (1945, 2:295). Plato's analogy for this movement from the ignorance of mere opinion to the certainty of true knowledge concerns the sudden transition from blindness to the gift of sight: "*inserting vision into blind eyes*" (*Republic* 518b6; my emphasis). In contrast to Socratic dialogue whose purpose is illumination, the purpose of Beckettian dialogue is to sustain "idle discourse" (WFG, 51) so that reason might thereby be protected from the risk of clarification and the difficult decisions that would follow. In this context, darkness is preferable to light: "But has it ['our reason'] not long been straying in the night without end of the abyssal depths?" (51). And blindness is preferable to vision. Indeed, the movement into deeper darkness, instead of toward greater illumination, is epitomized by the transition of Pozzo from having vision to blindness: "I used to have wonderful sight" (54).

Yet, though "confusion" (WFG, 51) brings its reward, it also entails frustration at not being able to know the truth—and, more fundamentally, not being able to know *why* truth remains inaccessible: "I don't know why I don't know!" (43). Ironically, the Boy, who encourages waiting for Godot, is the figure on whom Estragon physically vents his frustration at not being able to know the truth—or, conversely, to prove that a claim is false:

That's all a pack of lies. *(Shaking the Boy by the arm.)* Tell us the truth!

    Boy: *(trembling).* But it is the truth, Sir! (WFG, 33)

Estragon's rage at the inability to determine the truth epitomizes the predicament of philosophical reason in the world of the play. In the philosophies of both Berkeley and Plato, reason can successfully establish certainty, though it does so in opposite ways: either, with Berkeley, by postulating the primacy of sense perception, or, with Plato, by postulating the primacy of the nonsensory Ideas. But in the world of the play, reason is epistemologically challenged. It cannot achieve certainty ("Tell us the truth!") because its only available principle of verification is doubt or *un*certainty. In other words, as Estragon demonstrates, nothing is as certain as conviction in ignorance: "I don't know why I don't know!" Or, as Lucky exemplifies, nothing is certain but the inability of reason to understand its own limitations—to understand, that is, the reason for its own incompletion of thought: "left unfinished for reasons unknown" (WFG, 28–29).

In this context, the deeper significance of Estragon's physical abuse of Lucky emerges, along with another Platonic allusion. Just as, when shaking the Boy, Estragon was venting frustration at the inability to achieve certainty, so, when furiously "kicking" (WFG, 56) the fallen Lucky, Estragon is again, by implication, venting his consternation at the futility of thought. To begin with, in kicking Lucky, Estragon abuses the figure conspicuously associated with the hapless predicament of thought: "Think, pig!" (47). But the full resonance of Estragon's outburst emerges in the context of another Platonic dialogue (the *Protagoras*), where Socrates refers to knowledge or the reasoning faculty as a slave "which is kicked about" by unrestrained emotions: "Most people . . . do not think of knowledge as a force, much less a dominant or ruling force; they think a man may often have knowledge while he is ruled by something else, at one time anger, at another pleasure or pain, sometimes love, very often fear; *they really picture knowledge as a slave which is kicked about by all these other things*" (*Protagoras* 352bc, qtd. in Dodds 1951, 185; my emphasis).

There is perhaps no more succinctly penetrating evaluation of the mentality embodied by the primary couple than these words of Socrates. Vladimir and Estragon cannot achieve certainty ("No, nothing is certain" [WFG, 35]) because they know nothing but their own feelings, the most persistent of which is self-pitying boredom: "Nothing happens, nobody comes, nobody goes, it's awful!" (27). They allow emotion to overcome thought, just as Estragon allows emotion to provoke him into violence against Lucky—the incarnation of thinking. Indeed, obsession with their own feelings is precisely the factor that perpetuates their plight. Vladimir's reprehension of the blind Pozzo ironically rebounds upon himself: "He can think of nothing but himself!" (53). So does his subsequent pity: "Let him alone. Can't you see he's thinking of the days when he was happy" (55). Indeed, the fallen Lucky also represents the primary couple's own mentality, for the useless burden of "sand" (57) under which he collapses epitomizes their own preoccupation with the "misery" (41) of futility. Hence, it is appropriate that Estragon "hurts his foot" (56) when kicking Lucky, for he is confronting his own—and Vladimir's—refusal to know anything but the *pathos of purpose*: "alas alas abandoned unfinished" (29).[4]

The negation, in *Waiting for Godot*, of conviction in the purpose of life is illumined by another Platonic dialogue: the *Phaedo*. This dialogue contains three powerful and consecutive metaphors that recur, in distorted form, in the play. Though the correspondence of any one of them to an element in the play might be merely fortuitous, the correspondence of all three to respective elements strongly suggests that Beckett deliberately designed the parallels.

The first of these metaphors concerns the guard post. In the *Phaedo*, the watch or guard post is associated with the task of enduring life without deserting one's post through the act of suicide: "The allegory which the mystics tell us—that we are men put in a sort of

<hr>

4. In the context of the allusions in *Waiting For Godot* to the Platonic dialogues, the subtitle of the play, "a tragicomedy in two acts," gains further significance, for Socrates himself refers to "the whole tragicomedy of life" *(Philebus, 50b).*

guard post, from which one must not release oneself or run away—seems to me to be a high doctrine with difficult implications" (*Phaedo*, 62b). In *Waiting for Godot*, the task of standing guard is debased to keeping an appointment every evening with a party who never arrives: "We have kept our appointment and that's an end to that" (WFG, 51). Here, watching—the act on which security of life depends—is demoted to waiting, and waiting, in turn, is demoted to the procrastination of suicide: "We'll hang ourselves tomorrow. Unless Godot comes" (60).

Whereas in the *Phaedo* death is not to be preempted or prematurely induced, in *Waiting for Godot* it is the status quo, for life itself is construed as a posthumous exercise doomed by "habit" (WFG, 58) to recapitulate innumerably the same experience lived before: "To have lived is not enough for them." "They have to talk about it" (40). Indeed, Vladimir and Estragon are already pseudospectral, revisiting each evening the same futility, unable to impinge their action upon it. In fact, they perceive their environment as a "charnel-house" or, to interpolate a phrase from "For To End Yet Again," a "[p]lace of remains" (FTEYA, 11): "Where are all these corpses from?" "These skeletons" (WFG, 41). In *Waiting for Godot*, life is over when it begins: "They give birth astride of a grave, the light gleams an instant, then it's night once more" (57). As in "Afar a Bird," the only response to living is to "g[i]ve up before birth" (*AFAR*, 39). The only possible accomplishment is "to grow old" (WFG, 58). The image of human enterprise is the death's-head: "the skull fading fading fading" (29).[5]

The same passage in the *Phaedo* that construes life as a vigil at the guard post also foregrounds two more important metaphors. Just before the reference to the guard post, Socrates links the time before death with *sunset* and contemplation of the life after death or "the future life": "What else can one do in the time before sunset?" (*Phaedo*, 61e). Then, immediately after the guard post reference, Socrates as-

---

5. Mary Junker identifies the skull as the Turoe Stone in Connemara: "an anthropomorphic image of pagan worship, dating from around 279 B.C." (1995, 49).

sociates the notion of suicide with the action of *fleeing a good master:* "[A] stupid person might get the idea that it would be to his advantage to escape from his master" (62d). Both sunset and the possibility that a slave will flee from his master figure prominently in *Waiting for Godot.* Pozzo delivers a set speech on the sunset. Moreover, Pozzo also has a slave who, far from running away, tries to prevent his master from dismissing him: "He imagines that when I see how well he carries I'll be tempted to keep him in that capacity" (WFG, 21).

In each case, the moral earnestness implicit in the Socratic metaphors is debased. The sunset contemplation of the eschatological relation between the life to come and the life to end becomes a discourse on the irrelevance of preparation: "[N]ight is charging and will burst upon us pop! like that! just when we least expect it" (WFG, 25).[6] The metaphor regarding the temptation to flee a good master (i.e., to commit suicide) is inverted to concern the project to "cod" (21) the master into keeping the slave, as if intensification of suffering could, instead of prompting suicide, become the reason for living. This strategy epitomizes the plight of Vladimir and Estragon, who reduce life to excruciating futility in order to escape the responsibilities of purpose. Indeed, Lucky provides a gloss on their predicament: "labours abandoned left unfinished" (29).

Further consideration of Plato will clarify *Waiting for Godot.* In the *Meno* (97e–98a), Socrates employs the metaphor of the tether to distinguish knowledge from mere "opinion"—a term used by Vladimir in his first speech and a little later by Estragon (WFG, 7, 10). Knowledge can be relied upon, while opinion is prone to abscond:

> True opinions are a fine thing and do all sorts of good so long as they stay in their place, but they will not stay long. They run away from a man's mind; so they are not worth much until you *tether* them by working out the reason. That process, my dear Meno, is recollection, as we agreed earlier. Once they are tied down, they be-

6. According to Paul Davies, sunset "offers rest to the tired physical eye, so that imagination can free itself of the material world to which it is tied during the day" (1994, 205).

come knowledge, and are stable. That is why knowledge is something more valuable than right opinion. What distinguishes one from the other is *the tether (Meno,* 97e–98a).

The image of the tether is prominent in *Waiting for Godot,* for Lucky is tethered to Pozzo "by means of a rope passed round his neck" (WFG, 15), while Vladimir and Estragon, by their own admission, are tethered psychologically to Godot: "Tied to Godot! What an idea! No question of it" (14). Closer examination of the *Meno* passage perhaps strengthens the connection between the tether in that Platonic dialogue and the tether in Beckett's play. For Socrates introduces the notion of the tether by reference to "the statues of Daedalus" that, if left "untethered," will slip away *"like a runaway slave" (Meno,* 97d; my emphasis). Lucky, Pozzo's tethered slave, does indeed seem associated with this distinction between knowledge and mere opinion, for his supreme function is "to think" philosophically (WFG, 27) about the meaning of "man" (29).

We can conclude our consideration of Platonic allusions in *Waiting for Godot* with discussion of Godot's emissary, the Boy, who enters near the end of each act with the message that, though Godot "won't come this evening," he is sure to "come to-morrow" (WFG, 58). The figure of the Boy entrains a celebrated Platonic antecedent, even if the connection is only fortuitous. Early in Plato's *Republic,* Socrates and his companion are instructed by a boy to await the arrival of his master:

> After we had said our prayers and seen the spectacle we were starting for town when Polemarchus, the son of Cephalus, caught sight of us from a distance as we were hastening homeward and ordered his boy run and bid us wait for him, and *the boy caught hold of my himation from behind and said, Polemarchus wants you to wait.*
> And I turned around and asked where his master was.
> There he is, he said, behind you, coming this way. *Wait for him. (Republic,* 1:327b; my emphasis)

The great dialogue on justice that ensues after the brief waiting requested by the boy (Polemarchus's slave) contrasts starkly with

Vladimir's and Estragon's ever-renewing but inconclusive dialogue on their situation: "Yes, now I remember, yesterday evening we spent *blathering about nothing in particular.* That's been going on now for half a century" (WFG, 42; my emphasis). Whereas to Socrates, the purpose of dialogue is to train thought to recognize and overcome its own ignorance, for Vladimir and Estragon dialogue serves only to distract themselves from the responsibility of effective thinking.

### The Juxtaposition of Plato and Berkeley in *Waiting for Godot*

The preceding interpretation of *Waiting for Godot,* enabled by the allusions to Berkeley's *Treatise Concerning the Principles of Human Knowledge* and the Platonic dialogues, diverges from the popular reading, inaugurated by Martin Esslin and frequently reaffirmed. According to that view, *Waiting for Godot* dramatizes the absurdity of the "human" condition (WFG, 19), unfolding helplessly in a universe with neither intrinsic meaning nor purpose (Esslin 1969, 56).[7] An overlooked but extremely competent formulation of this prevailing view is offered by John J. Mood: "If there is anything Beckett *is* serious about, will *not* be disingenuous about, will *not* dissemble, it is this matter of helplessness" (1971, 263). But as we have found, there is abundant evidence that the plight of existence in the world of the play reflects not a universally objective condition, but a subjective attitude or perspective that prefers to perpetuate faith in futility. At the deepest level, the helplessness that afflicts Vladimir and Estragon is not generic but carefully planned. They wait for that which will never arrive because they are certain that it will never come. Their waiting awaits only its own continuation: "waiting for . . . waiting" ((WFG, 51, 50). They wait because it is all they know of life ("All my lousy life I've crawled about in the mud!" [39]) and all they *choose* to know: "You'd rather be stuck there doing nothing?" "Yes" (45).

That Vladimir and Estragon wait only on the condition that Godot will never come is indicated by their questioning of his emissary, the Boy, who arrives at the end of each evening to advise that, as

7. See O'Brien (1990, 16) and Butler (1991, 48–55).

Vladimir puts it, "[Godot] won't come this evening . . . [b]ut he'll come to-morrow" (WFG, 58). When the Boy arrives on first evening, Estragon asks: "What kept you so late?" (32). His query clearly shows that the object of the celebrated waiting is the Boy, not Godot. This emphasis on waiting for the Boy, instead of waiting for Godot, can be clarified by the insistence on the Boy's role as witness: "You did see us, didn't you?" (34); "You're sure you saw me, you won't come and tell me to-morrow that you never saw me!" (59). The proximate cause of this anxiety about not being seen is the fact that each evening a *different* boy arrives with Godot's message. Hence, each new Boy has no recollection of any previous meeting: "This is your first time?" "Yes, Sir" (33). "This is your first time." "Yes, Sir" (58).

Ironically, this situation suits Vladimir and Estragon perfectly, as further reference to Berkeley's metaphysics can clarify. As discussed earlier, the hallmark of Berkeley's philosophy is the proposition that to be is to be perceived. That is, objects exist only as ideas in the mind perceiving them. If Vladimir and Estragon remain uncertain about being perceived, they remain uncertain about their own existence: "Do you think God sees me?" (WFG, 49). But the project of Vladimir and Estragon *is* to remain uncertain of their own existence, to prove that existence is only an illusion that they themselves control: "We always find something, eh Didi, to give us the *impression* we exist?" (44; my emphasis). Indeed, on hearing the approach of intruders, Estragon's initial reflex is to hide behind the tree: "Your only hope left is to disappear" (47). Here avoidance of being seen indicates the wish to exist only in terms of the perplexity they sustain for each other: "That's the idea, let's contradict each other" (41).

We are ready now to explicate the fusion of Plato and Berkeley in *Waiting for Godot*. To begin with, these two philosophers uphold contradictory doctrines concerning the nature of reality. For Berkeley, reality is founded on sense perception, which in turn is a complex of ideas in the mind. For Plato, sense perception concerns only inconstant appearances, whereas genuine reality is to be founded on the changeless self-identity of the Ideal Forms, which remain "always constant and invariable, never admitting any alteration in any respect or in any sense" *(Phaedo,* 78d). Cassirer formulates the contrast between Plato and Berkeley compactly: "In order to affirm the reality of its objects, classical epistemology had to degrade sensation to subjective appearance, and ultimately set it down as a mere name. Now [with Berkeley] the opposite thesis is upheld: sensation has become the sole reality and matter is a mere name" (Cassirer 1957, 3:23).

*Waiting for Godot* conflates these two appraisals of reality. Here, reality is founded on perception, as in Berkeley's metaphysics, but perception always concerns "this immense confusion" (51R). Hence, unlike Berkeley's system where perception is "the only certain and utterly unproblematical . . . datum of all knowledge" (Cassirer 1957, 3:23), perception in the play confirms only a changeless indeterminacy that defies certain knowledge: "Nothing very definite" (WFG, 13). Hence constancy ("The essential doesn't change" [14]), instead of entailing truth, as in the Platonic metaphysics, simply confirms deception: "That's all a pack of lies" (33). In Beckett's universe, to be is to be deceived. It is to believe, despite available alternatives, that there is "[n]othing to be done" but continue the same futility, nothing to be known but the same perplexity: "What do we do now?" (12).

# 9

# Disintegrative Process in *Endgame*

*Endgame* is a play about process: "Something is taking its course" (13, 32). On one level, that elapsing process concerns the perform-ance of the play itself; as many critics have noted, *Endgame* fore-grounds its own status as a drama through a variety of devices: (a) Hamm's name (which, according to Hugh Kenner, denotes "an actor"; 1968, 00); (b) Hamm's reference to playing ("Me—to play" [END, 2]); (c) Clov's elaborate uncurtaining of the props and win-dows prior to speaking; and (d) the references to theatrical terms such as *dialogue* (58), *aside* (77), *soliloquy* (78), *underplot* (78), *exit* (81), and performative *technique* (59; Kenner 1968, 156). Hannah Copeland sums up this reflexive emphasis: "Here the focus upon the play as play is relentless" (1975, 48).[1]

But with his opening soliloquy, Clov indicates another kind of process, one whose commencement precedes his appearance on stage and does not rely on dramatic convention: "Finished, it's finished, nearly finished, it must be nearly finished. *(Pause.)* Grain upon grain, one by one, suddenly, there's a heap, a little heap, the impossible heap" (END, 1). Later, Hamm echoes these observations and deep-ens their significance: "It's finished, we're finished. Nearly finished"

---

1. Compare with Kenner: "its most persuasive metaphor, the play itself" (1968, 160). An even more famous metaphor linked with *Endgame* concerns chess. Indeed, as reported by Anthony Cronin and others, Beckett himself, during rehearsal for the 1967 Berlin production of *Endgame* (Endspiel), told one of the actors that Hamm sig-nified the king and that he was "a bad player." See Cronin (1996, 459–60).

(50); "Moment upon moment, pattering down, like the millet grains of . . . that old Greek, and *all life long you wait for that to mount up to a life*" (70; my emphasis). As Hamm's remarks suggest, this alternate process concerns the lived experience of time or, in alternate formulation, the temporality of living. Yet here the process of living entails not the continuous unfolding of the intrinsic meaning or value of the animate subject in question, but only the accumulation of temporal units that remain extraneous to the subject enduring through them.

## The Problematic Relation of Whole to Parts

The deeper implications of this view of life emerge when we investigate Hamm's allusion to "that old Greek." As several critics have noted, the philosopher cited is Zeno of Elea, who flourished around 450 B.C.[2] The imagery regarding falling grain occurs in one of Zeno's many arguments (technically, *reductiones ad absurdum*) against Pythagorean pluralism and in support of Parmenidean monism: If the *parts* (i.e., the grains) of a bushel of corn make no sound when falling, how can the *whole* (i.e., the entire bushel) make a sound when falling, since it is composed entirely of its parts? Through reasoning that Aristotle (who reports it) has no trouble refuting, Zeno here attempts (a) to demonstrate the logical absurdity of postulating parts, and hence, (b) to prove that reality is a plenum or indivisible and unitary whole *(Physics* 7.5.250a20–24).

An inversion of the same problem constitutes the thematic core of *Endgame*. Whereas Zeno problematized plurality and multiplicity, *Endgame* begins by problematizing indivisible wholeness. In this Beckettian context, life itself is the problematic whole. How can a whole life be made of such parts as both Clov and Hamm cite: "[A]ll life long you wait for that to mount up to a life"? Under these condi-

2. See Cohn (1980, 42) and Worton (1994, 80). Connor attributes the heap image to Sextus Empiricus (1988, 123). Worton also cites Eubulides of Miletus and "the *sorites* (or heap) paradox in which he proposed that there can be no such thing as a heap of sand, since one grain does not make a heap and adding one grain is never enough to convert a non-heap into a heap" (1994, 80).

tions, where the whole is negated by the meaningless accumulation of its temporal parts, life can no longer be construed as a continuous process of becoming by which the living individual progressively unfolds his or her significance: "Mean something! You and I, mean something! Ah that's a good one!" (END, 33). But if life comprises meaningless parts, or what Hamm terms "moments for nothing" (83), then the *time* in which life endures or elapses can no longer be defined as a cumulative succession of consecutive instants. In this sense, "time is over": "Moments for nothing, now as always, time was never and time is over, reckoning closed and story ended" (83). Instead of cumulative succession effecting continuous transition from past to future, time here paradoxically perpetuates its own irrelevance: "The end is in the beginning and yet you go on" (69).

In this context, as Clov indicates when answering Hamm's question, "What time is it?" time is always "[t]he same as usual" (END, 4). But if time merely perpetuates its own constancy and always remains the same as usual, then the passage of time can accomplish no more than the accumulation of identical units. Thus, instead of the eventual combination of parts into a whole (as in Hamm's waiting for granular moments "to mount up to a life"), the passage of time entails the continuous disintegration of the whole into its parts, which are then abandoned or withdrawn, as in one of Clov's "visions" (41): "I am so bowed I only see my feet, if I open my eyes, and *between my legs a little trail of black dust*" (81; my emphasis). This condition recalls Molloy's dictum: "To decompose is to live too" (MOL, 25).

Disintegrative process in *Endgame* is epitomized by sequential loss of parts. There are no more "bicycle wheels" (END, 8), "sugarplums" (55), "navigators" (65), "rugs" (67), or "coffins" (77). There is no more "pap" (9), "nature" (11), "tide" (62), or "painkiller" (71). Eventually, as Hamm indicates, "there'll be no more wall any more. Infinite emptiness will be all around you, all the resurrected dead of all the ages wouldn't fill it, and there you'll be like a little bit of grit in the middle of the steppe" (36). In this remarkable image of time as the agent of divestiture, the whole is evacuated of all content but a single residual part, "a little bit of grit in the middle of the steppe": subjectivity stranded in "infinite emptiness" (36). But the emptiness here indicated pertains not to the external world but to the internal one. The temporal process of divestiture or evacuation deprives subjectivity of its own content until all that remains is awareness of lack or deprivation. This is the quintessential suffering represented by Beckettian mimesis: "[Y]our heart bleeds you lose your heart drop by drop weep even an odd tear inward no sound" (HOW, 23, 66). It is graphically formulated Hamm: "There's something dripping in my head. A heart, a heart in my head" (END, 18).

**The Mimesis of a Mentality**

At this point, it is crucial to recognize that the setting of *Endgame* corresponds precisely to the paradigm of subjectivity stranded in "infinite emptiness." That is, the setting localizes a *mentality,* not a place, and the mentality in question is defined by preoccupation with loss and depletion. Of course, to situate the setting in a mental context is not a new suggestion, though it contradicts the opinion of such critics as Vivian Mercier, Theodore Adorno, and S. E. Gontarski, who have respectively identified the barren outer world in *Endgame* with postnuclear devastation; post-Holocaust depredation; and the war-ravaged Picardy-Normandy landscape, which Beckett himself—a volunteer ambulance driver for the Irish Red Cross—regularly drove through in 1945 (Mercier 1977, 174; Adorno 1969, 9–40; Gontarski 1985, 33). Regarding the relation between setting and mind, Hugh Kenner long ago noted that "the stage, with its high peepholes [seems] to be the inside of an immense skull" (1968, 155). Per Nykrog cites a nineteenth-century literary practice of construing "room" as a symbol for the mind (1998, 124). Moreover, Beckett's art makes frequent reference to mental as opposed to physical setting: "We are needless to say in a skull" (CAL, 38). The *Texts* narrator locates himself "inside an imaginary head" (TFN, 82) and then explicitly distinguishes that mental being from bodily existence: "What can have become then of the tissues I was, I can see them no more, feel them no more, flaunting and fluttering all about and inside me, pah they must be still on their old prowl somewhere, passing themselves

off as me" (TFN, 103). The narrator of "From an Abandoned Work"
applies a similar formula: "just went on, my body doing its best without me" (FAAW, 49).

Once it is recognized that the setting of *Endgame* is mental, the
obliteration of the external world ("[z]ero" [END, 29]) and the ex-
termination of everything living in it ("corpsed" [30]) gain new
meaning. For in this context, the emphasis on external vacancy signifies not the literal destruction of the outer world but the inability or
refusal of the mentality represented to acknowledge anything outside
the concerns preoccupying its own interiority: "To hell with the universe" (46). Since these concerns fundamentally involve awareness of
lack or depletion, the emptiness of the external world in the play is no
more than the objective correlative of internal awareness. That is, the
outer world becomes the reification of awareness of inner emptiness—an objectification of a habitual perspective or way of seeing. Indeed, the play foregrounds the role of perspective in defining the
outer world, as in the example of the madman who, when invited to
look through the window at "[a]ll that loveliness," recoiled
"[a]ppalled" for "[a]ll he had seen was ashes" (44). The role of perspective in determining the meaning of what is seen appears also in
Clov's observing through the wrong window: "Ah what a fool I am!
I'm on the wrong side!" (73). In noting his error, he associates it with
mental aberration: "Sometimes I wonder if I'm in my right senses.
Then it passes off and I'm as intelligent as ever" (73).

To observe that *Endgame* is (to adapt the Unnamable's phrasing) set in "a head abandoned to its ancient solitary resources" (UN,
361) is to approach the play as the mimesis of a mentality or psychological orientation toward life. Viewed from this angle, the characters
in the play constitute contrapuntal expressions of the same persistent
mentality. Indeed, according to James Knowlson, when Beckett directed a German production of *Endgame* (Endspiel) in 1967, he described the play as "full of echoes; they all answer each other" (1996,
551). The hallmark of this mentality is obsessive concern with interior distress to the exclusion of all other considerations. For example,
there is never anything in Hamm's world but the sense of its irrele-

vance: "It all happened without me" (END, 74).[3] The only object of his continuous attention is himself: "Well, there we are, there I am, that's enough" (83). No other object can compete with or displace preoccupation with his own suffering that abides "in the center" (25) of his awareness: "Can there be misery—loftier than mine?" (2). What never changes for Hamm is obsession with the malaise of his own interiority: "Last night I saw inside my breast. There was a big sore" (32).

### The Primacy of Habit

Experience in *Endgame* is dominated by the same principle of inescapable interiority as that formulated by Beckett in *Proust*: "We are alone. We cannot know and we cannot be known. 'Man is the creature that cannot come forth from himself, who knows others only in himself, and who, if he asserts the contrary, lies' " (P, 66). Yet, whereas according to the doctrine formulated in *Proust* isolation is imposed as an ontological condition of human being, in *Endgame* it arises from mental habit perpetuated over time. The play indicates that, at any age, Hamm resorts to the same mental habits—to the point that, as a character, he does not so much represent a person as incarnate a mental habit that can inhabit or, at least, influence any susceptible host. This dispensation reinforces our earlier observation that the play concerns the mimesis of an attitude or mentality.

However, the suggestion that the play dramatizes a persistent mental habit, regarding which (to interpolate Vladimir's phrase in *Waiting for Godot)* "The essential doesn't change" (WFG, 14), contradicts Jennifer Jeffers's claim (derived from the philosophical writings of Deleuze and Guatarri) that Beckett's art depicts "[t]he plane of immanence [which] does not represent an idea [but] . . . instead . . . presents the event, the discourse, the becoming or the flow" (Jef-

---

3. In a discussion of Robbe-Grillet's interpretation of Beckett, Bruce Morrissette employs a circumlocution for Hamm's absence: "the non-existence of his own presence." See Morrissette (1975, 69).

fers 1996, 65).[4] According to this view, Beckettian mimesis represents "thought . . . cut loose from representation," "an immanent plane where thinking is not restricted" by traditional categories of conceptualization, "where language stops and the pure image of thought begins" (Jeffers 1996, 66, 67). But far from concerning the pure flow of thought, abstracted from the structure of its own content, the mentality represented in *Endgame* remains imprisoned in its structure. Here thought can only reiterate through time the pattern of its own habitual operation.

The emphasis on habit in *Endgame* is relentless: "But I feel too old, and too far, to form new habits" (END, 81). Indeed, in response to Clov's question regarding repetitious practice ("Why this farce, day after day?"), Hamm identifies the cause as "[r]outine" (32). In *Proust,* Beckett defined habit as "An automatic adjustment of the human organism to the conditions of its existence" (P, 20). According to this theory, much invoked by critics, the life of an individual sustains routine patterns that insulate against the destabilizing intrusion of change, until factors beyond the control of the individual alter the circumstances of personal existence, requiring the construction of a new habit after an excruciating "period of transition" (P, 21).[5]

The relationship between Hamm and Clov corresponds to that between an individual and the habit by which "automatic adjustment of the human organism to the conditions of its existence" is achieved. In *Proust,* Beckett refers to habit as a "minister of dullness" and "agent of security" (P, 21) that is "tophatted and hygienic" (28). Clov is obsessed with domestic order ("I love order" [END, 57]) and, near the end of the play, sports a "Panama hat" (82). But the link between Clov and habit is reinforced in another way. In *Proust,* habit is compared to a "cook . . . who knows what has to be done, and will slave all day and all night rather than tolerate any redundant activity in the kitchen" (P, 20). When not with Hamm, Clov retires to

4. On immanence and becoming, see also Uhlmann (1999, 126).

5. The Beckett play most frequently related by critics to *Proust* is *Krapp's Last Tape.* See Brater (1987, 19); Henning (1988, 144–58); and Erickson (1991, 181–94).

his kitchen: "I'll go now to my kitchen" (END, 2). Since Clov is thus associated with the ministrations of habit, it follows that the departure of Clov, near the end of the play, signifies "the death of Habit and the brief suspension of its vigilance" (P, 23), initiating one of "the perilous zones in the life of the individual" suddenly bereft of habit (P, 19). Indeed, just before exiting, Clov refers to both reliance on habit ("But I feel too old, and too far, to form new habits" [END, 81]), and the sudden entry into the transitional period, "when for a moment the boredom of living [under the care of habit] is replaced by the suffering of being" (P, 19): "Then one day, suddenly, it ends, it changes" (END, 81). Hence, Hamm alone is Hamm without his "current habit of living" (P, 20). Hamm alone is Hamm suffering one of "these periods of abandonment" by habit, when the task is "to create a new habit that will empty the mystery of its threat" (P, 22).

But Hamm alone displays none of the suffering of being that Beckett in *Proust* associates with the period of transition. On the contrary, as soon as he realizes that Clov is gone, Hamm repeats the words with which, at the outset of the play, he initiated his "[r]outine" (32) with Clov: "Me—to play" (END, 2, 82). But this time, instead of issuing imperatives to Clov, he applies them to himself: "Discard" (82), "Take it easy" (82), "Raise hat" (82), "And put on again" (82), "Discard" (84), "speak no more" (84). Hamm concludes by covering his face with the handkerchief so that he resumes the "attitude" (55) with which, at the commencement of the play, he began. Hamm is immune to change because, as Clov observes, he perpetuates the same state, whatever his external circumstances: "All life long the same questions, the same answers" (5); "All life long the same inanities" (45). Hamm has always been like this, despite modification of local conditions. For no matter where he is, Hamm is never there: "Absent, *always*. It all happened without me" (74; my emphasis). His blindness epitomizes his obliviousness to change. As Pozzo declares in *Waiting for Godot*, "The blind have no notion of time. The things of time are hidden from them too" (WFG, 55). Indeed, the similarity between the series of imperatives uttered here by Hamm and the sequential stage directions reinforces the notion of immunity to change. For just as, on the theatrical level, the purpose of a play is to be performed again and again, so the purpose of habit is to ensure repetition of the thoughts and actions that constitute it.

## Habit and Automatism

In *Endgame,* character is reduced to habit, defined in *Proust* as "[a]n automatic adjustment of the human organism to the conditions of its existence" (P, 20). That is, according to Beckett, "Life is habit" (P, 19), and habit is determined by what Leo Spitzer, in a different context, refers to as "automatism": a mechanism with its own automatic—or, as we might say today, programmed—configuration of operation (1948, 149). In the play, that which is "taking its course" (END, 13, 32) is what the narrator of *How It Is* terms "the force of habit" (HOW, 47), construed here as automatic process, proceeding with the same mechanical inevitability as the ticking of the "alarm-clock" that Clov "hangs up" on the wall (END, 72). For, according to "the law of automatism," as formulated by Spitzer, "once the first step is taken the process must run its course" (1948, 149). To interpolate Hamm's phrasing, "The end is in the beginning" (END, 69), and once the process begins, it must continue to completion.

Ironically, the moment in the play where automatic process is most emphasized, reducing character to purely rote activity without emotional involvement, occurs when Clov responds "tonelessly" and with "fixed gaze" to Hamm's request to say "Something . . . from your heart" (END, 80). Here, just as, according to the *Proust* essay, "life is habit" (P, 19), so too love is habit—the operation of an impersonal automatism. More precisely, because life is habit whose pattern of response is "pre-established" (MOL, 62), there can be no love: "never loved anything" (HOW, 41). Similarly, in *Endgame* the love of God, as manifested through prayer, is also reduced to the operation of habit, understood as a pattern of response that continues automatically once initiated: "Off we go" (END, 55). Indeed, Nagg's mode of prayer parodies mechanical response, "Nagg (clasping his hands, closing his eyes, in a gabble): Our Father which art—" (55). An analogous instance of mechanical prayer (and one that, as Knowlson has noted, corresponds to an extant photograph of the very young Beckett with his mother on the veranda of Cooldrinagh, the family home) occurs in *How It Is*: "in a word bolt upright on a cushion whelmed in a nightshirt I pray according to her instructions" (Knowlson 1996, 462; HOW, 15).

With respect to automatism in *Endgame,* there are only two alternatives: "[w]inding up" (END, 72) and running down: "One day you'll say, I'm tired, I'll stop" (37); "Then one day, suddenly, it ends, it changes, I don't understand, it dies, or it's me, I don't understand, that either" (81). Love is irrelevant in this environment, for love here is not a feeling but just another activity performed according to memorized procedure: "Get out of here and love one another! Lick your neighbour as yourself!" (68). Moreover, love requires communication, and words themselves are the product of regularized intercourse, not spontaneous intimacy: "I use the words you taught me. If they don't mean anything any more, teach me others. Or let me be silent" (44); "I ask the words that remain—sleeping, waking, morning, evening. They have nothing to say" (83).[6] Nor can there be compassion in this environment, for when life is governed by a pattern of regularity, the suffering of others must either be assimilated to supervenient routine (as in the hospice for those "dying of their wounds" [80]) or ignored as efficaciously as possible: "Bottle him!" (10). Moreover, in a world ruled by automatism, emotion—the *sine qua non* of compassion—is subordinated to and eventually displaced by regularized performance: "Every man his specialty" (10).

Perhaps the supreme symbol in Beckettian art for the reduction of life to automatism is the timepiece, whether watch, clock, or timerbell. A short list of examples will foreground the issue: (a) Clov (as already noted) hanging an "alarm-clock" on the wall (END, 70) and then placing it "on lid of Nagg's bin" (79); (b) Pozzo referring to his watch ("A genuine half-hunter"), whose ticking, in the scene where

---

6. Compare, on this point, Jonathan Boulter: "Clov's complaint is that his experience of the world—or his linguistic representation of it—is bound by a language possibly defunct" (1998, 51).

Vladimir and Estragon attempt to locate it, is eventually confused with his own heartbeat: "It's the heart" (WFG, 30); (c) Winnie required to conduct her stationary existence "between the bell for waking and the bell for sleep" (HD, 21); (d) the narrator in *How It Is* referring to "Pim's timepiece" and the "ticking" of "a big ordinary watch with heavy chain" (HOW, 40, 58); (e) Molloy referring to his own life as a "[w]atch wound and buried by the watchmaker"—that is, as a "mechanism" that functions according to a "pre-established" pattern of operation, thus rendering personal responsibility for fulfillment in life irrelevant (MOL, 36, 51, 62).

In the context of automatism, Clov's placing of the alarm clock on the lid of Nagg's ashbin is especially significant. For time is indeed superfluous ("time is over" [END, 83]) in an environment where time is always "the same as usual" (4) because its moments are the measure of mechanical process, configured to follow a series of predetermined movements until concluding, as epitomized in "For To End Yet Again": "for to end yet again by degrees or *as though switched on*" (FTEYA, 15; my emphasis). Moreover, the primacy of automatism also clarifies the emphasis in *Endgame* on "the play as play" (to recall Copeland's phrase, quoted at the outset). For construed in strictly performative terms, a play *is* an automatism, designed to run to the end once it begins—and then to begin again on another occasion: "Through it who knows yet another end" (FTEYA, 15). Just as, to quote Hamm once again, "[t]he end is in the beginning" (END, 69), so the beginning of the next performance of the play is foreshadowed in the end. Hamm replaces the same handkerchief on his face at the end of the play as that which Clov removed from his face at the beginning.

Thus, in *Endgame*, automatism does not merely take its course. For once it has run down, it must begin again. Through this notion of redundant automatism, Beckett modifies the concept of habit enunciated in *Proust*: "[L]ife is a succession of habits, since the individual is a succession of individuals [each defined through the habits proper to him]" (P, 19). Whereas in *Proust* Beckett gave equal emphasis to habits and the "periods of transition" (P, 19) between them, in *Endgame,* by implication, he eliminates the transitional intervals between consecutive habits. Transition now has no significance other than the beginning of a new automatism—or the renewing of an old one: "To think that in a moment all will be said, all to do again" (CAL, 44).

The purpose of automatism in Beckettian mimesis is to reduce thinking to mechanical process ("But there is reasoning somewhere. . . . It's mechanical" [TFN, 117]) so that the mind can be excused from attending to its own content: "[W]hat's the matter with my head, I must have left it in Ireland, in a saloon" (TFN, 113). The celebrated upshot of this strategy is the predicament where the narrator's awareness is distracted by the audition of a voice whose identity he cannot determine but which, in fact, articulates his own thinking: "He knows they are words, he is not sure they are his" (UN, 354). This condition epitomizes the Beckettian "sense of absence" (MAL, 279)—a condition Hamm applies to himself ("Absent, always. It all happened without me" [END, 74]). When first citing this passage, we interpreted it in terms of Hamm's mental withdrawal from *external* circumstances. We can now see that, at a deeper level, it signifies Hamm's withdrawal from his *mental* circumstances. That is, Beckettian mimesis gives new meaning to the term *absent-mindedness.* For here absent-mindedness ("my mind absent, elsewhere" [TFN, 108]) ultimately pertains to the absence of the mind from its own thought in order thereby to achieve "flight from self" (UN, 367): "I say to the head, Leave it alone, stay quiet, it stops breathing, then pants on worse than ever. I am far from all that wrangle, I shouldn't bother with it" (TFN, 75).

## The Provenance of Automatist Process

The play appears to derive this strategy from childhood. Nagg recalls Hamm's nocturnal fear of abandonment: "Whom did you call when you were a tiny boy, and were frightened, in the dark? Your mother? No. Me. We let you cry. Then we moved you out of earshot, so that we might sleep in peace" (END, 56). Hamm refers to the habitual tactic of "the solitary child" to insulate itself from the threat of isolation: "Then babble, babble, words, like the solitary child who turns himself into children, two, three, so as to be together, and whisper together, in the dark" (70). After discovering that he has been abandoned by Clov, Hamm again invokes the plight of the solitary child: "You cried for night; it falls: now cry in darkness" (83).[7] The strategy of absent-mindedness through automatism can be construed as an elaboration of childhood recourse to conversation with imaginary friends. In this context, the "babble, babble" by which "the solitary child" populates his loneliness ultimately becomes the automatist flow of thought by which the mind withdraws attention, not only from the world of which it is aware, but also from its own awareness in order thereby to achieve complete insularity—a state symbolized by Hamm's retirement behind the bloody "Veronica," which he drapes over his face: "Old stauncher! You remain" (84).

The only factor that can overcome the need for subjective isolation is "compassion" (END, 76). But here we encounter a Beckettian double bind. Lack of compassion forces the subject to seek escape from his predicament. Yet compassion would condemn others to endure even longer their own plight. This unusual circumstance is dramatically expressed in Hamm's reproach of the peasant father who beseeched Hamm to "consent to take in" both the peasant father and his "child" (53): "He doesn't realize, all he knows is hunger, and cold, and death to crown it all. But you! You ought to know what the earth is like, nowadays. Oh I put him before his responsibilities!" (83).

Here Hamm indicates that the father's request for a shelter put his own need for survival before concern for the suffering that survival would force his son to endure. Yet, despite this opinion, Hamm apparently did admit Clov as a child into his abode. When he asks whether Clov can "remember when you came," the reply is "No. Too small you told me" (END, 38). As Hamm's ward, Clov has

7. According to Hersh Zeifman, Hamm's reference to nocturnal crying derives from one of Baudelaire's *fleurs du mal*: "Tu reclamais le Soir; il descend; le voici" (Zeifman 1999, 260).

learned his lesson well; he actually refines Hamm's rejection of compassion. Brief analysis of Clov's celebrated remark will clarify: "If I
don't kill that rat he'll die" (68). As an inversion of the tautology "If
I kill that rat he'll die," the statement epitomizes the Beckettian ethic
in *Endgame*. Compassion is meaningless. The preservation of life
only prolongs a condition of terminal futility. Hence, pity and cruelty
coincide.

There are only two types of people in *Endgame*: parents or
parental substitutes, and their children or wards. Nagg and Nell are
respectively Hamm's father and mother. Hamm "was a father to"
Clov (END, 38); Hamm's elaborate story concerns a father and son.
The figure of the abandoned or neglected child is especially emphasized: (a) Hamm as "a tiny boy" banished "out of earshot" at night so
that his parents "might sleep in peace" (56); (b) the peasant's child
temporarily left "all alone" while his father journeys to beg Hamm
for succor (52); and (c) the "small boy" suddenly spotted by Clov
and ignored by Hamm: "If he exists he'll die there or he'll come
here" (78). Thus established as a dominant motif, the abandoned or
neglected child is the ultimate source or *locus classicus* of the sense of
absence and "infinite emptiness" (36). In this context, Hamm's recourse to discarding possessions at the end of the play makes more
sense. The abandoned child has himself been discarded and so can
find protection only through identifying with discarding. All that he
retains is the sense of deprivation and the need to withdraw from the
uncaring world ("Outside of here it's death" [9]) into his own interiority—and ultimately, as we have seen, even *from* that interiority.

In Beckettian art, the supreme expression of parental indifference concerns the nativity scene in *Company*: "A mother stooping
over cradle from behind. She moves aside to let the father look. In his
turn he murmurs to the newborn. Flat tone unchanged. *No trace of
love*" (COM, 66; my emphasis). Here the utter absence of parental
love alters the project of the child, whose task is to satisfy "the craving
for company"—not through seeking the love forever withheld, but
by "devising figments to temper his nothingness" (COM, 77, 64).
The same project motivates the narrator of *Texts for Nothing*, in a pas-

sage that constitutes an apt gloss on Hamm's predicament at the conclusion of *Endgame*: "I'm in my arms, I'm holding myself in my arms, without much tenderness, but faithfully, faithfully. Sleep now, as under that ancient lamp, all twined together, tired out with so much talking, so much listening, so much toil and play" (TFN, 79).

Paradoxically, in the Beckettian universe the greatest need of the mentality formed by the sense of abandonment and neglect suffered by "the solitary child" is to sustain the state of isolation. In that circumstance no further rejection can ever intrude, since the only companions are the figures whom "the solitary child turns himself into" through fantasy (END, 70). In alternate formulation, the isolation experienced in childhood simply becomes a habit that experience cannot break. On the model of the parent-child relationship, intimacy is construed as reciprocal estrangement, as in the *Texts* narrator's account of walks with his father as a boy: "[W]e walked together, hand in hand, silent, sunk in our worlds, each in his worlds, the hands forgotten in each other" (TFN, 79). Analogous accounts occur in *The Unnamable* ("each one in his little elsewhere" [UN, 403]) and *Ohio Impromptu* ("so long alone together" [OI, 14]).

### The Problematics of Love

The fundamental source of the "misery" (END, 2) in the play concerns love or, more precisely, its lack. The overwhelming power of love to affect the mind is formally enunciated in *Words and Music*: "Love is of all the passions the most powerful passion and indeed no passion is more powerful than the passion of love. That is the mode in which the mind is most strongly affected and indeed in no mode is the mind more strongly affected than this" (WM, 24). In the Beckettian environment, as indicated by the narrator of *How It Is*, love cannot be distinguished from the fear of abandonment: "love fear of being abandoned a little of each no knowing" (HOW, 66). That is, because of "the well-known mechanism of association" (MOL, 48), whose operation is founded on bitter experience (obliquely suggested in the examples cited above), the need for love is associated with the pain of rejection. Thus, love is construed as the relation between "tormentor" and "victim" (HOW, 129). Elsewhere in the Beckettian canon, love is associated with extreme personal danger whose immediate analogue is the risk of death. Indeed, when reflecting on his sudden terror, the *Texts* narrator confuses love with the threat of murder and then reassures himself of absolute isolation in the Gobi desert—an image recalling Hamm's reference to "a little bit of grit in the middle of the steppe" (END, 36): "And to start with stop palpitating, no one's going to kill you no one's going to love you and no one's going to kill you, perhaps you'll emerge in the high depression of Gobi, you'll feel at home there" (TFN, 86). The linking of love and mortal danger perhaps derives from the child's dependence on parental figures whose inadequate love implies the threat of abandonment: "We let you cry. Then we moved you out of earshot, so that we might sleep in peace" (END, 56).

In *Endgame,* the problem of love ultimately entrains the problem of God. Here the supreme expression of love withheld pertains to the Deity, who refuses to exist even though the plight of those on "earth" (END, 53, 68, 81) sorely requires him: "The bastard! He doesn't exist!" (55). Closer inspection of the hilarious prayer scene will deepen our understanding of the play. According to well-established custom ("Again!"), Hamm instructs Clov and Nagg to join him in prayer: "Let us pray to God" (54). They adopt appropriate "[a]ttitudes of prayer" (55), but after a few moments each desists, "discouraged": "Sweet damn all!" (55). Here prayer entails the expectation of prompt reward for good action, just as Nagg, in a synchronous context, expects the reward that Hamm promised him for listening to his story: "Me sugar-plum!" (54, 55). But as Hamm advises Nagg, in the midst of the prayer scene, "There are no more sugar-plums!" (55). In response, Nagg accepts responsibility for his own disappointment, attributing its cause to his own mistreatment of Hamm during early childhood:

> It's natural. After all I am your father. It's true if it hadn't been me it would have been someone else. But that's no excuse. (Pause.) Turkish Delight, for example, which no longer exists, we all know

that, there is nothing in the world I love more. And one day I'll ask you for some, in return for a kindness, and you'll promise it to me. One must live with the times. (Pause.) Whom did you call when you were a tiny boy, and were frightened, in the dark? Your mother? No. Me. We let you cry. Then we moved you out of earshot, so that we might sleep in peace. (END, 56)

With extraordinary compression, the prayer scene conflates the unresponsiveness of God to human entreaty with the reciprocal unresponsiveness of father and son. Just as God the Father ("Our Father which art—" [END, 55]) does not answer prayers, so Nagg the father did not answer his son's nocturnal cries nor, in retaliation for paternal abandonment, does Hamm reward his father's "kindness" or good action.[8] Here the economy of the "universe" (46) is interpreted after the model of dysfunctional father-son love. In alternate formulation, in the world of the play familial love has no more reality than God. Yet there is something deeper here. God does not answer because he does not exist. But he does not exist because he is a "bastard"—that is, too uncaring and selfish to exist. According to this illogical theology, the first principle of being is not the existence of God, as in traditional Christian ontology, but the nonexistence of God, which expresses God's indifference and lack of compassion.

These are the originary qualities in the universe of *Endgame*. In the human sphere, they derive from defective parental love and create, in "the solitary child," the need for autonomy: the need, that is, not to need the love that never responds ("I don't need you any more" [END, 79]). The ultimate means of achieving this autonomy—of satisfying "the need never to need" (W, 202)—is recourse to automatism. In this way, the need for love ("Whom did you call when you were a tiny boy, and were frightened, in the dark?" [END, 56]) is transformed into the need for abandonment so that the com-

8. According to Joseph Smith, who relates Hamm to God, "In *Endgame* God is not dead. He is not permitted death. He is merely profoundly weary of it all but uncertain that he can be done with it" (1991, 199). For a related study, see Wicker (1998, 39–51).

pensatory mechanism of automatism can take its course. Yet recourse to automatism reduces life to the temporal process of divestiture, where each beginning signifies only the inevitability of running down until the end, again and again. Hence, to live is to disintegrate.

# 10

Krapp's Last Tape and the
Beckettian Mimesis of Regret

Perhaps no drama more deserves to be called a "memory play" (to invoke Ruby Cohn's designation) than *Krapp's Last Tape*—a play that, through pairing the aged Krapp with what Martin Esslin terms an "autobiographical library of annual recorded statements," unfolds a series of rememorations (Cohn 1975, 194; Esslin 1969, 56). In this regard, *Krapp's Last Tape*, like *The Glass Menagerie* as described by its author, Tennessee Williams, appears as a work in which nostalgia is "the first condition" (Williams 1972, 26). This impression is reinforced by the abundant connections, expertly charted by James Knowlson, between the lives of Krapp and Samuel Beckett, his author (Knowlson 1996).[1] In *Krapp's Last Tape*, the relentless emphasis on

1. A short list of these links will illustrate: (a) the girl in the punt connected with Ethna MacCarthy with whom Beckett fell in love soon after enrolling at Trinity College in October 1923 (Knowlson 1996, 442–43); (b) Krapp's "girl in a shabby green coat" (KLT, 17) associated with Peggy Sinclair, a cousin with whom Beckett fell in love in the summer of 1928 (Knowlson 1996, 81); (c) Miss Beamish (whom Beckett first met when he came to Rousillon in 1942) as the model for "Old Miss McGlome" (KLT, 15; Knowlson 1996, 330–31); (d) Krapp's outdoor "vision, at last" (KLT, 20) derived from Beckett's own indoor vision in his mother's room during the summer of 1945 (Knowlson 1996, 352); (e) the "house on the canal where mother lay a-dying, in the late autumn, after her long viduity" (KLT, 18) connected with Merrion Nursing Home where Beckett's mother, May, died of Parkinson's disease on August 25, 1950 (Knowlson 1996, 384). For a relating of Krapp's account of his "vision" to Schopenhauer's account of artistic genius, see Uhlmann (1999, 19).

memory as the agent of negative retrospection on life has prompted many critics to construe the play in generically mimetic terms, and hence to interpret Krapp as the Beckettian version of Everyman. For example, according to Joseph Smith, the play treats "the question whether *any* life can be said to have been lived for other than naught" (1991, 197). According to Anthony Kubiak, the play consummates the mimetic tradition of "Western drama" with respect to the inevitability of "pain, failure, and hopelessness" in life (1991, 121). Daniel Katz transposes this universalizing tendency to a more theoretical plane, by interpreting Krapp in poststructuralist terms as a representation of "the interminable denial of subjective appropriation which makes up 'Not I' " (1999, 9).

But to construe the play, in generically mimetic terms, as the representation of some aspect or quality universally applicable to human life is to construe Krapp's plight as irreversibly inevitable, and not as one that could, by any means, be averted. In such interpretation, Krapp cannot be judged responsible for his predicament; its cause concerns the intrinsic nature of life, not the intrinsic nature of Krapp. Yet, the upshot of such interpretation is to suppress or obscure the *moral* dimension of the play—a dimension memorably formulated, in another context by Matthew Arnold, as entailing the question of "[h]ow to live," how to apply "ideas to life" (Arnold 1959, 539) so that it is not "abandoned to passion or allowed to drift at hazard" (Arnold 1938, 1085). But in thus demanding the avoidance of *irresponsibility*, the moral question of how to live presupposes the recognition of *responsibility*—the obligation, that is, to direct life toward its proper goal, however defined.

The moral dimension is not only fundamental to *Krapp's Last Tape* but also fundamentally *ambiguous*. From one perspective, Krapp displays *irresponsibility* in becoming the victim of his own psychological mechanism or habitual attitude to life, which reduces his existence to the state of regret regarding an event he obsessively remembers: "Be again, be again. (Pause.) All that old misery. (Pause.) Once wasn't enough for you. (Pause.) Lie down across her" (KLT, 26–27). Yet from another perspective, through precisely this lapse into regret, Krapp displays *responsibility* by conducting his life toward the Beckettian goal of abandonment—a state of vacancy beyond the reach of regret: "Regretting, that's what helps you on . . . regretting what is, regretting what was . . . that's what transports you, towards the end of regretting" (UN, 371). Ironically, *neither* alternative confirms the conventional view that the play represents the futility of life. If Krapp is construed in terms of irresponsibility, then his plight, by definition, cannot be attributed to universally impinging forces over which he has no control. But if Krapp is construed in terms of responsibility and successful achievement of the Beckettian goal, then his plight cannot be deemed an example of "failure, and hopelessness" (to retrieve Kubiak's characterization).

The ambiguity of Krapp's predicament, with respect to the alternatives of irresponsibility and responsibility, is epitomized by the *time* indicated in the stage directions. Though the accumulated tapes suggest Krapp's concern with the *past*, and though his observance of this particular birthday (his sixty-ninth) emphasizes his situation in the *present*, the first stage direction of the play indicates "(A late evening in the *future*)" (KLT, 9; my emphasis). Since Krapp is in a present that rememorates various pasts, the designation of an evening in the future becomes problematic. But the problem can be solved when we realize that the temporal designation is not chronological but symbolic. That is, it indicates not a date not yet reached on a calendar, but an inevitability toward which Krapp is always tending. But is this inevitability the result of factors that Krapp cannot control or to factors for which he is responsible? On the one hand, Krapp's predicament seems to stem from the mentality or perspective on life that he embodies at any age, but which in principle he could modify. On the other hand, Krapp appears caught in a cycle whose momentum cannot be altered.

The first alternative—irresponsibility or failure to properly address the problem of how to live—can be introduced by contrasting the view of age in *Krapp's Last Tape* with that in Samuel Johnson's *Rasselas*. Our intention here is simply to foreground an important aspect of Beckett's play, not to adduce any theories of literary influence on his work—though, as Knowlson indicates, in late 1936, Beckett conceived the never-executed plan of writing a play concerning Dr. Johnson and Mrs. Thrale (Knowlson 1996, 269). *Rasselas* begins with the admonition that disappointment in life is inevitable; age cannot "perform the promises of youth": "Ye who listen with credulity to the whispers of fancy, and pursue with eagerness the phantoms of hope; who expect that age will perform the promises of youth, and that the deficiencies of the present day will be supplied by the morrow; attend to the history of Rasselas prince of Abissinia" ([1952] 1958, 505). To Johnson, the problem of unhappiness in old age is generic. The individual bears no responsibility for it. But from the point of view we shall now adopt, this is not the situation in *Krapp's Last Tape*, where Krapp's plight results from his own choices. Here, to invoke the Heracleitean dictum, character is man's fate (Heracleitus 1966, 32).

The notion of deficient self-control and failure to assume responsibility for one's actions is localized in Krapp's relation to bananas (though critics who discuss the bananas treat them as phallic symbols, ultimately indicative of Krapp's masturbatory narcissism).[2] Despite repeated resolutions over the years to "Cut 'em out!" (KLT, 14), Krapp continues gorging: "Have just eaten I regret to say three bananas and only with difficulty refrained from a fourth" (14). Ironically, the compulsivity of Krapp's banana bulimia is conspicuously analogous to the compulsivity of his rememoration. Moreover, his much-emphasized discarding of banana peels is obviously analogous to his tendency to reject or forget memories.[3] He "nearly falls" after treading on the first skin, and then "finally pushes it, still stooping, with his foot over the edge of stage into pit." After peeling the second banana, he "tosses skin into pit" (11). He treats memories in the same way as he treats banana skins. No longer interested in rememo-

2. See, for example, Astro (1990, 155); Henning (1988, 153); and Erickson (1991, 187).

3. For critics noting Krapp's tendency to forget or disremember, see Mercier (1977, 197) and Henning (1988, 147).

rating the year just concluded, Krapp first discards the envelope on which he has scrawled his notes—"Crumples it and *throws it away*" (24; my emphasis)—and then discards the tape he is recording so that he might gorge once more on the more distant memory of the girl in the punt—"He suddenly bends over machine, switches off, wrenches off tape, *throws it away*, puts on the other, winds it forward to the passage he wants, switches on, listens staring front" (27; my emphasis).

The problem of disposal common to bananas and memories suggests that, like bananas, memories are "[f]atal things for a man with [Krapp's] condition" (KLT, 14), for compulsive consumption of them constipates his life: "What's a year now? The sour cud and the iron stool" (25). Here movement toward the future is formulated in terms of preoccupation with the past: "These old P.M.s are gruesome, but I often find them—(Krapp switches off, broods, switches on)—a help before embarking on a new . . . (hesitates) . . . retrospect" (16). Krapp's relation to memory entails a further paradox. On the one hand, Krapp's life is a repudiation of his own previous or earlier selves and their respective experiences: "Well out of that, Jesus yes!" (17); "Just been listening to that stupid bastard I took myself for thirty years ago, hard to believe I was ever as bad as that. Thank God that's all done with anyway" (24). This disposal of the past seems to serve the project of advancing toward fulfillment in the future: "Perhaps my best years are gone. When there was a chance of happiness. But I wouldn't want them back. Not with the fire in me now. No, I wouldn't want them back" (28). But on the other hand, the consequence of discarding the past is eventually to reduce life to regret—"drowned in dreams" (25)—with the result that Krapp is, to interpolate Beckett's words from *Proust*, "present at his own absence" (P, 27).

From this perspective, Krapp does indeed appear irresponsible in his failure to control a pattern of thought that dooms him to nostalgia. Originally, Krapp's retrospective project was not to return to the past, but to define his identity through the annual progression of perspectives on the past. But eventually this retrospective project back-

fires such that Krapp has no identity except through regretting the
past and abdicating responsibility to constitute his identity through
striving toward the future: "Sometimes wondered if a last effort
mightn't—(Pause.) Ah finish your booze now and get to your bed.
Go on with this drivel in the morning. Or leave it at that. (Pause.) Lie
propped up in the dark—and wander. Be again in the dingle on a
Christmas Eve, gathering holly, the red-berried. All that old misery"
(KLT, 26).

Yet from another perspective, Krapp's relation to memory enables him to evade the great hazard enunciated in the theory of life
formulated by Beckett in his study of Proust. In this theory (summa-
rized in chapter 9), the life of an individual is governed by habits or
routine patterns of existence that sustain their own continuity and
enable the individual to adapt to his or her environment until dis-
rupted by a period of transition, during which "for a moment the
boredom of living is replaced by the suffering of being" (P, 19).[4]
Here, Beckett construes life in terms of a process of *decantation*
whereby the habits and forms of life established by the individual in
the past must inevitably yield to changing circumstances and conditions in the future: "The individual is the seat of a constant process of
decantation, decantation from the vessel containing the fluid of future time, sluggish, pale and monochrome, to the vessel containing
the fluid of past time, agitated and multicoloured by the phenomena
of its hours" (P, 15). As a result of the continual impingement of
change and the need to adapt to it, life is here construed as "a succession of habits, since the individual is a succession of individuals"
(P, 19).

As Esslin has noted, the annual tapes recorded by Krapp foreground this notion of the individual as a succession of individuals
(1969, 56). But it has never before been noticed that *Krapp's Last
Tape* actually *stages* the process of temporal decantation wherein, according to the passage from *Proust* already cited, this succession finds

4. For treatments of the relevance of *Proust* to *Krapp's Last Tape,* see Brater
(1987, 19); Henning (1988, 144–58); and Erickson (1991, 181–94).

its originating cause. On three occasions Krapp disappears "( . . . backstage into darkness . . . )" (KLT, 12, 17, 24), where he is heard uncorking bottles and decanting their contents: "( . . . Sound of bottle against glass, then brief siphon . . . )" (24). Significantly, on each of these occasions, the passage of time is emphasized: "( . . . Ten seconds. Loud pop of cork. Fifteen seconds . . . )" (12). The link between the passage of time and decantation is reinforced by Krapp's habit of consulting his prominently displayed "( . . . [h]eavy silver watch . . . )" (9) just before each trip backstage to decant (10, 17, 23).

Ironically, Krapp himself constitutes a dramatic refutation or, more precisely, counter example of the theory of life expressed by Beckett in *Proust*. In the play, character finally supercedes the "constant process of decantation" that individual identity necessarily undergoes. Here we reach the deeper significance of the play's title. The notion of life as *succession* is displaced by the notion of life as *regression*. There will be no more tapes—not because Krapp will not live another year (as Vivian Mercier suggests), but because Krapp has found a way to overcome the process of decantation whereby, through the passage of time, the individual becomes a succession of individuals (1977, 184). By fixating exclusively on past moments, Krapp reduces the present to the site of rememoration and thus fortifies his life against change. Through regretting the past that can never return, Krapp renders the future irrelevant. This is his last tape because there will never be anything new to record: "Leave it at that" (KLT, 26). Originally, the purpose of "retrospect" (16) was to mark annual progress away from the past: "Well out of that, Jesus yes!" (17); "Thank God that's all done with anyway" (24). But now the only retrospect concerns the importunity of regret: "Be again, be again" (26). In discarding the new tape—"( . . . wrenches off the tape, throws it away . . . )" (27)—Krapp discards the very process by which he confirms his identity as a succession of individuals. Henceforth, he will be himself only through interrogating his loss: "Could have been happy with her, up there on the Baltic, and the pines, and the dunes. (Pause.) Could I?" (25). By this means, Krapp

triumphs over the decantation of time. This triumph can be clarified
through examination of the scene most obsessively rememorated by
Krapp—the one concerning the girl in the punt: "We drifted in
among the flags and stuck. The way they went down, sighing, before
the stem! (Pause.) I lay down across her with my face in her breasts
and my hand on her. We lay there without moving. But under us
all moved, and moved us, gently, up and down, and from side to
side" (27).

The passage narrates a remarkable opposition between flux and
immobility. Krapp and the girl are unmoving, but beneath them "all
moved." A related opposition closes the play, as Krapp sits "motionless" while "( . . . [t]he tape runs on in silence)" (KLT, 28). Here
Krapp makes love to motionlessness in his life by giving all his passion
to regret.

Further analysis of this opposition between motion and motionlessness will clarify the implications of regret in the play. As a character, Krapp is positioned between two principles of movement: one
concrete—the tapes revolving in the tape recorder—the other abstract—the passage of time, suggested by both the setting "( . . . in
the future)" and the repeated action of decantation (KLT, 9). Recourse to the tape recorder is the primary means by which Krapp
negates the movement of time. He does this not merely by focusing
on the past in order to ignore the movement of time toward the future. More profoundly, the tapes enable him to replace *continuity*
with *atomicity*—that is, to replace the experience of time as an unbroken flow of becoming with the experience of time as a series of
discrete, disposable parts, which can be discarded or rememorated at
will: "Happiest moment of the past half million" (25). In his earlier
phases, Krapp construed life as a series of escapes from involvement
with either a loved one ("Well out of that, Jesus yes!" [17]) or his
own emotional turmoil ("Thank God that's all done with anyway"
[24]). The hidden motive of the tape-recording ritual is to detach
Krapp from implication in the continuity of his own life, by reducing
it to a series of disposable and fixed memories whose relation to the
present Krapp, as he moves through time, can always be repudiated.

Conversely, by fixating on one of those memories, Krapp repudiates his very location in the present.

This paradoxical project to repudiate the past by discarding memories, and to repudiate the present by obsessive remembering, entails a remarkable deconstruction of the theory of life as a succession of individuals, which Beckett formulated in *Proust*. As typified by his response to his mother's death, Krapp's reaction, after completing every stage of his life, is relief that it is "All over and done with, at last" (KLT, 20). By this means, he reduces life to the mere succession of moments ("Moments. Her moments, my moments. The dog's moments" [20]), but *without* the excruciating intervals of transition when, according the schema in *Proust*, "the boredom of living is replaced by the suffering of being." Yet at the end of the play, as Krapp sits "( . . . motionless . . . )" while "( . . . [t]he tape runs on in silence)" (28), it becomes apparent that his ultimate project is not merely to reduce life to a succession of moments without the inconveniently intervening intervals postulated in *Proust*, but to empty time of the succession of moments by which its movement is punctuated. Thus, through regret, Krapp simulates a state where time is no longer threatening because its movement, divested of succession, simply perpetuates the same unchanging preoccupation. He discards women ("living on and off with Bianca in Kedar street" [16]) just as he discards his past selves. But this refusal of continuity, with either himself or others, is precisely the factor that inevitably makes his life prey to the futility of regret.[5]

Yet in the Beckettian universe, a paradoxical transvaluation of values occurs, such that futility becomes the only valid goal. Indeed, in an utterance that could serve as Krapp's epitaph, the Unnamable explicitly posits futility as a raison d'être: "No, one can spend one's life thus, unable to live, unable to bring to life, and die in vain, having done nothing, been nothing" (UN, 358). The Beckettian protago-

5. However, some critics link the predicament of the aged Krapp with too much concern for the future (in the mode of artistic ambition), not too little. See Mercier (1977, 85); Abbott (1996, 65); and Pilling (1976, 85).

nist is always "a monster of the solitudes" (HOW, 13), and Beckett's minimalist art always concerns "the little that's left of the little whereby man continues" (HOW, 26). In this context, to assess Krapp on the conventional "moral plane" (HOW, 57) is a labor in irrelevance. For in Beckettian terms, through enduring the decantation of time by which he is "aged out of recognition" (HOW, 107), Krapp is simply a Beckettian "paradigm of human kind" (TFN, 108), suffering "in obedience to the unintelligible terms of an incomprehensible damnation" (UN, 308). Ineluctably, in the Beckettian universe, existence is "senseless, speechless, issueless misery" (MOL, 13).

The relation of *Krapp's Last Tape* to the conditions prevailing in the Beckettian universe can reveal the undiscovered implications of the stage directions concluding the play: "(Krapp motionless staring before him. The tape runs on in silence)" (KLT, 28). Like the couple in *Ohio Impromptu,* Krapp is now "[b]uried in who knows what profounds of mind" (OI, 18). Indeed, Paul Lawley has noted that the relation between "the taped voice of Krapp-at-thirty-nine" and "Krapp-at-sixty-nine" corresponds to that between Reader and Listener in *Ohio Impromptu* (Lawley 1994, 91). In this circumstance, lapsed in silence indefinitely prolonged, Krapp approaches the Beckettian ideal as formulated in *The Unnamable*: "I don't mind failing, it's a pleasure, but I want to go silent. Not as just now, the better to listen, but peacefully, victorious, without ulterior object. Then it would be a life worth having, a life at last" (UN, 310). As "[t]he tape runs on in silence" (28), it is almost as if Krapp were listening to a recording of silence—listening, that is, to a transcription of ultimate reality in the Beckettian universe: "And the ticking of an invisible alarm-clock was as the voice of that silence which, like the dark, would one day triumph too. And then all would be still and dark and all things at rest for ever at last" (MAL, 203).

Hence, Krapp remains a radically ambiguous character. In terms of the eudaemonistic assumption that the supreme task in life is to achieve "happiness" (KLT, 16, 28), Krapp is a dismal failure. But viewed in terms of the Beckettian ideal regarding silence "without ulterior object" (UN, 310), wherein "all things [are] at rest for ever at last" (MAL, 203), Krapp achieves resounding success. For in that silence, lost in reverie about the punt experience that the recorded voice intoned, it almost seems as if Krapp has fulfilled the Beckettian narrator's project to become him whom the words recall: "Will they succeed in slipping me into him, the memory and dream of me, into him still living" (TFN, 134). In that impossible circumstance, silence is the supreme—and indeed only—felicity: "[I]t will be the silence . . . the lasting one" (UN, 414). To apply Malone's words, Krapp here approaches "the blessedness of absence" (MAL, 222). For in the nostalgia induced by "old words back from the dead" (to invoke Bom's apt formula in *How It Is* [HOW, 95]), Krapp is not here and now; he is only there and then.

Yet, at bottom, what Krapp wants is not the return of the past, but the passionate abandon of the present to the importunity of "retrospect"(KLT, 16): "Once wasn't enough for you. (Pause.) Lie down across her" (27). In this context, the irony of Krapp's relation with Fanny, the "[b]ony old ghost of a whore" (25), emerges: "I told her I'd been saving up for her all my life" (26). Through reducing his life to a series of retrospects on discarded selves and relationships, Krapp tends inevitably toward the stage where all that remains is regret. But through that regret, epitomized by obsessive rememoration of lovemaking in the canoe, Krapp gives all his yearning to ghosts—to the perseveration, that is, of moments long departed, whose rememoration Krapp pursues with more consistency of attachment than he ever gave to anything or anyone in the past. In this sense, he has indeed been saving up for ghosts all his life, allocating to dead moments a fidelity that he never accorded to living ones: "Thank God that's all done with anyway" (24). As Dr. Johnson wrote in an *Idler* essay, "[H]e to whom the present offers nothing will often be looking backward on the past" ([1952] 1958a, 191). But in Krapp's case, the present offers nothing precisely because his deepest wish is to be "a memory come alive" (to borrow a phrase from Kafka's diary entry for October 15, 1921 [1974, 203]). Krapp's need is to have no life but to rememorate the one(s) that he rejected—a project epitomized by the narrator of "Enough": "It is then I shall have lived then or never"

(E, 57). The only way for Krapp to be free of attachment is to be attached, through regret, to loss.

Krapp's failure to find fulfillment through the forward movement of life can be clarified through reference to *Waiting for Godot.* Whereas in *Krapp's Last Tape* the refusal of forward movement is expressed through regretting a past that will never return, in *Waiting for Godot* it is expressed through waiting for a future that will never arrive. The future will never happen because it already has happened, as evident in Estragon's amplification of his observation regarding "Another day done with": "For me it's over and done with, no matter what happens" (WFG, 38). Whereas Krapp focuses on events already concluded, Estragon focuses on inevitable conclusion. By opposite means, each rejects the notion of novelty in life—an attitude articulated in the opening sentence of *Murphy*: "The sun shone, having no alternative, on the nothing new" (MUR, 1). In consequence, all that remains is repetition, as epitomized in Krapp's imperative, "Be again" (KLT, 26). In this context, Krapp's immunity to moral evaluation is confirmed. His recourse to regret here appears not as a character fault, but—to retrieve a formula from *Proust*—as "[a]n automatic adjustment of the human organism to the conditions of its existence" (P, 20). In the Beckettian universe, reality is reduced to a recurring cycle that prevents creative advance: "the endless April showers and the crocuses and then the whole bloody business starting all over again" (W, 47). Viewed from this angle, Krapp's regret results not so much from choice as from mechanical and involuntary adaptation to the unavoidable circumstances of life. Indeed, the mechanical aspect of Krapp is suggested by his close relation with his "machine" (KLT, 13), the tape recorder. In fact, as Lawley points out, Beckett instructed actor Pierre Chabert to "[b]ecome as much as possible one with the machine" (1994, 93).

But, regardless of such emphasis, Krapp is a man, not a machine—one who has abdicated responsibility to control his own compulsion toward mechanical repetition with respect to both bananas and the recourse to rememoration that they symbolize. Indeed, as noted earlier with respect to his banana bulimia, Krapp himself acknowledges his failure to control compulsive consumption: "Cut 'em out!" (KLT, 14). But his resolution soon lapses. Indeed, Krapp's frequent intervals of vacuity are prominently associated with the very bananas he undertakes to forswear. For example, twice on the same page the same description of his action is repeated: "puts end of banana in his mouth and remains motionless, staring vacuously before him" (11). Virtually the same description pertains to Krapp's immersion in nostalgia at the end of the play ("Krapp motionless staring before him") as the "tape runs on in silence" (28). We reach here the deeper implication of Krapp's identification with the tape recorder emphasized by Beckett when directing the play. Krapp wants to become one with the machine—to merge, that is, with reiterated memory—so that the effort of living is replaced by surrender to regret.

Krapp's contribution to his own predicament can be gauged by considering the remarkable moment when the present Krapp (age sixty-nine) and a past Krapp (age thirty-nine) share laughs regarding a Krapp from an earlier year:

> Hard to believe I was ever that young whelp. The voice! Jesus! And the aspirations! (Brief laugh in which Krapp joins.) And the resolutions! (Brief laugh in which Krapp joins.) To drink less, in particular. (Brief laugh of Krapp alone.) (16)
>
> Sneers at what he calls his youth and thanks God that it's over. (Pause.) False ring there. (Pause.) Shadows of the opus . . . magnum. Closing with a—(brief laugh)—yelp to Providence. (Prolonged laugh in which Krapp joins.) (KLT, 17)

The key to understanding this shared laughter is to consider first the sole instance when only Krapp laughs: "Brief laugh of Krapp alone." The topic on that occasion concerns the resolution "[t]o drink less." It is obvious that the younger Krapp still takes that resolution seriously, though he is unable to fulfill it. But in the years since then, Krapp has abandoned all his resolutions and can laugh as readily at that one as at all the others. As Ruby Cohn observes, "The laughter is inspired by the futility of aspiration and resolution" (1974, 94). Similarly, Steven Connor argues that Krapp's laugh alone "adds a layer of disillusion" (1990, 6). But as the end of the play suggests, this defeatist and weak-willed attitude has the last laugh on Krapp.

Perhaps a deeper implication of this laughter is indicated by the celebrated typology of laughter in *Watt*: (a) "the bitter laugh," which "laughs at that which is not good"; (b) the "hollow laugh," which "laughs at that which is not true"; and (c) "the mirthless laugh," which "laughs . . . at that which is unhappy" (W, 48).[6] Ultimately, the laughter in *Krapp's Last Tape* pertains to this third category: the laugh that "sneers" (to use the younger Krapp's term) at unhappiness—that is, at disappointment, surrender, lapse of will, and defeat. For the perfect defense against these calamities is to mock the suffering of them. Yet the deeper irony of Krapp's laughter is that he shirks the effort to achieve happiness. It is much easier to cry about happiness lost, forfeited, or never achieved: "Scalded the eyes out of me reading *Effie* again, a page a day, with tears again. Effie . . . (Pause.) Could have been happy with her, up there on the Baltic, and the pines, and the dunes. (Pause.) Could I?" (KLT, 25).

Krapp refuses to face his predicament in the present and take responsibility for his feelings about it. Through self-pitying regret, Krapp repudiates his present life, just as he repudiates and repudiated his past selves. His present suffering is never his fault. It can be blamed on the past, and the decisions made or avoided then. That is the "belief [he has] been going on all [his] life" (KLT, 21).

The irony of Krapp's predicament can be further clarified. In an earlier phase, on the occasion of his "vision" (KLT, 20), he believed in the "unshatterable association until my dissolution of storm and night with the light of the understanding and the fire" (21). On one level, Krapp has obviously failed to fulfill the promise of his vision, for his creative life never fructified. But on a more profound level, he did indeed fulfill the implications of his vision regarding the fusion of light and darkness. Through reducing his life to the agony of regret, he has inundated "the light of the understanding" with anguished

6. Ruby Cohn (1975, 185) draws attention to Watt's anatomy of laughter, but does not apply it specifically to *Krapp's Last Tape*.

nostalgia so that "the fire" in him is now explicitly linked with yearning for death: "drowned in dreams and *burning* to be gone" (25; my emphasis). At the moment of his spectacular vision, Krapp did not expect that this would be its result. But he never achieves recognition or anagnorisis regarding his plight. Just as he recognizes the problem of his "bowel condition" (13) yet refuses to control the banana bulimia that aggravates it, so he recognizes the sense of "misery" (26) that has always dogged his life, but refuses to take responsibility for its cause: obsessive-compulsive regret—the need to define himself through "retrospect" (16).

# Conclusion
## The Beckettian Absolute Universal

In Beckettian mimesis, there are no definitive conclusions in the sense of either termination or comprehension. Instead of termination, there is only the tedious continuation of that which cannot be stopped because that which continues is "finality without end" (MOL, 111). Instead of comprehension, there is the persistence of confusion: "always the same thing proposing itself to my perplexity" (TFN, 121). In this context, to end is to initiate movement toward "yet another end" (FTEYA, 15). To end is to confirm the inevitability of resuming: "I knew that all was about to end, or to begin again, it little mattered which, and it little mattered how, I had only to wait" (MOL, 161). Nothing ends because the prevailing predicament never changes: "and always the same old thing the same old things" (HOW, 107). Nothing is understood because experience provokes the same perplexity: "all is inexplicable, space and time, false and inexplicable" (TFN, 113). The impossibility of concluding, in the dual sense of termination and comprehension, is spectacularly expressed in the quintessential Beckettian metaphor concerning the reciprocal estrangement of speaker and auditor (or consciousness and its own content): "[O]ne who speaks saying, *without ceasing* to speak, Who's speaking?, and one who hears, mute, *uncomprehending,* far from all" (TFN, 134; my emphasis). An analogous metaphor involves the reciprocal estrangement of sight and its object: "perpetually looking at something while at the same time wondering what that something could possibly be" (MAL, 282).

This emphasis on unrelenting confusion constitutes a stunning inversion of metaphysics, for whereas the task of metaphysics, according to Etienne Gilson, is "to grasp, beyond all particular sciences, the conditions that make knowledge itself possible" (1965, 5), in Beckettian mimesis, the fundamental task is to struggle endlessly with the conditions that make knowledge impossible. More precisely, the fundamental task is to ensure the continuity of conditions that make knowledge impossible and perpetuate "[d]ear incomprehension" (UN, 325). Yet the knowledge here to be thwarted ultimately concerns self-knowledge: "[N]o one here knows himself it's the place without knowledge" (HOW, 123).

The Beckettian predicament is to have no identity but awareness of nonidentity, no being but awareness of inexistence: "the knowing non-exister" (TFN, 134). But, at bottom, this predicament is an "imposed task" (UN, 314) or project whose purpose is "the alleviations of flight from self" (UN, 367). The need to have no identity derives from the ineradicable guilt attached to identity: "to be is to be guilty" (TFN, 95). The proximate cause of this guilt is the pain of experience, whose unrelenting intensity invokes the notion of punishment for existing: "I was given a pensum, at birth perhaps, as a punishment for having been born perhaps" (UN, 310). In this context, self-pity becomes self-exculpation. To be obsessed with the pain of experience is to repudiate responsibility for suffering it: "[I]t's not my turn to know what, to know what I am, where I am, and what I should do to stop being it" (UN, 413). To brood on the sense of punishment is to confirm innocence ("punished for having been punished" [UN, 394]) and ignorance of fault ("[W]hat is required of me that I am tormented thus" [HOW, 63]). But the strategy requires tireless vigilance regarding the content of awareness: "[J]ust be vigilant, the eyes staring behind the lids, the ears straining for a voice not from without, were it only to sound an instant, to tell another lie" (TFN, 95–96). Here, awareness is progressively drained of all content but the registration of enduring exhaustion: "past bearing it, going on bearing it" (UN, 385).

Hence, Beckettian mimesis represents the attempt to approximate purely *conceptual* existence: to have no existence, that is, but a mode of awareness whose sole purpose is to reduce experience to fixation on an unchanging *idea*. That idea or mental construct concerns the intensity of suffering: "For anything worse than what I do, without knowing what, or why, I have never been able to conceive" (MOL, 46). The strategy of reducing experience to the idea of suffering *than which no worse can be conceived* exactly inverts the reasoning in St. Anselm's celebrated ontological argument regarding the idea of a Being *than which no greater can be conceived*. Brief consideration of that argument will clarify the issue under consideration.

❧

According to the ontological argument, as the being than which no greater can be conceived, God must exist, for if he did not exist, then he would not be the being than which no greater can be conceived. As Gilson explicates, that ultimate status would belong to the being that, in addition to being the greatest that can be *conceived,* also *exists* in reality: "For indeed, to exist in reality is greater than to exist in the intellect only" (1955, 133). Therefore, to be the being than which no greater can be conceived, God must actually exist. Whereas St. Anselm's ontological argument proves the *existence* of God through reference to the *idea* of him as the being than which there is no greater, Beckettian reasoning seeks to prove "inexistence" (HOW, 69) through reference to the idea of suffering a predicament than which there is no worse, for in this case, the experience than which there is no worse concerns awareness of lack of identity: "And even my sense of identity was wrapped in a namelessness often hard to penetrate" (MOL, 31).

The unexpected connection with St. Anselm's ontological argument has more profound implications, but their excavation will first require explicating the presuppositions of medieval realism implicit in Anselm's argument. According to medieval realism, a philosophy grounded in the logical relations of concepts, *reality* is defined in terms of *truth,* and truth, in turn, is defined in terms of *universality.* Hence, as Wilhelm Windelband notes, that which is most true, and hence most real, is that which is most universal: "The more universality, the more Reality" (1958, 1:292). Universality pertains to range of predictability. Alfred North Whitehead explains: "The notion of a universal is of that which can enter into the description of many particulars" (1978, 48). For example, the universal term *species* applies to (or can be predicated of) all members of a given species, but the universal term *genus* applies to all species comprising that genus. Hence, as Jacques Maritain notes, since the notion of genus entails a higher order of abstraction than that of species, "to arrive at the genus you eliminate whatever is distinctive of the species" (1971, 37). The more universal the term or class, the more general becomes its content, with the result that the absolute universal (God) has no content or specific determination at all. Windelband elaborates: "[A]ccording to a law of formal logic . . . concepts become poorer in contents or intension in proportion as their extension increases so that the content 0 must correspond to the extension ∞ [such that] the absolutely universal is also the concept of the 'First,' void of all content" (1958, 1:250). Thus, as the absolutely universal, God can be defined only in terms of negation. Again Windelband verifies: "Hence this doctrine becomes identical with the old 'negative theology,' according to which we can predicate of God *only what he is not*" (1958, 1:290; my emphasis).

Molloy explicitly invokes the *via negativa* of negative theology: "What I liked in anthropology was its inexhaustible faculty of negation, its relentless definition of man, as though he were no better than God, *in terms of what he is not*" (MOL, 39; my emphasis). The irony of this remark has long been overlooked. For as we shall now find, this reference to the procedure for defining the absolute universal provides an unexpected gloss on the celebrated Beckettian tendency toward lessness, evacuation, Nothing, and minimalism.[1] On the level now under consideration, the reductive thrust in Beckettian mimesis relates to the law of *abstraction*, whereby (to retrieve Windelband's

1. Beckettian minimalism has attracted much attention. For representative commentary, see Brater (1987); James Knowlson and John Pilling (1980, 103); Gontarski (1985, 3); and Amiran (1993, 13).

explanation) "concepts become poorer in contents or intension in proportion as their extension increases" (1958, 1:250).

In medieval realism, the absolute universal is construed as an ultimate form or supreme genus *with no content* (i.e., in Maritain's phrase, with no specific "determinations which particularize it"), because by definition it cannot be described by anything less universal than itself (1971, 37). Here, absence of *content* is the reciprocal of universal presence (or extension) of *form*. Like medieval realism, Beckettian mimesis also associates diminishing content with increasing universality or abstraction. The most obvious example of this situation occurs when Moran, like a Beckettian Narcissus, peers at his reflection in a pool and sees not his own particular face but a species-face from which all particularizing notes have been removed: "nothing to show if it was a man's face or a woman's face, a young face or an old face" (MOL, 149). Yet, even as Beckettian mimesis mimics—and even invokes—the abstractive procedure of medieval realism, it inverts the very function of abstraction. As we have seen, in the logical hierarchy of medieval realism, divestiture of particulars corresponds to the degree of abstraction, and degree of abstraction corresponds to what Whitehead terms a "phase of generalization [which] exhibits its own peculiar simplicities which stand out just at that stage, and at no other stage" (1978, 16). He elaborates: "[T]here are certain simplicities concerning the behaviour of men which are obscured if we refuse to abstract from the individual peculiarities of particular specimens" (1978, 16–17). But in Beckettian mimesis, instead of allowing "simplicities" or universal forms to stand out, divestiture of particulars allows "formlessness" to stand out: "The forms are many in which *the unchanging* seeks relief from its *formlessness*" (MAL, 197; my emphasis).

This formless "changelessness" (TFN, 118) is the Beckettian equivalent of the absolute universal. Whereas the absolute universal is ordinarily construed in terms of absence of *content,* the Beckettian absolute universal is construed in terms of absence of *form.* Here the ultimate form is contradiction of form, as encountered, for example, in Murphy's Third Zone: "Here there was nothing but commotion and the pure forms of commotion" (MUR, 112). Beckettian mimesis

200 I Trapped in Thought

confutes the principle of abstraction, even in invoking it. As we have seen, the function of abstraction is to allow form—an "internal determination" (Whitehead's term) common to all relevant particulars—to stand out (1978, 47). Thus, abstraction proceeds from the manifold *differences* among particulars to the essential *sameness* of form that they all share. But Beckettian mimesis stymies this procedure. For the particulars it represents display no differences. Here, experience concerns particulars without individual differences. As such, they are not particulars at all because they lack differentiation. Examples abound, as in *Murphy*: "big blooming buzzing confusion" (MUR, 245); *Malone Dies*: "one vast continuous buzzing" (MAL, 207); and *Molloy*: "I drown in the spray of phenomena" (MOL, 111). The most explicit formulation of this lack of differentiation among particulars occurs in *The Unnamable*: "[T]here is no great difference here between one expression and the next, when you've grasped one you've grasped them all" (UN, 388).

The Beckettian assault on abstraction concerns the particulars of not only *perception* but also *conception*: "[I]deas are so alike, when you get to know them" (MAL, 225). Here difference is literally inconceivable because the ideas that would enable such conception are themselves indistinguishable from one another. Yet, without *difference* there can be no *sameness* to abstract. Abstraction presupposes difference (what Whitehead, in a passage quoted earlier, terms "the individual peculiarities of particular specimens"). We reach now a key to Beckettian mimesis. Instead of abstracting sameness from disparate particulars, the Beckettian representation of experience foregrounds or detaches the sameness already implicit in particulars bereft of difference: "And if all muck is the same muck that doesn't matter . . ." (MOL, 41). The most striking example of the displacement of difference by sameness concerns the representation of time. In Beckettian mimesis, the distinct moments comprising the continuity of time are identical, with the result that time itself collapses into "one enormous second" (TFN, 82), as in Pozzo's enraged response to the question concerning when he went blind and Lucky went dumb: "When! When! One day, is that not enough for you, one day he went dumb, one day I went blind, one day we'll go deaf, one day we were born, one day we shall die, the same day, the same second, is that not enough for you?" (WFG, 57).

Yet, the status of abstraction in Beckettian mimesis is eminently ambiguous. On the one hand, the mimesis *thwarts* abstraction by suppressing the differences required in order to detach therefrom some form or factor representative of the whole. On the other hand, through this emphasis on sameness, the mimesis ironically *presupposes* abstraction—the cognitive isolation of some property common to the particulars concerned. To say, with the Unnamable, that "there is no great difference here between one expression and the next" (388) is to assume the abstractive process of correlation and comparison. The extraordinary opposition in Beckettian mimesis between *thwarting* and *presupposing* abstraction is epitomized by the polarity between Watt and Worm. Whereas Watt is denied recourse to abstraction, Worm (in *The Unnamable*) exists only as an abstraction.

In *Watt*, mimesis depicts a world without universals: "For Watt now found himself in the midst of things which, if they consented to be named, did so as it were with reluctance" (W, 81). In this context, to name is to abstract a universal from a particular so as to identify that particular as belonging to a given class or set. Gilson elaborates: "[T]he universals are virtually present in individuals, from which they are abstracted by our intellect" (1965, 67). Without abstraction of universals, there can be no conception of the object perceived, for conception, in this context, entails the abstraction of some identifying universals(s) from the object perceived. A celebrated example of this resistance to abstraction concerns Watt's encounter with the pot that refuses to be named—that is, to be the subject of some identifying predicate. The same resistance to abstraction applies equally to himself: "[H]e made the distressing discovery that of himself too he could no longer affirm anything that did not seem as false as if he had affirmed it of a stone" (W, 82). The most explicit example of perception bereft of explicative conception concerns Watt's perplexed perception of Mr. Knott: "But what conception have I of Mr. Knott? None" (120).

Whereas Watt cogitates without conception (that is, without the ability to abstract an identifying universal from the particular), Worm is nothing but a conception: "Feeling nothing, he exists nevertheless, but not for himself, for others, others conceive him and say, *Worm is, since we conceive him,* as if there could be no being but being conceived, if only by the beer" (UN, 346; my emphasis). Worm is only an idea; Watt has no ideas. But, as an idea, Worm simply *objectifies* Watt's own subjective condition, taken to its logical terminus. Further analysis of each will clarify. As an *object* of thought, Worm is no more than the idea of an awareness or subjectivity, *deprived of both sentience and thought*: "What he does not know is that there is anything to know. His senses tell him nothing, nothing about himself, nothing about the rest, and this distinction is beyond him" (UN, 345). As a *subject,* Watt approximates the momentary experience of precisely the same state: "He lay on the seat, *without thought or sensation,* except for a slight feeling of chill in one foot" (W, 232; my emphasis).

Thus, Beckettian mimesis approximates its own version of Ophelia's madness—awareness without clear and distinct idea, but with much negative affect: "[T]here might be thought, / Though nothing sure, yet much unhappily" *(Hamlet,* 4.5.12–13). Here thought is reduced to reciprocal modes of attention without cognition—what might respectively be termed *positive* and *negative* ignorance: "to know that you are beyond knowing anything" (MOL, 64) vs. not to know "that there is anything to know" (UN, 346). By this means, Beckettian mimesis transcends the Classical Skepticism with which it is often associated.[2] Skepticism affirms the impossibility of affirmation. More precisely, in Windelband's phrasing, according to Skeptic doctrine of *aphasia* (a term invoked by Lucky in *Waiting for Godot*), "nothing can be affirmed as to the things themselves" (WFG, 28; Windelband 1958, 1:167). Yet, as just suggested, Beckettian mimesis commingles the positive ignorance, characteristic of Skepticism, where "nothing is known" (W, 21), with the negative ignorance of not knowing that there is or can be knowing.

An echo of this negative ignorance appears in the Unnamable's query: "Can one be ephectic otherwise than *unawares*?" (UN, 291; my emphasis). Brief explication will clarify. The term *ephectic* means

2. See, for example, Plonowska (1996) and Mooney (1982).

pertaining to *epoche*—a term, in Skepticism, denoting suspension of judgment regarding truth or falsehood (for, if nothing can be affirmed, then no judgment can be verified). In Skepticism, *epoche* presupposes positive ignorance (accepting "that you are beyond knowing anything") and hence entails *deliberate* abstention from judgment. In this context, an *epoche* executed "unawares" is a contradiction in terms. But in the context of negative ignorance, *epoche* cannot be exercised "otherwise than unawares," as the Unnamable says. For if there is no knowing "that there is anything to know," there can be no knowing that there is any judgment concerning it to suspend.

Viewed from this angle, the defining project of Beckettian mimesis, in such works as *The Unnamable* and *Texts for Nothing*, is to convert positive ignorance into negative ignorance through the metaphor of a voice compelled to speak and an auditor compelled to hear: "[T]here's a voice without a mouth, and somewhere a kind of hearing, something compelled to hear" (TFN, 137). Ultimately, voice and auditor constitute reciprocal functions of the same awareness, reduced to epistemological vacancy. Compulsion to speak releases the expressive pole of that awareness from obligation to attend to what it is saying: "This voice that speaks . . . indifferent to what it says . . . not listening to itself but to the silence that it breaks" (UN, 307). Compulsion to hear releases the auditory pole from the obligation to understand: "I don't try to understand, I'll never try to understand any more" (TFN, 78). The project is to continue this circumstance until both the capacity to express and the capacity even to register incomprehension lapse: "hoping to wear out a voice, to wear out a head" (TFN, 112).

By this "metaphor" concerning "the matter of voices" (UN, 325), Beckettian mimesis reduces introspective awareness—the most individual of all intellectual acts—to an abstract universal, from which all particularizing notes or determinations have been eliminated. As we have seen, in medieval realism the abstract universal is God, who can be defined only in terms of negation. In Beckettian mimesis, the abstract universal is the act of introspection, which also can be defined only in terms of negation: "Where I am there is no one but me, who am not" (UN, 355).

But here we encounter an abstract universal of a self-negating type that will require some explanation. Conventionally, if the act of introspection is treated as an abstract universal, it must be represented in terms common to all particular acts of introspection but not qualified by the peculiarities of any one of them. For, as John Locke indicated in his *Essay Concerning Human Understanding*, "Words become general by separating from them the circumstances of time and place, and any other ideas that may determine them to this or that particular existence" (Locke, qtd. in Cassirer 1957, 1:136n. 29). Thus, to interpolate Ernst Cassirer's comments on abstraction, considered as an abstract universal, the act of introspection must be represented "free from all particularities," such that it is described "as it is, *not from the standpoint of this man or that man, but from the standpoint of no one*" (Cassirer 1957, 3:478; my emphasis). Beckettian introspection satisfies precisely these conditions. Following Locke's prescription for universals, the Unnamable's self-reflection unfolds separated from "the circumstances of time and place, and any other ideas that may determine [it] to this or that particular existence": "Where now? Who now? When now?" (UN, 291). Following Cassirer's designation, the Unnamable's self-reflection is expressed "not from the standpoint of this man or that man, but from the standpoint of no one": "Nothing to do but stretch out comfortably on the rack, in blissful knowledge you are nobody for all eternity" (UN, 338).

The paradoxical implications of Beckettian introspection as an abstract universal, one that foregrounds the factor common to introspecting subjects while excluding what pertains to them only individually, can be clarified through reference to a celebrated precedent: the Cartesian *cogito*.[3] Though the Cartesian *cogito* is expressed in terms of first person cogitation *(I* think), and though, in his *Meditations,* Descartes invests the *cogito* with details proper to himself alone, at bottom the *cogito* is construed impersonally in terms of the rational

3. For earlier Cartesian applications, see Kenner (1968a, 117–32).

faculty common to all individuals belonging to the same species: "I am therefore, to speak precisely, only a thinking being, that is to say, *a mind,* an understanding, or a reasoning being" *(Meditations,* 84). Thus construed as a representative mind, the *cogito* is an abstract universal. At bottom, it is not a particular mind but the faculty of reflexive understanding distinctive of the species *man*: "Nevertheless, I must remember that *I am a man,* and that consequently I am accustomed to sleep and in my dreams to imagine the same things that lunatics imagine when awake, or sometimes things which are even less plausible" *(Meditations,* 74). Moreover, the universality of the *cogito* (its applicability to all members of the human species) is reinforced by its identity as a reflective consciousness whose proposition, *cogito ergo sum,* is equally valid for whatever particular consciousness pronounces it. In this context, the *cogito* is not a particular consciousness, but rather the capacity of reflection or self-awareness implicit in *any* particular consciousness in so far as it is a consciousness. Paul Ricoeur amplifies: "[R]eflection tends to posit itself as a universal constituting ego, which is supposed to transcend the limitations of the empirical subject" (1978b, 9).

Whereas Cartesian introspection applies in principle to every particular consciousness and indeed constitutes the reflection by which each consciousness affirms its own singular existence, Beckettian introspection negates the very notion of particular consciousness ("here all self to be abandoned" [HOW, 83]) and contradicts the notion of singularity presupposed by that notion: "in this being which is called me and is not one" (TFN, 131). This circumstance can be clarified by examining the reflexivity proper to the Cartesian *cogito*. As Sartre explains, the *cogito* is immediately reflective: "I cannot *think* that I am speaking without *knowing that I think that I am speaking*" (1948, 195). In contrast, in Beckettian introspection, the reflexive relation between thought and awareness of thought has lapsed: "He knows they are words, he is not sure they are not his" (UN, 354). To the Cartesian formula of reflexivity, "I think therefore I am," the Beckettian riposte is "I say it as I hear it" (HOW, 7). Understanding the implications of this loss of reflexivity will be facilitated by refer-

206 | Trapped in Thought

ence to Kierkegaard's formulation of the relation between selfhood
and reflexivity. But in making this reference, our purpose is not to develop a Kierkegaardian interpretation of Beckettian introspection,
but rather to employ a valuable intellectual tool in advancing our own
investigation.[4]

Kierkegaard's formulation of selfhood entails the paradoxical notion of a relation relating itself to itself: "The self is a relation which
relates itself to its own self" (1954, 146). This lapidary account of reflexivity can be explicated through brief consideration of a subject
confronting its reflection in a mirror. In order for the subject to recognize the image in the mirror as its own reflection (that is, an expression of its own identity), the subject must relate itself to the
relation between itself and that image. Unless the subject relates itself
to that relation, the subject and the image remain related only by opposition—one *here* in front of the mirror, the other *there* in the glass.
A superb example of precisely this condition occurs in *Wuthering
Heights,* when the delirious Catherine, while talking with Nelly Dean,
does not recognize her own reflection in the mirror: " 'Don't you see
that face?' she enquired, gazing earnestly at the mirror. And say what
I could, I was incapable of making her comprehend it to be her own;
so I rose and covered it with a shawl" (Brontë 1963, 161). Just as,
with respect to her reflection, Catherine cannot "comprehend it to
be her own"—cannot, that is, relate herself to the relation between
herself and "that face"—so the Unnamable cannot relate himself to
the relation between what he says and what he hears: "I'm neither
one side nor the other. I'm in the middle, I'm the partition" (UN,
383).

Under these conditions, the poles of Cartesian reflexivity (thinking and knowing that I am thinking) are reciprocally estranged, and
the Unnamable's relation to them is radically problematized—indeed, *pluralized*: "I say what I hear, I hear what I say, I don't know,
one or the other, or both, that makes three possibilities" (UN, 412).

4. For readings relating Beckett to Kierekegaardian existentialism, see Sharma
(1993, 275–79) and Bove (1982, 185–221).

Far from displaying the Kierkegaardian reflexivity through which self-hood relates itself to itself, Beckettian introspection disintegrates self-hood into a series of problematic relations: "I who am here, who cannot speak, cannot think, and who must speak, and therefore perhaps think a little, cannot *in relation to* me who am here, to here where I am, but can a little, sufficiently, I don't know how, unimportant, *in relation to* me who was elsewhere, who shall be elsewhere, and to those places where I was, where I shall be" (UN, 301; my emphasis).

In this passage explicitly, selfhood or identity is expressed in terms of a proliferating series of relations whose constitutive terms multiply to the point of ambiguity. Whereas for Kierkegaard selfhood is defined as self-relation to relation ("The self is a relation which relates itself to its own self"), in Beckettian introspection selfhood disintegrates into relations whose terms are unstable and readily confused: "I'm getting mixed, confusing here and there, now and then" (TFN, 120). Though Moran claims, in another context, that "the falsity of the terms does not necessarily imply that of the relation" (MOL, 111), no relation—and *a fortiori* no relation to relation—can be sustained when its constitutive terms are perpetually "meeting, mingling, falling asunder" (UN, 386). For relation presupposes distinctness: If the terms related are not distinct, there can be no relation between them. F. H. Bradley elaborates: "But if you come to what is distinct, you get relations at once" (1930, 22).

Beckettian introspection is notorious for blurring the fundamental relations on which the notion of self is founded. One of these concerns the relation between self and world: "[M]y personal system was so distended at the period of which I speak that the distinction between what was inside it and what was outside it was not at all easy to draw" (W, 43). Another concerns the reflexivity by which the self relates itself to itself. At bottom, Beckettian introspection seeks not to confirm reflexive relation, as in the Cartesian and Kierkegaardian paradigms, but to abandon all relations on which the confirmation of selfhood depends: "time to forget all lose all be ignorant of all

whence I come whither I go" (HOW, 110). By this means, Beckettian introspection achieves the supreme abstraction by which it "falls
half out of species" (HOW, 110) and identifies through a form more
universal than species. That is, Beckettian introspection simulates
(one might almost say "parodies") on the experiential level—the
level of lived mental awareness—the process of abstraction by which
medieval realism, on the ontological level, approached God as the ultimate universal or supreme genus.

As noted earlier, in that process of abstraction the ultimate universal is approached through increasing *extension* or range of predictability, thereby minimizing *intension* or particularizing content.
Maritain clarifies: "To reach this supreme genus you will be obliged
to eliminate all the varieties of being, all the determinations which
particularize it. In short to arrive at the genus being you will be compelled to eliminate everything which is and you will thus reach a
being indistinguishable from nothing" (1971, 37).

Just as abstracting the supreme genus reaches "a being indistinguishable from nothing," so Beckettian introspection concerns an
awareness "indistinguishable from nothing": "[T]here's nothing
here, nothing to see, nothing to see with" (UN, 375).[5] From this perspective, the Beckettian preoccupation with nothing takes to its final
stage the process whereby, to cite Aquinas, "[T]he universal [is] abstracted from particulars in so far as the intellect knowing it derives its
knowledge from things" (*Summa Theologica*, 1, Q56, A1, obj. 1). In
Beckettian mimesis, the ultimate universal thus abstracted, according
to "the laws of the mind," pertains to "senseless, speechless, issueless
misery": "free to do what, to do nothing, to know, but what, the laws
of the mind perhaps, of my mind, that for example water rises in pro-

---

5. Critics often link the Beckettian notion of Nothing with philosophical precedents. For Sartrian readings, see Butler (1984, 74–113); Hesla (1971, 184–92); and
Cohn (1973, 111). For a Heideggerean account, see Barker (1996, 125–56). For linkage with chaos theory, see Uhlmann (1999, 21); Meriwether (1994); S. Levy (1996);
Dearlove (1982); and Federman (1965). For connection with Democritus, see Pilling
(1976, 124). For association with Zen Buddhism, see Kundert-Gibbs (1999).

portion as it drowns you and that you would do better, at least no worse, to obliterate texts than to blacken margins, to fill in the holes of words till all is blank and flat and the whole ghastly business looks like what is, senseless, speechless, issueless misery" (MOL, 13).

In this passage, the Beckettian universal is expressed through literary analogy: The unrelenting "misery" of life is compared to a blackened page where "all is blank and flat." Whatever particulars the words on the page might express, their ultimate referent is that immutable universal: "[W]hatever I say, it will always as it were be the same thing" (MOL, 45–46). Indeed, this emphasis on the abstract universal or form is foregrounded in Molloy's account of his own cognition: "I saw the world . . . in a way inordinately *formal*" (MOL, 50; my emphasis).

Molloy's ability to perceive universal forms *immediately,* rather than abstracting them *discursively* from the particulars of sense perception, has a precedent in the history of ideas, which will help illumine Beckettian mimesis. In Thomist angelology, angels are endowed with a higher "power of understanding" *(Summa Theologica,* 1, Q55, A2, resp.) by which they know, not through abstraction from particulars, but through what is termed "innate" or "connatural" species. That is, at the moment of their creation, angels "received from God the species [or universal forms] of things known" *(Summa Theologica,* 1, Q55, A2, resp.). To interpolate Gilson's explication, whereas the human mind is like a "blank tablet" on which knowledge of universals must be inscribed through abstraction from particulars, the angelic mind is "like a canvas covered with its painting or, better, like a mirror reflecting the luminous essences of things" (Gilson 1956, 169–70).

Just as, according to Thomist angelology, the angelic mind is created with the universal forms of reality already intact within it, so the Beckettian mind is represented in terms of an innate "attitude of dejection" (MAL, 230) whose mode of interpreting experience remains constant. It is an attitude that resents life—"That's not a life worth living either" (UN, 368)—as bitterly as it fears death—"And to dread death like a regeneration" (MOL, 140). From the perspective of this attitude, "the whole ghastly business"—what the Unnamable terms "the meaning of life" (UN, 353)—reduces to "senseless, speechless, issueless misery" (MOL, 13). The *Texts* narrator formulates this unvarying condition alliteratively: "nothing ever but nothing and never" (TFN, 135). This is the Beckettian abstract universal: the idea of unchanging "formlessness" (MAL, 197) bereft of purpose—a "coming and being and going in purposelessness" (W, 58). No matter what appears to be happening, at bottom nothing is happening. More precisely, according to "the laws of the mind" (MOL, 13) operant in Beckettian mimesis, nothing is happening but preoccupation with emptiness: "[T]here was never anything, never can be, life and death all nothing, that kind of thing, only a voice dreaming and droning on all around, that is something, the voice that was once in your mouth" (FAAW, 49).

✻

The status and role of the Beckettian abstract universal can be clarified by reference to Bishop Berkeley, whose epistemology expressly denies the existence of abstract universals. The link between Beckett and Berkeley is foregrounded by direct citation of the philosopher's name in the course of Lucky's spectacular speech in *Waiting for Godot* (WFG, 29).[6] Critics have sometimes proclaimed a *similarity* between the epistemologies of Beckett and of Berkeley. But the connection between these two writers is instead founded on *contradiction*. Whereas Berkeley denies the existence of abstract ideas, Beckettian mimesis seeks to empty experience of everything but an abstract idea—in this case, the misery of emptiness. Explication of this matter can begin with brief recapitulation of Berkeley's position.

Berkeley's famous ontological dictum, *esse est percipi* (to be is to be perceived), rests on the impossibility of abstraction. If abstraction is impossible, then unperceived existence is also impossible, for such

---

6. For earlier applications of Berkeley to Beckett, see F. Smith (1998); Kroll (1995); and Henning (1982).

existence would constitute the ultimate abstraction: "For can there be a nicer strain of abstraction than to distinguish the existence of sensible objects from their being perceived, so as to conceive them existing unperceived? Light and colors, heat and cold, extension and figures—in a word, the things we see and feel—what are they but so many sensations, notions, ideas, or impressions on the sense? And is it possible to separate, even in thought, any of these from perception?" (Berkeley 1957, 25).

According to Berkeley, the mind cannot "frame a general notion by abstracting from particulars" because, in order to be conceived, every general idea (such as the general idea of a triangle or a man) must contain particulars (1957, 10). Consider his account of the idea of a man: "But then whatever hand or eye I imagine, it must have some particular shape and color. Likewise the idea of a man that I frame to myself must be either of a white, or a black, or a tawny, a straight, or a crooked, a tall, or a low, or a middle-sized man. I cannot by any effort of thought conceive the abstract idea above described" (1957, 9–10).

It has never before been noted that Moran's encounter with his own reflection constitutes a stunning counterexample to Berkeley's claim. For here Moran literally perceives a general human face from which all particulars have been abstracted: "nothing to show if it was a man's face or a woman's face, a young face or an old face" (MOL, 149). A similar encounter with the general idea of man occurs one page later, when Moran meets a stranger: "I was face to face with a dim man, dim of face and dim of body, because of the dark" (MOL, 150). In thinking of this stranger, Moran literally frames an abstract general idea of man. That is, he perceives the stranger not as an *individual* but as the manifestation of a *type* characterized by the abstract relationships of its "various parts": "But little by little *I formed an idea of the type of individual it was.* And indeed there reigned between his various parts great harmony and concord, and it could truly be said that his face was worthy of his body, and vice versa. And if I could have seen his arse, I do not doubt I should have found it on a par with the whole" (MOL, 150; my emphasis).

The profound implications of the Beckettian refutation of Berkeley's denial of abstraction will emerge after further explication of Berkeley's ontological doctrine. According to Berkeley, reality comprises two kinds of being: ideas and the agents or minds that have them. Agents are defined as "spiritual substances, or human souls, which will or excite ideas in themselves at pleasure" (1957, 39). In this schema, there can be no *idea* of an agent, mind, or spirit. Since the existence of an idea "consists in being perceived," there cannot be "an image and likeness of an agent subsisting by itself" (1957, 93). Moreover, as "the very being of an idea implies passiveness and inertness," while the being of an agent implies activity and movement, ideas and agents are contraries: "Hence there can be no *idea* formed of a soul or spirit; for all ideas whatever, being passive and inert, they cannot represent unto us, by way of image or likeness, that which acts" (1957, 35–36).

As we shall now see, through the "matter of voices" (UN, 325), Beckettian mimesis paradoxically confutes Berkeley's claims while invoking the assumptions on which they are based. Explication can proceed step by step. To begin with, whereas Berkeley claims that there can be no idea of an agent because agents are active, while ideas are inert and passive, Beckettian mimesis boldly represents an agent characterized by the "passiveness and inertness" that Berkeley attributes to ideas: "[H]e understands nothing, can't take thought, doesn't know what they want, doesn't know they are there, feels nothing, ah but just a moment, he feels, he suffers, the noise makes him suffer, and he knows, he knows it's a voice, and he understands, a few expressions here and there" (UN, 360).

Here the inert agent is Worm, a subject explicitly construed as an idea: "Worm is, since we conceive him" (UN, 346). But Worm's auditory predicament simply objectifies that of the Unnamable who invents him: "A second later, I'm a second behind them, I remember a second, for the space of a second, that is to say long enough to blurt it out, as received, while receiving the next, which is none of my business either" (UN, 368). Thus, through the "bold metaphors" (UN, 333) of voice and auditor, Beckettian mimesis reduces the agent (construed, according to Berkeley's definition, in terms of the ability to perceive and produce ideas) to precisely the "passiveness and inertness" proper to ideas.

But Beckettian mimesis goes farther in its violation (one might almost say parody) of Berkeley's doctrine. In reducing the agent to the status of a Berkelean idea, Beckettian mimesis also deprives the agent of its defining function: perception of ideas. At bottom, the Beckettian agent perceives nothing: "[T]here's nothing here, nothing to see, nothing to see with" (UN, 375). But in Berkelean terms, to perceive nothing is not to be an agent. Whereas for ideas, to be is to be perceived, for agents, not to perceive—or equivalently, to perceive nothing—is not to be: "Where I am there is no one but me, who am not" (UN, 355). This is the Beckettian alternative to suicide. To be or not to be becomes to perceive or not to perceive. Not to perceive confers not death, but "inexistence" (TFN, 131). What dies in "inexistence" is a particular identity: "towards an even vainer death than no matter whose" (TFN, 115). In the Berkelean paradigm, agents are particularized by their perceptions. In the Beckettian paradigm, agents ultimately perceive nothing. But an agent that perceives nothing lacks the principle of individuation and is no more than an unidentifiable awareness: "Who now?" (UN, 291). More precisely, an agent that perceives nothing is less than an unidentifiable awareness because it is estranged from its own agency: "It's a voice, and it speaks to me. In inquiring boldly, if it is not mine. In deciding, it doesn't matter how, that I have none" (UN, 354).

The ramifications of this predicament emerge when we remember that, at bottom, the nothing perceived is the Beckettian abstract universal: "senseless, speechless, issueless misery" (MOL, 13). Perceiving this ultimate universal ensures that agency, construed in moral terms as the capacity to formulate and pursue purposes, has neither reality nor efficacy, for the condition of purposelessness cannot be transcended. To interpolate Malone's apt remark, "That is what comes from the taste for generalization" (MAL, 253). In this context, the "metaphor" (UN, 325) of voices achieves its deepest meaning. The disintegration of reflexivity into the estranged components of voice and auditor consummates the absolute futility—and irrelevance—of agency, where the only purpose is to negate purpose: "But little by little with a different aim, no longer in order to succeed, but in order to fail" (MAL, 195). This insistence on negation of purpose—on directing purpose toward failure, not achievement—is the ultimate Beckettian defense mechanism against "senseless, speechless, issueless misery." Insofar as the misery concerns the "moral anguish" (MAL, 267) caused by "hope blighted" (HOW, 32) and consequent despair, the only solace is complete loss of purposive yearnings: "I have suffered must have *suffered morally hoped more than once despaired to match* your heart bleeds you lose your heart drop by drop" (HOW, 23; my emphasis).

Further investigation of this notion of moral suffering will clarify the import of the Beckettian abstract universal of "senseless, speechless, issueless misery" (MOL, 13). Through reference to "[c]atastrophe in the ancient sense" (MAL, 254), Beckettian mimesis explicitly opposes its own notion of moral suffering with that in Greek tragedy. In the works of Sophocles, suffering at once illumines human vulnerability and human greatness. Werner Jaeger elaborates: "To know oneself is thus for Sophocles to know man's powerlessness; but it is also to know the indestructible and conquering majesty of suffering humanity" (1945, 1:284). This view of moral suffering is sneeringly invoked by Malone, in the same passage mentioning "[c]atastrophe in the ancient sense": "To be buried in lava and not turn a hair, it is then then a man shows what stuff he is made of." Beckettian mimesis abandons this notion of nobility through moral suffering in favor of its contrary. The heroic struggle with catastrophe is replaced by a lapse into futility: "who could not be and gave up trying" (UN, 347). In other words, "To be buried in lava and not turn a hair" (MAL, 254) becomes to be "buried in who knows what *profounds of mind*" (OI, 18; my emphasis).

In those profounds of mind, thought focuses exclusively on the Beckettian universal: "senseless, speechless, issueless misery" (MOL,

13). Experience is reduced to the awareness of pain, and pain, in turn, is shorn of all particularizing determinations, such as cause, purpose, duration, intensity, even sensation and registration: "labyrinthine torment that can't be grasped, or limited, or felt, or suffered, no, not even suffered" (UN, 314). In these circumstances, all that remains of pain is "lassitude, perplexity, consternation" (TFN, 97). By this means, subjectivity is relieved of the burden of identity and achieves "the alleviations of flight from self" (UN, 367). Instead of relating itself to its own self, subjectivity relates itself to awareness of pointless misery: a misery with no content because it is no more than the objectification of a perspective that refuses to acknowledge anything but deficiency, absence, or loss. As such, Beckettian mimesis represents the contrary of the sublime. According to George Santayana, the sublime consists in contemplative immersion of the subject in an object immeasurably more grand and powerful than itself: "But when in thus translating ourselves we rise and play a higher personage, feeling the exhilaration of a life freer and wider than our own, then the experience is one of sublimity" (1961, 168). Whereas through contemplation of the sublime, according to Santayana, subjectivity is enabled to "escape" its habitual boundaries and "live as it were in the object itself, energizing in imitation of its movement" (Santayana 1961, 168), in Beckettian mimesis subjectivity is compelled or "driven" (UN, 374) to sustain preoccupation with misery in order, through the sheer persistence of this obsession, to be eventually deprived of all awareness: "That's right, wordshit bury me, avalanche, and let there be no more talk of any creature, nor of a world to leave, nor of worlds to reach, in order to have done, with worlds, with creatures, with words, with misery, misery" (TFN, 118).

As a result of this obsessive reiteration of misery, "Nothing is more real than nothing" because nothing is left of the real but the wish for its absence: "But my notes have a curious tendency . . . to annihilate all they purport to record (MAL, 192, 259). Through preoccupation with the ultimate misery, than which no worse can be conceived, Beckettian mimesis abstracts from experience everything but the exhaustingly tedious futility of suffering it. The role of abstraction in constructing this predicament can be clarified by reference to a remarkably apt passage from Thomas Hardy's *Tess of the d'Urbervilles*: "With these natures, corporeal presence is sometimes less appealing than corporeal absence; the latter creating *an ideal presence, that conveniently drops the defects of the real*" (Hardy 1960, 216; my emphasis). Whereas in Hardy's account, "an ideal presence" is constructed by *dropping* "the defects of the real," the Beckettian absolute universal is constructed by *emphasizing* the defects of the real until all that remains is the desire to flee it: "I'm trying to see where I am, so as to be able to go elsewhere" (TFN, 121). By this means, Beckettian mimesis achieves the representation of "Life, we dare almost say, in the abstract" (MPTK, 105).

References

Index

# References

## Beckett's Works

Beckett, Samuel. 1949. "Bram Van Velde." In *Proust, and Three Dialogues with Georges Duthuit*. London: John Calder.

———. 1954. *Waiting for Godot*. Translated by Samuel Beckett. New York: Grove Press.

———. 1957a. "All That Fall." In *Krapp's Last Tape, and Other Dramatic Pieces*. New York: Grove Press.

———. 1957b. "Krapp's Last Tape." In *Krapp's Last Tape, and Other Dramatic Pieces*. New York: Grove Press.

———. 1957c. *Murphy*. New York: Grove Press.

———. 1958a. *Endgame*. Translated by Samuel Beckett. New York: Grove Press.

———. 1958b. "Malone Dies." In *Three Novels: Molloy, Malone Dies, The Unnamable*, translated by Samuel Beckett, with Patrick Bowles assisting with the translation of *Molloy*. New York: Grove Press.

———. 1958c. "Molloy." In *Three Novels: Molloy, Malone Dies, The Unnamable*, translated by Samuel Beckett with Patrick Bowles assisting with the translation of *Molloy*. New York: Grove Press.

———. 1958d. "The Unnamable." In *Three Novels: Molloy, Malone Dies, The Unnamable*, translated by Samuel Beckett, with Patrick Bowles assisting with the translation of *Molloy*. New York: Grove Press.

———. 1959. *Watt*. 1953. Reprint. New York: Grove Press.

———. 1961. *Happy Days*. New York: Grove Press.

———. 1964. *How It Is*. Translated by Samuel Beckett. New York: Grove Press.

———. 1965. "Proust." In *Proust, and Three Dialogues with Georges Duthuit*. London: John Calder.

———. 1967a. "Eh Joe." In *Eh Joe and Other Writings*. London: Faber and Faber.

———. 1967b. "Film." In *Eh Joe and Other Writings*. London: Faber and Faber.

———. 1967c. "Texts for Nothing." In *Stories and Texts for Nothing*, translated by Samuel Beckett. New York: Grove Press.

———. 1967d. "The Calmative." In *Stories and Texts for Nothing*, translated by Samuel Beckett. New York: Grove Press.

———. 1967e. "The Expelled." In *Stories and Texts for Nothing*, translated by Samuel Beckett. New York: Grove Press.

———. 1968a. "Words and Music." In *Cascando, and Other Short Dramatic Pieces*. 1962. Reprint. New York: Grove Press.

———. 1968b. "Cascando." In *Cascando, and Other Short Dramatic Pieces*. 1963. Reprint. New York: Grove Press.

———. 1968c. "Play." In *Cascando, and Other Short Dramatic Pieces*. 1964. Reprint. New York: Grove Press.

———. 1972a. "Dante . . . Bruno. Vico..Joyce." *Our Exagmination Round His Factification For Incamination of Work in Progress*. London: Faber.

———. 1972b. *The Lost Ones*. Translated by Samuel Beckett. London: Calder and Boyars.

———. 1973. *Not I*. London: Faber and Faber.

———. 1974a. "Enough." In *First Love, and Other Shorts*, translated by Samuel Beckett. New York: Grove Press.

———. 1974b. "First Love." In *First Love, and Other Shorts*, translated by Samuel Beckett. New York: Grove Press.

———. 1974c. "From an Abandoned Work." In *First Love, and Other Shorts*, translated by Samuel Beckett. New York: Grove Press.

———. 1974d. "Imagination Dead Imagine." In *First Love, and Other Shorts*, translated by Samuel Beckett. New York: Grove Press.

———. 1974e. *Mercier and Camier*. Translated by Samuel Beckett. London: Calder.

———. 1974f. *More Pricks Than Kicks*. 1934. Reprint. London: Pan Books.

———. 1976a. "Afar A Bird." In *For To End Yet Again, and Other Fizzles*, translated by Samuel Beckett. London: John Calder.

———. 1976b. "For To End Yet Again." In *For To End Yet Again, and Other Fizzles*, translated by Samuel Beckett. London: John Calder.

———. 1976c. "He is barehead." In *For To End Yet Again, and Other Fizzles*, translated by Samuel Beckett. London: John Calder.

———. 1976d. "Horn came always." In *For To End Yet Again, and Other Fizzles,* translated by Samuel Beckett. London: John Calder.

———. 1976e. "I Gave Up Before Birth." In *For To End Yet Again, and Other Fizzles,* translated by Samuel Beckett. London: John Calder.

———. 1976f. "Old Earth." In *For To End Yet Again, and Other Fizzles,* translated by Samuel Beckett. London: John Calder.

———. 1976g. "Peintres de l'empêchment." In *Samuel Beckett,* edited by Tom Bishop and Raymond Federman. Paris: Editions de l'Herne.

———. 1976h. "Still." In *For To End Yet Again, and Other Fizzles,* translated by Samuel Beckett. London: John Calder.

———. 1979. *Company.* London: John Calder.

———. 1981a. *Ill Seen Ill Said.* Translated by Samuel Beckett. New York: Grove Press.

———. 1981b. "Rockaby." In *Rockaby, and Other Short Pieces by Samuel Beckett.* New York: Grove Press.

———. 1983. *Disjecta: Miscellaneous Writings and a Dramatic Fragment.* Edited by Ruby Cohn. London: John Calder.

———. 1984. "Ohio Impromptu." In *Three Plays: Ohio Impromptu, Catastrophe, and What Where.* New York: Grove Press.

**All Other Works**

Abbott, H. Porter. 1988. "The Harpooned Notebook: Malone Dies." In *Samuel Beckett's Molloy, Malone Dies, The Unnamable,* edited by Harold Bloom, 71–79. New York: Chelsea House.

———. 1996. *Beckett Writing Beckett: The Author in the Autograph.* Ithaca: Cornell Univ. Press.

Acheson, James. 1997. *Samuel Beckett's Artistic Theory and Practice: Criticism, Drama and Early Fiction.* London: Macmillan.

Ackerley, C. J. 1993. "The Unnamable's First Voice." *Journal of Beckett Studies* 2, no. 2:53–58.

Adorno, Theodore. 1969. "Towards an Understanding of *Endgame*." In *Twentieth Century Interpretations of "Endgame,"* edited by Bell Chevigny, translated by Samuel Weber, 82–114. Englewood Cliffs, N.J.: Prentice-Hall.

Alighieri, Dante. 1970. "Inferno." Vol. 1 of *The Divine Comedy,* translated by Charles S. Singleton. Bollingen Series 80. Princeton, N.J.: Princeton Univ. Press.

Alter, Jean. 1987. "Waiting for the Referent: Waiting for Godot?" In *On Re-*

*ferring in Literature,* edited by Anna Whiteside and Michael Is-sacharoff, 42–56. Bloomington: Indiana Univ. Press.

Alvarez, A. 1973. *Samuel Beckett.* New York: Viking.

Amiran, Eyal. 1993. *Wandering and Home: Beckett's Metaphysical Narrative.* University Park: Pennsylvania State Univ. Press.

Aquinas, St. Thomas. 1947. *The Summa Theologica.* Translated by Fathers of the English Dominican Province. 1923. Reprint. New York: Benziger Brothers.

Aristotle. 1941a. "Metaphysics." Translated by W. D. Ross. *The Basic Works of Aristotle.* Edited by Richard McKeon. New York: Random House.

———. 1941b. "Nicomachean Ethics." Translated by W. D. Ross. *The Basic Works of Aristotle.* Edited by Richard McKeon. New York: Random House.

———. 1941c. "Physics." Translated by R. P. Hardie and R. K. Gaye. *The Basic Works of Aristotle.* Edited by Richard McKeon. New York: Random House.

———. 1941d. "Poetics." Translated by Ingram Bywater. *The Basic Works of Aristotle.* Edited by Richard McKeon. New York: Random House.

———. 1952. *Metaphysics.* Translated by Richard Hope. Ann Arbor: Univ. of Michigan Press.

Armstrong, A. H., and R. A. Markus. 1960. *Christian Faith and Greek Philosophy.* London: Darton, Longman, and Todd.

Arnold, Matthew. 1938. "Marcus Aurelius." In *Essays in Criticism, First Series, in English Prose of the Victorian Era,* edited by Charles Frederick Harrold and William D. Templeman, 1085–1100. New York: Oxford Univ. Press.

———. 1959. "Wordsworth." In *Victorian Poetry and Poetics,* edited by Walter E. Houghton and G. Robert Stange, 534–544. Boston: Houghton Mifflin.

Astro, Alan. 1990. *Understanding Samuel Beckett.* Columbia: Univ. of South Carolina Press.

Auerbach, Erich. 1961. *Dante: Poet of the Secular World.* Translated by Ralph Mannheim. Chicago: Univ. of Chicago Press.

Augustine. 1951. *The Confessions of Saint Augustine.* Translated by Edward B. Pusey. New York: Washington Square.

Aurelius, Marcus. 1961. *The Communings With Himself of Marcus Aurelius Antonius.* Translated by C. R. Haines. Loeb Classical Library. Cambridge: Harvard Univ. Press.

Bair, Deirdre. 1978. *Samuel Beckett: A Biography.* London: Harcourt.

Baker, Phil. 1997. "Beckett Beyond the Pleasure Principle." In *Beckett and the Mythology of Psychoanalysis,* 128–144. London: Macmillan.

Barker, Stephen. 1990. "Conspicuous Absence: Trace and Power in Beckett's Drama." In *Rethinking Beckett: A Collection of Critical Essays,* edited by Lance St. John Butler and Robin J. Davis, 181–205. New York: St. Martin's Press.

———. 1996. *Recovering the Néant: Language and the Unconscious in Beckett, The World of Samuel Beckett.* Edited by Joseph H. Smith. Baltimore: Johns Hopkins Univ. Press.

Becker, Barbara S., and Charles R. Lyons. 1985–86. "Directing/Acting Beckett." *Comparative Drama* 19, no. 4:289–304.

Beckerman, Bernard. 1986. "Beckett and the Act of Listening." In *Beckett at 80/Beckett in Context,* edited by Enoch Brater, 149–167. Oxford: Oxford Univ. Press.

Begam, Richard. 1996. *Samuel Beckett and the End of Modernity.* Stanford: Stanford Univ. Press.

———. 1997. "Samuel Beckett and Antihumanism." *REAL: Yearbook of Research in English and American Literature* 13:299–312.

Berkeley, George. 1957. *A Treatise Concerning the Principles of Human Knowledge.* Edited by Colin Colin M. Turbayne. 1710. Reprint. Indianapolis: Bobbs-Merrill.

Berlin, Normand. 1986. "The Tragic Pleasure of *Waiting for Godot.*" In Beckett at 80/ Beckett in Context. Edited by Enoch Brater, 46–66. Oxford: Oxford Univ. Press.

Blackham, H. J. 1952. *Six Existentialist Thinkers.* New York: Harper.

Blanchot, Maurice. 1979. "Where now? Who now?" In *Samuel Beckett: The Critical Heritage,* edited by Lawrence Graver and Raymond Federman, translated by Richard Howard, 678–86. London: Routledge and Kegan Paul. Originally published in Nouvelle Revue Francaise, October 1953.

Blau, Herbert. 1991. "Quaquaquaqua: The Babel of Beckett." In *The World of Samuel Beckett,* edited by Joseph H. Smith, 1–15. Baltimore: Johns Hopkins Univ. Press.

Bochenski, I. M. 1965. *Contemporary European Philosophy.* Translated by Donald Nicholl and Karl Aschenbrenner. Berkeley: Univ. of California Press.

Boulter, Jonathan. 1998. " 'Speak no more': The Hermeneutical Function of Narrative in Samuel Beckett's *Endgame*." In *Samuel Beckett: A Casebook*, edited by Jennifer M. Jeffers, 39–62. New York: Garland.

Bove, Paul A. 1982. "Beckett's Dreadful Postmodern: The Deconstruction of Form in *Molloy*." In *De-Structing the Novel: Essays in Applied Postmodern Hermeneutics*, edited by Leonard Orr, 185–221. Troy, N.Y.: Whitson.

Bradley, F. H. 1930. *Appearance and Reality: A Metaphysical Essay*. 2d ed. Ninth impression (corrected). Oxford: Oxford Univ. Press.

———. 1951. *Ethical Studies*. New York: The Liberal Arts Press.

Brater, Enoch. 1987. *Beyond Minimalism: Beckett's Late Style in the Theater*. New York: Oxford Univ. Press.

Brentano, Franz. 1960. "The Distinction between Mental and Physical Phenomena." In *Realism and the Background of Phenomenology*, edited by Roderick M. Chisolm. New York: Free Press.

Brewer, Maria Minich. 1987. "A Semiosis of Waiting." In *Samuel Beckett Waiting for Godot*, edited by Ruby Cohn. London: Macmillan.

Broer, Lawrence. 1987. "Beckett's Heroic Vision: Sounds of Hope, Exclamations of Grief in *Waiting for Godot*." In *From the Bard to Broadway*, edited by Karelisa V. Hartigan. Lanham, Md.: Univ. Press of America.

Brontë, Emily. 1963. *Wuthering Heights*. Edited by David Daiches. London: Penguin.

Brooks, Peter. 1984. *Reading For the Plot: Design and Intention in Narrative*. New York: Alfred A Knopf.

Butler, Lance St. John. 1984. *Samuel Beckett and the Meaning of Being: A Study in Ontological Parable*. London: Macmillan Press.

———. 1991. "*Waiting for Godot* and Philosophy." In *Approaches to Teaching Beckett's "Waiting for Godot,"* edited by June Schlueter and Enoch Brater, 48–55. New York: Modern Language Association.

Büttner, Gottfried. 1984. *Samuel Beckett's Novel "Watt."* Translated by Joseph P. Dolan. Philadelphia: Univ. Of Pennsylvania Press.

Cassirer, Ernst. 1944. *An Essay on Man*. New York: Yale Univ. Press.

———. 1957. *The Philosophy of Symbolic Forms*. 3 vols. Translated by Ralph Mannheim. New Haven and London: Yale Univ. Press.

———. 1981. *Kant's Life and Thought*. Translated by James Haden. New Haven: Yale Univ. Press.

Catanzaro, Mary F. 1989. "The Voice of Absent Love in *Krapp's Last Tape* and *Company*." *Modern Drama* 32, no. 3:401–12.

Cavell, Stanley. 1969. *Must We Mean What We Say?* New York: Scribner's.

Clausius, Claudia. 1987. "Bad Habits While Waiting for Godot." In *Myth and Ritual in the Plays of Samuel Beckett,* edited by Katherine H. Burkman, 124–43. Cranbury, N.J.: Associated Univ. Press.

———. 1991. *"Waiting for Godot* and The Chaplinesque Comic Film Gag." In *Approaches to Teaching Beckett's "Waiting for Godot,"* edited by June Schlueter and Enoch Brater, 71–78. New York: Modern Language Association.

Cochrane, Charles Norris. 1940. *Christianity and Classical Culture.* London: Oxford Univ. Press.

Cohn, Ruby. 1973. *Back to Beckett.* Princeton: Princeton Univ. Press.

———. 1975. "The Laughter of Sad Sam Beckett." In *Samuel Beckett Now.* 2d ed. Edited by Melvin J. Friedman, 185–97. Chicago: Univ. of Chicago Press.

———. 1980. *Just Play: Beckett's Theater.* Princeton: Princeton Univ. Press.

Coleridge, Samuel Taylor. 1952. *On the Principles of Genial Criticism Convening the Fine Arts. Criticism: The Major Texts.* Edited by Walter Jackson Bate. New York: Harcourt.

Collins, Michael J. 1991. " 'Let's Contradict Each Other': Responding to *Godot."* In *Approaches to Teaching Beckett's "Waiting for Godot,"* edited by June Schlueter and Enoch Brater, 31–36. New York: Modern Language Association.

Connor, Steven. 1988. *Samuel Beckett: Repetition, Theory and Text.* Oxford: Blackwell.

———. 1990. " 'What? Where?' Presence and Repetition in Beckett's Theater." In *Rethinking Beckett: A Collection of Critical Essays,* edited by Lance St. John and Robin J. Davis, 1–19. New York: St. Martin's Press.

———. 1997. "The Modern Auditory." In *Rewriting the Self: Histories from the Renaissance to the Present,* edited by Roy Porter, 203–23. London: Routledge.

Copeland, Hannah Case. 1975. *Art and the Artist in the Works of Samuel Beckett.* The Hague: Mouton.

Corfariu, Manuela, and Daniela Roventa-Frumusana. 1984. "Absurd Dialogue and Speech Acts: Beckett's *En Attendant Godot." Poetics* 13, nos. 1–2:119–33.

Cousineau, Thomas J. 1979. " 'Watt': Language as Interdiction and Consolation." *Journal of Beckett Studies* 4, no. 2:1–13

Cronin, Anthony. 1996. *Samuel Beckett: The Last Modernist.* London: HarperCollins.

Davies, Paul. 1994. *The Ideal Real: Beckett's Fiction and Imagination.* Rutherford: Fairleigh Dickinson Univ. Press.

Dearlove, J. E. 1982. *Accommodating the Chaos: Samuel Beckett's Nonrelational Art.* Durham, N.C.: Duke Univ. Press.

de Man, Paul. 1983. *Blindness and Insight: Essays in the Rhetoric of Contemporary Criticism.* Minneapolis: Univ. of Minnesota Press.

Democritus of Abdera. 1966. *Ancilla to the Pre-Socratic Philosophers: A Complete Translation of the Fragments in Diels.* Fragmente der Vorsokratiker. Translated by Kathleen Freeman. Cambridge: Harvard Univ. Press.

Derrida, Jacques. 1976. *Of Grammatology.* Translated by Gayatri Chakravorty Spivak. 1974. Reprint. Baltimore and London: Johns Hopkins Univ. Press.

Descartes, Rene. 1964a. *Discourse on the Method of Rightly Conducting the Reason and Seeking Truth in the Field of Science, Philosophical Essays.* Translated by Laurence J. Lafleur. New York: Bobbs-Merrill.

———. 1964b. *The Meditations Concerning First Philosophy.* In *Philosophical Essays.* Translated by Laurence J. Lafleur. New York: Bobbs-Merrill.

Dewey, John. 1934. *Art As Experience.* New York: Putnam.

Dobrez, Livio. 1973. "Samuel Beckett's Irreducible." In *Southern Review: An Australian Journal of Literary Studies* 6:221.

Dodds, E. R. 1951. *The Greeks and the Irrational.* Berkeley: Univ. of California Press.

Duffy, Brian. 1998. "The Prisoners in the Cave and Worm in the Pit: Plato and Beckett on Authority and Truth." *Journal of Beckett Studies* 8, no. 1:51–71.

Edie, James M. 1967. "Transcendental Phenomenology and Existentialism." In *Phenomenology: The Philosophy of Edmund Husserl and Its Interpretation,* edited by Joseph J. Kockelmans, 244. Garden City, N.Y.: Doubleday.

Eliot, T. S. 1963. "The Waste Land." In *Collected Poems: 1909–1962.* London: Faber.

Erickson, Jon. 1991. "Self-Objectification and Preservation in Beckett's *Krapp's Last Tape.*" In *The World of Samuel Beckett,* edited by Joseph H. Smith, 181–94. Baltimore: Johns Hopkins Univ. Press.

Esslin, Martin. 1961. *The Theatre of the Absurd.* New York: Doubleday.

Federman, Raymond. 1965. *Journey to Chaos: Samuel Beckett's Early Fiction.* Berkeley: Univ. of California Press.

———. 1970. "Beckettian Paradox: Who is Telling the Truth?" In *Samuel*

*Beckett Now,* edited by Melvin J. Friedman, 103–18. Chicago: Univ. of Chicago Press.

Fletcher, Beryl S., and John Fletcher. 1978. *A Student's Guide to the Plays of Samuel Beckett.* London: Faber.

Fletcher, John, and John Spurling. 1972. *Beckett: A Study of his Plays.* London: Methuen.

Foster, Paul. 1989. *Beckett and Zen: A Study of Dilemma in the Novels of Samuel Beckett.* London: Wisdom.

Frend, W. H. C. 1972. *The Rise of the Monophysite Movement: Chapters in the History of the Church in the Fifth and Sixth Centuries.* Cambridge: Cambridge Univ. Press.

Freud, Sigmund. 1984. "On Narcissism: An Introduction." In *On Metapsychology: The Theory of Psychoanalysis,* edited by Albert Dickson, translated by James Strachey. Vol. 11 of The Penguin Freud Library. 15 vols. 1973–1986. New York: Pelican.

Garzilli, Enrica. 1986. "Myth, Word, and Self in *The Unnamable.*" In *Critical Essays on Samuel Beckett,* edited by Patrick A. McCarthy 87–91. Boston: G. K. Hall.

Gilson, Etienne. 1936. *The Spirit of Medieval Philosophy.* Translated by A. H. C. Downes. Notre Dame, Ind., and London: The Univ. of Notre Dame Press.

———. 1938. *The Philosophy of St. Bonaventure.* Translated by Dom Illtyd Trethowan and F. J. Sheed. New York: Sheed and Ward.

———. 1952. *Being and Some Philosophers.* 2d ed. Toronto: Pontifical Institute of Medieval Studies.

———. 1955. *History of Christian Philosophy in the Middle Ages.* New York: Random House.

———. 1956. *The Christian Philosophy of St. Thomas Aquinas.* Translated by L. K. Shook. New York: Octagon.

———. 1960. *The Christian Philosophy of Saint Augustine.* Translated by L. E. M. Lynch. New York: Random House.

———. 1965. *The Unity of Philosophical Experience.* New York: Scribner's.

Gleik, James. 1987. *Chaos: Making a New Science.* New York: Viking/ Penguin.

Gontarski, S. E. 1985. *The Intent of Undoing in Samuel Beckett's Dramatic Texts.* Bloomington: Indiana Univ. Press.

Graver, Lawrence. 1989. *Samuel Beckett: "Waiting for Godot."* Cambridge, Eng.: Cambridge Univ. Press.

Grillmeier, Aloys. 1975. *Christ in Christian Tradition*. Translated by John Bowden. 2 vols. Rev. ed. Atlanta: John Knox.

Hamilton, Edith. 1930. *The Greek Way*. New York: W. W. Norton.

Hardy, Thomas. 1960. *Tess of the d'Urbervilles*. Edited by William E. Buckler. 1891. Reprint. Boston: Houghton Mifflin.

Henning, Sylvie Debevec. 1982. " 'Film': A Dialogue between Beckett and Berkeley." *Journal of Beckett Studies* 7:89–99.

———. 1988. *Beckett's Critical Complicity: Carnival, Contestation, and Tradition*. Lexington: Univ. Press of Kentucky.

Heracleitus of Ephesus. 1966. *Ancilla to the Pre-Socratic Philosophers: A Complete Translation of the Fragments in Diels*. Fragmente der Vorokratiker. Edited and translated by Kathleen Freeman. Cambridge: Harvard Univ. Press.

Hesla, David. 1971. *The Shape of Chaos: An Interpretation of the Art of Samuel Beckett*. Minneapolis: Univ. of Minnesota Press.

Hill, Leslie. 1990. *Beckett's Fiction: In Different Words*. Cambridge: Cambridge Univ. Press.

Hobson, Harold. 1956. "Samuel Beckett, Dramatist of the Year." In *International Theatre Annual*. London: Calder.

Hoffman, Frederick J. 1964. *Samuel Beckett: The Language of Self*. New York: Dutton.

Homan, Sidney. 1984. *Beckett's Theatres: Interpretations for Performance*. Lewisburg: Bucknell Univ. Press.

Husserl, Edmund. 1931. *Ideas: General Introduction to Pure Phenomenology*. Translated by W. R. Boyce Gibson. New York: Collier.

———. 1960. *Cartesian Meditations: An Introduction to Phenomenology*. Translated by Dorion Cairns. The Hague: Martinus Nijhoff.

Hutchings, William. 1991. *"Waiting for Godot* and the Principle of Uncertainty." In *Approaches to Teaching Beckett's "Waiting for Godot,"* edited by June Schlueter and Enoch Brater, 26–30. New York: Modern Language Association.

Ilie, Paul. 1967. *Unamuno: An Existential View of Self and Society*. Madison: Univ. of Wisconsin Press.

Iser, Wolfgang. 1974. *The Implied Reader: Patterns of Communication in Prose Fiction from Bunyan to Beckett*. Baltimore: The Johns Hopkins Univ. Press.

———. 1989. *Prospecting: From Reader Response to Literary Anthropology*. Baltimore: Johns Hopkins Univ. Press.

Jaeger, Werner. [1934.] 1945. *Paideia: The Ideals of Greek Culture.* Translated by Gilbert Highet. 2d ed. 3 vols. New York: Oxford Univ. Press.

———. 1962. *Aristotle.* Translated by Richard Robinson. 2d ed. London: Oxford Univ. Press.

Jaspers, Karl. 1955. *Reason and Existenz.* Translated by William Earle. New York: Noonday Press.

Jeffers, Jennifer M. 1996. "The Image of Thought: Achromatics in O'Keefe and Beckett." *Mosaic: A Journal for the Interdisciplinary Study of Literature* 29, no. 4: 59–67.

Johnson, Samuel. [1952.] 1958a. "Essay for *Idler* No. 72, September 1, 1759." In *Rasselas, Poems, and Selected Prose,* edited by Bertrand H. Bronson, 189–91. New York: Holt, Rinehart, and Winston.

———. [1952.] 1958b. "Rasselas." In *Rasselas, Poems, and Selected Prose,* edited by Bertrand H. Bronson, 505–612. New York: Holt, Rinehart, and Winston.

Joyce, James. 1992a. *A Portrait of the Artist as a Young Man.* Edited with introduction and notes by Seamus Deane. 1914–15. Reprint. London: Penguin.

———. 1992b. *Ulysses.* Introduction by Declan Kiberd. London: Penguin.

Junker, Mary. 1995. *Beckett: The Irish Dimension.* Dublin: Wolfhound Press.

Kafka, Franz. 1974. "Diaries 1914–1923." In *I am a Memory Come Alive: Autobiographical Writings by Franz Kafka,* edited by Nahum N. Glatzer, translated by Martin Greenberg and Hannah Arendt. New York: Schocken Books.

Kant, Immanuel. 1963. "Analytic of the Beautiful." In *Analytic of the Beautiful from The Critique of Judgment with excerpts from Anthropology From a Pragmatic Viewpoint, Second Book,* translated by Walter Cerf. Indianapolis: Bobbs-Merrill.

Katz, Daniel. 1999. *Saying I No More: Subjectivity and Consciousness in the Prose of Samuel Beckett.* Evanston, Ill.: Northwestern Univ. Press.

Kennedy, Andrew. 1989. *Samuel Beckett.* Cambridge: Cambridge Univ. Press.

Kenner, Hugh. 1968. *Samuel Beckett: A Critical Study.* Berkeley: Univ. of California Press.

Kern, Edith. 1986. "Beckett's Modernity and Medieval Affinities." In *Critical Essays on Samuel Beckett,* edited by Patrick A. McCarthy, 145–52. Boston: G. K. Hall.

Kierkegaard, Søren. 1954. *The Sickness Unto Death, in Fear and Trembling and The Sickness Unto Death.* Translated by Walter Lowrie. Garden City, N.Y.: Doubleday.

Knight, Alan E. 1971. "The Medieval Theatre of the Absurd." *PMLA* 86, no. 2:183–89.

Knowlson, James. 1996. *Damned to Fame: The Life of Samuel Beckett.* London: Bloomsbury.

Knowlson, James, and John Pilling. 1980. *Frescoes of the Skull: The Later Prose and Drama of Samuel Beckett.* New York: Grove Press.

Kockelmans, Joseph J. 1967. "What Is Phenomenology: Some Fundamental Themes of Husserl's Phenomenology." In *Phenomenology: The Philosophy of Edmund Husserl and Its Interpretation,* edited by Joseph J. Kockelmans, 24–36. Garden City, N.Y.: Doubleday.

Kojeve, Alexandre. 1969. *Introduction to the Reading of Hegel.* Edited by Allan Bloom. Translated by James H. Nichols, Jr. Ithaca and London: Cornell Univ. Press.

Kristeva, Julia. 1980. "Postmodernism?" *Bucknell Review* 25:136–41.

Kroll, Norma. 1995. "Berkeley Inside Out: Existence and Destiny in *Waiting for Godot.*" *Journal of English and Germanic Philology* 94, no. 4:530–53.

Kubiak, Anthony. 1991. "Post Apocalypse with Out Figures: The Trauma of Theater in Samuel Beckett." In *The World of Samuel Beckett,* edited by Joseph H. Smith, 107–24. Baltimore: Johns Hopkins Univ. Press.

Kundert-Gibbs, John Leeland. 1999. *No-Thing Is Left To Tell: Zen/ Chaos Theory in the Dramatic Art of Samuel Beckett.* Madison, N.J.: Fairleigh Dickinson Univ. Press.

Kwant, Remy C. 1967. "Merleau-Ponty and Phenomenology." In *Phenomenology: The Philosophy of Edmund Husserl and Its Interpretation,* edited by Joseph J. Kockelmans, 375–94. Garden City, N.Y.: Doubleday.

Lacan, Jacques. 1978. *The Four Fundamental Concepts of Psycho-analysis.* Translated by Alan Sheridan. New York: Norton.

Lamont, Rosette. 1975. "Beckett's Metaphysics of Choiceless Awareness." In *Samuel Beckett Now,* edited by Melvin J. Friedman, 199–218. 2nd ed. Chicago: Univ. of Chicago Press.

Lauer, Quentin. 1967. "On Evidence." In *Phenomenology: The Philosophy of Edmund Husserl and Its Interpretation,* edited by Joseph J. Kockelmans, 150–57. Garden City, N.Y.: Doubleday.

Lawley, Paul. 1983. "Counterpoint, Absence and the Medium in Beckett's *Not I.*" *Modern Drama* 26, no. 4:407–14.

———. 1994. "Stages of Identity: From *Krapp's Last Tape* to *Play*." In *The Cambridge Companion to Beckett,* edited by John Pilling, 88–105. Cambridge: Cambridge Univ. Press.

Levy, Eric. P. 1976. "Existence Searching Essence: The Plight of The Unnamable." *Mosaic* 10, no. 1:103–14.

———. 1980. *Beckett and the Voice of Species: A Study of the Prose Fiction.* Totawa, N.J.: Gill and Macmillan.

———. 1982. *"Company:* The Mirror of Beckettian Mimesis." *Journal of Beckett Studies* 8:95–104.

———. 1994. "Self-Pity Neurosis." *San Jose Studies* 20, no. 1:18–30.

———. 1998. " 'defeated joy': Melancholy and Eudaemonia in *Hamlet*." *The Upstart Crow: A Shakespeare Journal* 18:95–109.

———. 1999. " 'Nor th'exterior nor the inward man': The Problematics of Personal Identity in *Hamlet*." *University of Toronto Quarterly* 68, no. 3:711–27.

Levy, Shimon. 1996. "Does Beckett 'Admit the Chaos'?" *Journal of Beckett Studies* 6, no. 1:81–95.

Locatelli, Carla. 1990. *Unwording the World: Samuel Beckett's Prose Works After the Nobel Prize.* Philadelphia: Univ. of Pennsylvania Press.

Lossky, Vladimir. 1957. *The Mystical Theology of the Eastern Church.* Translated by Fellowship of St. Alban and St. Sergius. Cambridge: Clarke.

Malcolm, Norman. 1966. "Wittgenstein's *Philosophical Investigation*." In *Wittgenstein: The Philosophical Investigations,* edited by George Pitcher, 65–103. Garden City, N.Y.: Doubleday.

Maritain, Jacques. 1948. *Existence and the Existent.* Translated by Lewis Galantiere and Gerald B. Phelan. New York: Pantheon.

———. 1971. *A Preface to Metaphysics: Seven Lectures on Being.* 1939. Reprint. Freeport, N.Y.: Book For Libraries Press.

McCandless, David. 1988. "Beckett and Tillich: Courage and Existence in *Waiting for Godot*." *Philosophy and Literature* 12, no. 1:48–57.

Meche, Jude R. 1995. *Obsessive-Compulsive Behavior in Samuel Beckett's Trilogy.* Huntington, W.Va.: University Editions.

Mercier, Vivian. 1977. *Beckett/Beckett.* New York: Oxford Univ. Press.

Meriwether, James. 1994. "Chaos and Beckett's 'Core of Murmurs': Toward a Contemporary Theoretical Structure." *SubStance* 73:95–108.

Mood, John J. 1971. " 'The Personal System'—Samuel Beckett's *Watt*." *PMLA* 86, no. 2:255–65.

232 | References

Mooney, Michael E. 1982. "Presocratic Scepticism: Samuel Beckett's *Murphy* Reconsidered." *ELH* 49, no. 1:214–34.

Moorjani, Angela B. 1982. *Abyssmal Games in the Novels of Samuel Beckett.* Chapel Hill: Univ. of North Carolina Press.

———. 1992. *The Aesthetics of Loss and Lessness.* London: Macmillan.

Morot-Sir, Edouard. 1984. "Grammatical Insincerity and Samuel Beckett's Non-Expressionism: Space, Subjectivity, and Time in *The Unnamable.*" In *Writing in a Modern Temper: Essays on French Literature and Thought in Honor of Henri Peyne,* edited by Mary Ann Caws, 225–39. Saratoga, Calif.: Anna Libri.

Morrissette, Bruce. 1975. "Robbe-Grillet as a Critic of Samuel Beckett." In *Samuel Beckett Now,* edited by Melvin J. Friedman, 59–72. 2d ed. Chicago: Univ. of Chicago Press.

Murphy, P. J. 1990. *Reconstructing Beckett: Language for Being in Samuel Beckett's Fiction.* Toronto: Univ. of Toronto Press.

Nykrog, Per. 1998. "In the Ruins of the Past: Reading Beckett Intertextually." In *The Critical Response to Samuel Beckett,* edited by Cathleen Culotta Andonian, 120–43. Westport, Ct.: Greenwood Press.

O'Brien, Eoin. 1986. *The Beckett Country.* Dublin: Black Cat Press.

O'Hara, J. D. 1992. "Freud and the Narrative of 'Moran.' " *Journal of Beckett Studies* 2.1:47–63.

———. 1997. *Samuel Beckett's Hidden Drives: Structural Uses of Depth Psychology.* Gainesville: Univ. Press of Florida.

Owens, Joseph. 1951. *The Doctrine of Being in the Aristotelian Metaphysics.* Toronto: Pontifical Institute of Medieval Studies.

Parmenides. 1966. *Ancilla to the Pre-Socratic Philosophers: A Complete Translation of the Fragments in Diels.* Fragmente der Vorsokratiker. Translated by Kathleen Freeman. Cambridge: Harvard Univ. Press.

Pegis, Anton. 1939. *St. Thomas and the Greeks.* Milwaukee: Marquette Univ. Press.

Penrose, Roger. 1994. *Shadows of the Mind: A Search for the Missing Science of Consciousness.* Oxford: Oxford Univ. Press.

Pilling, John. 1976. *Samuel Beckett.* London: Routledge and Kegan Paul.

Plato. 1961a. "Apology." In *The Collected Dialogues of Plato Including the Letters,* edited by Edith Hamilton and Huntington Cairns, translated by Hugh Tredennick. Bollingen Series 71. New York: Bollingen.

———. 1961b. "Charmides." Translated by Benjamin Jowett. In *The Col-*

*lected Dialogues of Plato Including the Letters,* edited by Edith Hamilton and Huntington Cairns. Bollingen Series 71. New York: Bollingen.

———. 1961c. "Euthydemus." Translated by W. H. D. Rouse. In *The Collected Dialogues of Plato Including the Letters,* edited by Edith Hamilton and Huntington Cairns. Bollingen Series 71. New York: Bollingen.

———. 1961d. "Gorgias." Translated by W. D. Woodhead. In *The Collected Dialogues of Plato, Including the Letters,* edited by Edith Hamilton and Huntington Cairns. Bollingen Series 71. New York: Bollingen.

———. 1961e. "Lesser Hippias." Translated by Benjamin Jowett. In *The Collected Dialogues of Plato, Including the Letters,* edited by Edith Hamilton and Huntington Cairns. Bollingen Series 71. New York: Bollingen.

———. 1961f. "Meno." Translated by W. K. C. Guthrie. In *The Collected Dialogues of Plato, Including the Letters,* edited by Edith Hamilton and Huntington Cairns. Bollingen Series 71. New York: Bollingen.

———. 1961g. "Phaedo." Translated by Hugh Tredennick. In *The Collected Dialogues of Plato, Including the Letters,* edited by Edith Hamilton and Huntington Cairns. Bollingen Series 71. New York: Bollingen.

———. 1961h. "Philebus." Translated by R. Hackforth. In *The Collected Dialogues of Plato, Including the Letters,* edited by Edith Hamilton and Huntington Cairns. Bollingen Series 71. New York: Bollingen.

———. 1961i. "Republic." Translated by Paul Shorey. In *The Collected Dialogues of Plato, Including the Letters,* edited by Edith Hamilton and Huntington Cairns. Bollingen Series 71. New York: Bollingen.

———. 1961j. "Theaetetus." Translated by F. M. Cornford. In *The Collected Dialogues of Plato, Including the Letters,* edited by Edith Hamilton and Huntington Cairns. Bollingen Series 71. New York: Bollingen.

Plonowska, Ewa. 1996. *The Rhetoric of Failure: Deconstruction of Skepticism, Reinvention of Modernism.* Albany: State Univ. of New York Press.

Plotinus. 1964. "Enneads." *The Essential Plotinus.* Translated by Elmer O'Brien. New York: New American Library.

Rabillard, Sheila. 1992. "The Body in Beckett: Denegation and the Critique of a Depoliticized Theatre." *Criticism* 34, no. 1:99–118.

Rabinovitz, Rubin. 1992. *Innovation in Samuel Beckett's Fiction.* Chicago: Univ. of Illinois Press.

Ramsay, Nicola. 1985. "*Watt* and the Significance of the Mirror Image." *Journal of Beckett Studies* 10:21–36.

Renton, Andrew. 1994. "Disabled figures: from the *Residua* to *Stirrings*

*Still.*" In *The Cambridge Companion to Beckett,* edited by John Pilling, 167–83. Cambridge: Cambridge Univ. Press.

Rickels, Milton. 1962. "Existential Themes in Beckett's *Unnamable.*" *Criticism* 4:134–47.

Ricoeur, Paul. 1978a. "Existential Phenomenology." In *The Philosophy of Paul Ricoeur: An Anthology of his Work,* edited by Charles E. Reagan and David Stewart, translated by Edward G. Nallard and Lester E. Embree, 75–85. Boston: Beacon Press.

———. 1978b. "The Unity of the Voluntary and the Involuntary as a Limiting Idea." In *The Philosophy of Paul Ricoeur,* edited by Charles E. Reagan and David Stewart, translated by Daniel O'Connor, 3–19. Boston: Beacon Press.

Ross, Sir David. 1949. *Aristotle.* 5th ed. London: Methuen.

Ryle, Gilbert. 1949. *The Concept of Mind.* New York: Barnes and Noble.

Saint-Martin, Fernande. 1976. *Samuel Beckett et L'Univers de la Fiction.* Montreal: Les Presses de l'Université de Montréal.

Santayana, George. 1961. *The Sense of Beauty: Being the Outline of Aesthetic Theory.* 1896. Reprint. New York: Collier.

Sartre, Jean-Paul. 1948. *The Psychology of Imagination.* Translated by Bernard Frechtman. New York: Washington Square Press.

———. 1952. "Being and Nothingness." Quoted and translated by H. J. Blackham. *Six Existentialist Thinkers.* New York: Harper.

———. 1955. *Literary and Philosophical Essays.* Translated by Annette Michelson. New York: Collier.

———. 1963. *Search for a Method.* Translated by Hazel E. Barnes. New York: Random House.

———. 1967. "Consciousness of Self and Knowledge of Self." In *Readings in Existential Phenomenology,* edited by Nathaniel Lawrence and Daniel O'Connor, translated by Mary Ellen and Nathaniel Lawrence, 113–42. Englewood Cliffs: Prentice-Hall.

Scanlon, Robert. 1992. "Mimesis Praxeos in the Works of Samuel Beckett." *Journal of Beckett Studies* 1, nos. 1–2:5–14.

Scheler, Max. 1967. "Towards a Stratification of the Emotional Life." In *Readings in Existential Phenomenology,* edited by Nathaniel Lawrence and Daniel O'Connor, 19–30. Englewood Cliffs: Prentice-Hall.

Schopenhauer, Arthur. 1967. *The World as Will and Idea, Philosophy of Recent Times.* Vol 1. Edited by James B. Hartman. New York: McGraw-Hill.

Schrag, Calvin O. 1967. "Phenomenology, Ontology, and History in the

Philosophy of Heidegger." In *Phenomenology: The Philosophy of Edmund Husserl and Its Interpretation*, edited by Joseph J. Kockelmans, 277–93. Garden City, N.Y.: Doubleday.

Shakespeare, William. 1982. *Hamlet*. Edited by Harold Jenkins. London: Methuen.

Sharma, Anurag. 1993. "*Waiting for Godot*: A Beckettian Counterfoil to Kierkegaardian Existentialism." *Samuel Beckett Today/Aujourd'hui* 2:275–79.

Sherzer, Dina. 1998. "Samuel Beckett, Linguist and Poetician: A View from *The Unnamable*." *SubStance* 17, no. 2:87–98.

Smith, Frederik N. 1998. "Beckett and Berkeley: A Reconsideration." *Samuel Beckett Today/Aujourd'hui* 7:331–47.

Smith, Joseph H. 1991. "Notes on Krapp, Endgame, and 'Applied' Psychoanalysis." In *The World of Samuel Beckett*, edited by Joseph H. Smith, 195–203. Baltimore: Johns Hopkins Univ. Press.

Spitzer, Leo. 1948. *Linguistics and Literary History: Essays in Stylistics*. Princeton: Princeton Univ. Press.

Strauss, Walter A. 1959. "Dante's Belacqua and Beckett's Tramps." *Comparative Literature* 11, no. 3:250–61.

Strawson, P. F. 1959. *Individuals: An Essay in Descriptive Metaphysics*. London: Methuen.

Thiher, Allen. 1983. "Wittgenstein, Heidegger, the Unnamable, and Some Thoughts on the Status of Voice in Fiction." In *Samuel Beckett: Humanistic Perspectives*, edited by Stan Gontarski, 80–90. Columbus: Ohio State Univ. Press.

Tillich, Paul. 1963. *Systematic Theology*. 3 vols. Chicago: Univ. of Chicago Press.

Thomas, Ronald R. 1989. "The Novel and the Afterlife: The End of the Line in Bunyan and Beckett." *Modern Philology* 86, no. 4:385–97.

Todorov, Tzvetan. 1989. "The Structural Analysis of Literature: The Tales of Henry James." In *Critical Tradition: Classical and Contemporary Trends*, edited by David H. Richter, 900–917. New York: St. Martin Press.

Trezise, Thomas. 1990. *Into the Breach: Samuel Beckett and the Ends of Literature*. Princeton: Princeton Univ. Press.

Uhlmann, Anthony. 1999. *Beckett and Poststructuralism*. Cambridge: Cambridge Univ. Press.

Webb, Eugene. 1972. *The Plays of Samuel Beckett*. Seattle: Univ. of Washington Press.

Whitehead, Alfred North. 1978. *Process and Reality: An Essay in Cosmology.* Edited by David Ray Griffin and Donald W. Sherburne. 1929. Reprint. New York: Free Press.

Wicker, Brian. 1998. "Samuel Beckett and the Death of the God-Narrator." In *The Critical Response to Samuel Beckett,* edited by Cathleen Culotta Andonian, 39–51. Westport, Ct.: Greenwood Press.

Williams, Tennessee. 1972. *The Glass Menagerie.* 1945. Reprint. New York: New American Library.

Windelband, Wilhelm. 1958. *A History of Philosophy.* Translated by James H. Tufts. 2 vols. 1901. Reprint. New York: Harper.

Wittgenstein, Ludwig. 1958. *Philosophical Investigations.* Translated by G. E. M. Anscombe. 3rd ed. New York: Macmillan.

Woods, M. J. 1967. "Problems in *Metaphysics.*" In *Aristotle: A Collection of Critical Essays,* edited by J. M. E. Moravcsik, 215–38. Garden City, N.Y.: Doubleday.

Worthen, William B. 1983. "Beckett's Actor." *Modern Drama* 26, no. 4: 415–24.

Worton, Michael. 1994. *"Waiting for Godot* and *Endgame*: Theatre as Text." In *The Cambridge Companion to Beckett,* edited by John Pilling, 67–87. Cambridge: Cambridge Univ. Press.

Yuan, Yuan. 1997. "Representation and Absence: Paradoxical Structure in Postmodern Texts." *Symposium: A Quarterly Journal in Modern Literatures* 51, no. 2:124–41.

Zaller, Robert. 1986. "Waiting for Leviathan." In *Critical Essays on Samuel Beckett,* edited by Patrick A. McCarthy, 160–73. Boston: G. K. Hall.

Zeifman, Hersh. 1999. "From *That Time* To No Time: Closure in Beckett's Drama." In *Beckett and Beyond,* edited by Bruce Stewart, 260–67. Gerrards Cross, U.K.: Colin Smythe.

# Index

101; ignorance as precondition for
knowledge in, 3, 4; Pure Ideas or
Forms and, 16, 152; true/false
judgments of objects and, 151–52;
*Waiting for Godot* and
juxtaposition of Berkeley and,
159–61; *Waiting for Godot* and
relation to Berkeley and, 144–61;
*Waiting for Godot* and relevance of
dialogues from, 150–59
*Play* (Beckett), 1, 122
Plotinus, 109, 110
*Poetics* (Aristotle), 76
*Portrait of the Artist as a Young Man,
A* (Joyce), 62
Pozzo (fictional character), 7, 17, 124,
130, 144; blindness and, 136, 137,
140, 142, 155, 169; couples
analogy between Estragon/
Vladimir and Lucky and, 132–36;
habit and, 134, 135; *hubris* and,
63; pain and, 132; tether image
and, 158; tragic *anagnorisis,* or
recognition of, 142
Presence, 50, 51, 53, 55, 59
Process: *Endgame* and provenance of
automatist, 173–76; *Endgame* as
disintegrative, 162–79
*Proust* (Beckett), 28, 184; habit and
automatism in, 170, 172; primacy
of habit in, 167, 168; theory of life
in, 186

*Rasselas* (Johnson), 182, 183
Reader (fictional character), 64
Reason, 49, 61–62, 67–69, 71,
72, 74, 77, 78, 87, 103, 197,
204–5
Renton, Andrew, 43, 51
*Republic* (Plato), 72, 153, 158

Ricoeur, Paul, 23, 90
*Rockaby* (Beckett), 112
Ross, Sir David, 121
Ryle, Gilbert, 104

Santayana, George, 215
Sartre, Jean-Paul, 79, 80, 205
Satire, 70
Scheler, Max, 22
Schopenhauer, Arthur: critics on
Beckett and, 31; inversion of
mimesis of pain from, 30–32;
Uhlmann on Beckett and, 30n. 5;
will of endless striving and, 31
Schrag, Calvin, 88
Self-knowledge, 3, 4, 6, 12, 17, 71,
103, 110, 111, 196
Sherzer, Dina, 2, 101n. 4
Silence, 37, 59, 109, 203; avoidance
of, 104, 126; consciousness of,
98–99; Lawley and, 189; meaning
of, 189–90; polarity of noise and,
103, 105, 106; stage directions and
end-of-play, 189; Unnamable and,
108–9; *Waiting for Godot* and,
122, 125, 150
Sisyphus (fictional character), 102
Smith, Joseph, 181
Socrates, 71, 72, 153, 154–55, 158
Spitzer, Leon, 170
Stephen Dedalus (fictional character),
62
"Still" (Beckett), 36
St. John Butler, Lance, 145
Subjectivity, 9–10, 90, 99, 159, 202,
215; disintegrative process,
mimesis of mentality and, 165–67;
perception and, 8; sublimity and,
215; transcendentals, mimesis of
inexistence and, 88–89

differences/sameness in, 200;
dissolution of identity in, 6;
existential incapacity or ineptitude
in, 18; experience in, 215; feeling
and knowing nothing in, 19;
futility as raison d'être in, 189–90;
identity in, 100–122, 196, 207;
inexistence in, 85, 86, 91, 93, 94,
95, 96, 97, 98, 99; introspection
in, 204, 205; knowing in, 202,
203; living without life in, 66, 68,
70, 72, 73, 74, 77, 81; mentality
personified in, 12; metaphysics of
Beckettian introspection in,
100–122; mimesis of regret and,
182; moral suffering in, 5, 214;
pain in, 21, 22–23, 24–28, 29, 31,
32, 33, 35; persistence of
confusion in, 196; philosophical
terminology and, 9; problem of
incorrigibility in, 24–25;
provenance of automatist process
in, 176; pure verbal structures in,
2; raison d'être for futility in,
189–90; reciprocals of narration in,
25, 26–27; relation between
thought and pain in, 29; risk of
fallibility in, 1; seeing nothing in,
37, 41, 42, 44, 46; self-
preoccupation in, 10; silence in,
189, 190; subjectivity in, 10

Vanni Fucci, 14, 34
van Velde, Bram, 51
Vladimir (fictional character): couples
analogy between Pozzo/Lucky
and Estragon and, 132–36;
deadening influence of habit and,
127, 129, 156; false innocence
and, 123–43; futility of life and,

124–26, 127–28, 148–49, 150,
152–53, 159–61; habit and
automatism and, 172;
inaccessibility of truth by, 155;
inexistence and, 85; introspection
and, 121; pain and, 131–35; tether
image and, 158; as theatrical
spectator/actor, 129–30

*Waiting for Godot* (Beckett): absence
in, 51, 52, 63; avoidance of silence
in, 126; blindness and, 136–37,
140, 142, 153, 155, 169;
compulsive use of words in, 125,
126, 159; confusion and
uncertainty in, 125–26; couples
analogy in, 132–36; critics on,
123–24; differences/sameness in,
200–201; direction that never
arrives in, 6; Esslin on, 68, 144,
159; false innocence in, 123–43;
function of thought in, 125–26;
God in, 52, 130, 145–50; habit in,
127, 129, 133, 134, 135, 156;
Hutchings on, 69; ignorance and,
126, 127; inaccessibility of truth in,
153–54; inexistence in, 85;
juxtaposition of Berkeley and Plato
in, 159–61; Knight on, 148; life as
abstraction in, 16; life's futility in,
124–26, 127–28, 146, 148–49,
150, 152–53, 159–61; living
without life in, 68, 69, 70, 75, 79,
80; metaphysics of introspection in,
118, 121; Mood on, 159; moral
sorrow or *acedia* in, 139; pain in,
21, 131–35; primacy of habit in,
167; refusal of forward movement
in, 191; relation of Berkeley and
Plato to, 144–61; relevance of